YOUR
CHINESE
ROOTS

YOUR
CHINESE
ROOTS

The Overseas Chinese Story

Thomas Tsu-wee Tan

Times Books International
Singapore ● Kuala Lumpur

For my daughter, Ariel Bing-shi

[Frontispiece]. 'Street of the Gamblers' by Arnold
Genthe. San Francisco Chinatown in the early days
attracted many gambling activities.
(California Historical Society, San Francisco)

© **1986 TIMES BOOKS INTERNATIONAL**
Times Centre
1 New Industrial Road
Singapore 1953

2nd Floor
Wisma Hong Leong Yamaha
50 Jalan Pencala
46050 Petaling Jaya
Selangor, Malaysia

Reprinted 1989

Printed by Kim Hup Lee Co. Pte Ltd

ISBN 9971 65 310 9

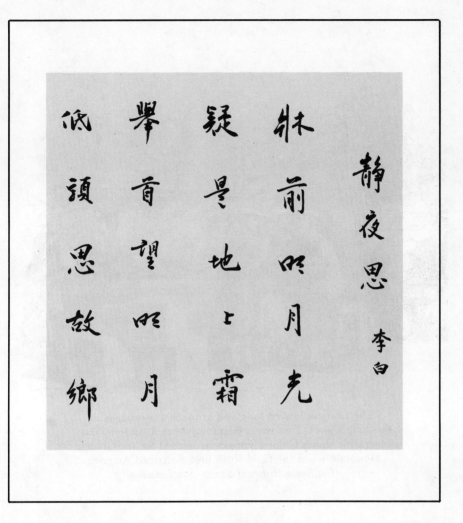

静夜思 李白

牀前明月光
疑是地上霜
舉頭望明月
低頭思故鄉

Silent Night

The moonlight lies bright before my couch;
I wonder if it were frost on the ground?
I raise my head and gaze at the bright moon;
I hang my head, thinking of my native land.

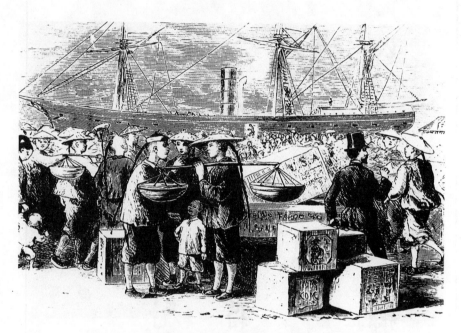

The Chinese braved long and arduous sea voyages to
far-flung shores. This wood engraving from a contemporary
magazine shows Chinese emigrants headed for the Golden
Mountain when the Gold Rush first electrified America.
(California Historical Society, San Francisco)

CONTENTS

PREFACE

THE *raison d'être* for writing this book is to present to readers a portraiture of *huaqiao* (overseas Chinese) life in countries as diverse as Singapore, America, Australia, New Zealand and Britain. There have been many previous publications, each dealing individually with one country, but most of these are highly specialized material, written by and for academics. Thus topics on Chinese emigration, overseas community structure, principal institutions and interests of the *huaqiao* have not enjoyed as much publicity as they deserved.

A few selected parts of this book, principally on Singapore, is based on my Ph.D. dissertation. Much editing and enlargement of the dissertation have since taken place so as to make the original unrecognizable. New chapters have been added, including chapters on the Chinese in America, Australia, New Zealand and Britain.

The language and style of the dissertation have undergone a change. Most dissertations are unreadable by ordinary standards. It seems impossible according to academic strictures, not to avoid footnoting every paragraph and cross-referencing every other sentence.

I have consciously attempted to cut down on jargon and the use of specialized terms. It is hoped that this will result in eliminating or reducing impediments to readability and comprehension. I have also reduced the use of references to sources; instead a comprehensive list of books and material consulted is given at the end of the book.

With regard to the usage of Chinese names and characters, the originals that have been made popular by general usage are kept so as to avoid confusing the general reader. Thus Tan Kah Kee remains as Tan Kah Kee instead of Chen Jiageng, and Mao Tse-tung instead of Mao Zedong. Only when names and characters have no generally accepted local spelling, are they romanized according to the Hanyu Pinyin system.

A book of this magnitude covering both the historical developments and community organizations of the Chinese in several countries owes much to the work of scholars working in such diverse fields as sociology, history, political science and anthropology. I have benefited greatly from their published works and points of view, no matter whether they are congruent with my own views or not. Whatever is of value in this book owes much to their past labour. Should I have for some reason failed to acknowledge my debt to any of them, I ask for their forgiveness. However, any wrong interpretations or inaccuracies in this book are solely my own responsibilities.

I wish especially to thank Stanford M. Lyman who, as professor in the New School for Social Research in New York, first sparked my interest in Chinese community organization. To Professor Paul H. Wilken, I owe a great debt for his diligent and wholehearted supervision of my dissertation. I wish to thank Peng Song Toh who guided me through the intricacies of the Singapore Chinese associational life, Kenny Lau who gave fully of his knowledge of Hong Kong society, Professor Stephen H. K. Yeh and Dr Chiew Seen Kong for their faith in my abilities and for their friendship.

The University of Virginia and the Lee Foundation have my gratitude for their generous grants. The staff of several libraries: the National Library, the United States Information Service Library and the Haymarket Street Library in Sydney have been most helpful and diligent in sourcing materials for my use.

Tzi-yan, who was my editor for a short period, did an excellent job on my first draft. Fiona who saw this book through was erudite, meticulous and analytical – in short, everything that an author would want in an editor. In addition, her superior knowledge of the Chinese language and culture did much to improve the quality of this work. Her arduous and painstaking research on Chinese surnames together with the contribution from the Bilingual section of the *Straits Times* deserves the highest accolades.

I also wish to convey my thanks to Philip Hu who did the maps and the drawings on China, and the Fujian and Guangdong provinces. Mrs Dorothy Hu provided a rare surprise by contributing a hitherto unpublished photograph of Tan Kah Kee in Beijing in 1949. Ivy Ho, my long-time friend, did most of the typing for this book. Tsu Haung read part of the draft and provided invaluable suggestions.

Finally, I would like to acknowledge my parents and my wife, Lai Sim, who, from beginning to end, have made the contribution that count the most.

Thomas Tsu-wee Tan

San Francisco Chinatown in the 1930s, looking down Grant Avenue. Photograph by Piggott.
(California Historical Society, San Francisco)

Part I

BEING CHINESE

We enter the High Hall. It opens upon the courtyard by screen doors of lattice which fold back, leaving all one side open. It is windowless. The walls are panelled in dark wood. Light streams in from the court, direct, dramatic, in a broad flood, upon the portraits of the ancestors on the wall opposite and the shelves of spirit tablets inscribed with the names of all the dead. My father's tablet is among them. On a great slab of redwood, facing the doors, are the words, 'Loyalty and filial piety continue in the family'.

Han Suyin
Destination Chungking

A Chinese grocer in New York Chinatown exhibiting his produce. Circa 1890.

1
PERSONAL ACCOUNT

I AM a second-generation Singapore-born Chinese. My grandfather hailed from Jinmen (Quemoy) island which is administratively part of Fujian (Fukien) province. Jinmen is strategically located in Xiamen harbour and from this island stronghold, Koxinga, the Ming dynasty supporter, was able to control much of the Fujian coast from 1646 to 1658. The island is now held by nationalist forces based in Taiwan.

My grandfather was originally a Howe (侯), though my surname is Chen (陈). The reason he came to change his surname is itself an interesting account and throws some light into the workings of the Chinese mind. It transpired that years ago a member of the Chen clan from northern Fujian came to Jinmen on business. While in Jinmen, he met and was betrothed to a daughter of the Howe family. Soon after he took ill and did not recover. His fiancée, then only 18, took a vow of chastity. Such an act was not unknown in China. Since time immemorial, arches have been erected on village squares to commemorate the virtues of young widows who choose a life of loneliness and austerity in order to keep untarnished the memory of their husbands and their clans.

One of her own brothers then took pity on her and gave his second son, my grandfather, to be brought up as if he were her own son. (By tradition, the eldest son cannot be given away to another family of a different clan. He is needed to extend the lineage and to tend to the duties of ancestor worship.) My grandfather's surname was then changed from Howe (侯) to Chen (陈).

Years passed and my grandfather reached adulthood. Like millions of others, he followed the stream of immigrants attracted by the economic opportunities in the Nanyang. For a time, he worked as a sailor ferrying logs from Indonesia to Singapore for the sawmills. He subsequently went back to Jinmen, got married and brought my grandmother over to Singapore. Here, in this country, my grandmother gave birth to five children, two boys and three girls. My father is the eldest son.

My grandfather was by this time working as a clerk and bill-collector for a sawmill in Tanjong Rhu. By my family's accounts, he was not an exemplary father. One recollection had it that when my grandmother was in labour, a relative had to be sent to look for him in one of many brothels he frequented. He died in 1953 at the age of 78, some relatives say of venereal disease.

My grandmother, in contrast, was a saint. She nursed her children and grandchildren during long illnesses; slogged and slaved for the family. Money was scarce then, much of it profligated away by my opium-loving grandfather. In her later years, she became a vegetarian, spending long hours in prayer and meditation. When she died in 1974, it was one of the saddest moments in my life.

My father grew up in the Singapore of the 1920s and 1930s, at the height of British colonialism. He had very little opportunity for education, only managing six years of primary school. Times were hard and jobs difficult to come by. He had to go to Malaya, to Muar to work as a timber merchant. After he married my mother in 1945, six children came in quick succession. (I am the second of three boys.) Financially we were even more strapped for cash. My father had to work at two or three jobs at one time – a store clerk in the day and accounts clerk in two or three Chinese companies in the night. I remember my mother waiting anxiously for his bonuses every year, as the Lunar New Year approached, before we could go out to buy new clothes and shoes.

My eldest brother was smart enough to earn a bursary while in the university. I was not that bright and had to depend on my father's scholarship. I could barely make the university fees on my father's salary. But one point I never forgot is my father's commitment to learning. He regretted his own lack of education and wanted all his children – including his daughters – to go as far as possible in education. It was years later before I realized that respect for education is one legacy of Chinese culture and I am thankful that my father felt the way he did back in those lean years.

My Chinese roots, however, really caught up with me in America. In 1977 I resigned from my job and went to New York for further studies. How do I describe New York City? I remember walking through Central Park. It was such a long, dark park, as big as Singapore it seemed, while I am accustomed to the smaller, intimate spaces of a little island. Not infrequently people get mugged, raped, murdered, and once in a while dismembered corpses are found. It is a place one can easily get lost in – but there is another side to New York City. Out of the darkness of the park one can easily walk into the lighted jungle of concrete and steel – great concrete block piled on concrete block, a testimony to the achievements and ingenuity of man.

New York City brought me up short with the truth Kant spelt out ages ago. 'We see things not as they are but as we are.' All that I saw and learnt was coloured by my oriental upbringing. I marvelled at the freedom of the American people which expresses itself in so many forms, from the free enterprise on the streets to the rights of the individual. I was shocked and continue to be by the seeming rudeness of some American students, who would noisily pack their bags and leave the class even in the middle of an absorbing lecture. In the East, the teacher has always been held in high reverence. Such an affront, I thought, would never have occurred in my own country.

Here in this magnificent city I spent two years living in a dingy basement room. Next door lived an old bachelor – one of the many victims of America's past exclusion policy which kept out the women-folk and of international politics – the closure of China to overseas Chinese after 1949. Uncle Li, for he is truly an uncle to me, took me in hand; taught me how to cook rice, Chinese style, how to take the subway, what places to avoid and to see. In the dingy basement we spent many happy hours together.

I remember coming home in the night after school, and he would be sitting at his table, his skinny, spare frame hunched over the table taking his dinner, or, magnifying glass in hand, reading the Chinese newspaper. One day I caught him in the toilet, crying at the wash-basin. He had received a letter from China – his sister had died. He had never met his family again, so many years ago after coming to America to study. And in the end he had only me to tell the news. His friendship and the experience we shared together underline for me the importance of family life – which is the bedrock of Chinese culture.

The manifestations of Chinese culture are abundantly clear in New York City. Though I was very engrossed in my studies, I had many occasions to enjoy Chinatown. Though gloomy and impassive, it is one of the most picturesque quarters of New York. Before you approach Chinatown, you can smell it – the earthy smells of vegetables and fruits, exotic delicacies brewing on the sidewalks, and the sweat mingled with the smell of incense and oriental perfume. One is struck by the colours everywhere, the rich hues which the Chinese love, and the more subdued shades of a western metropolis. Nostalgia flooded over when near Canal Street or East Broadway, one caught the first stirrings of the Chinese tongue.

Often I had walked through Chinatown's narrow cobbled alley-ways drinking in the sights – the telephone booth with its vermilion red pagoda roof, the tangy smell of salted fish and shrimps, the curio shops with their oddest claptrap, beautiful garments, fans and shoes, the restaurants with their Chinese characters emblazoned in bright neon lights.

What fascinated me most were the curio shops, with their beautiful, fanciful and oddest exhibits – flowery paper lanterns, gaily coloured garments for women and men, porcelain dolls, thin bamboo back scratchers, and all sizes of gorgeous embroidered shoes. They were enough to send me into a reverie lasting several minutes.

I remember passing through Canal Street one wintry evening. Out of the stillness of the air and the shuffling of Chinese feet, came the tinkling of distant musical instruments, the clash of cymbals thin and high and the shrill dissonance of strings. The haunting little tune weaved a strange spell, recalling memories of some distant idyll, of a landscape weirdly different from what I saw before me – of terraced rice fields, misty mountains, bamboo groves and temples with their graceful sloping roofs and curved eaves.

Later, for a while, I was to work in a Chinese shop, and the practical side of the Chinese presented itself. My job was to make and sell bean curd. My sister, who was staying with me while on vacation, worked in a garment factory for about three months. Of the Chinese employers, all I can say is that they work you very hard and pay you only a pittance. I could not keep up with the pace of work and had to 'resign'. My employer thrust a bundle of dollar bills into my hand and told me I was too much of a scholar – a dubious compliment I am sure.

I worked later in a garment factory, ironing clothes and collecting them in large bins at the end of the day. Though the pay was low and the work hard I enjoyed working in Chinatown. Chinese businesses are run like one big family – the bosses and the employees eat together, children frolic around the workplace and the rancorous Cantonese dialect blasted at you the whole day – from the radio and your fellow workers; made worse by the fact that I do not understand Cantonese.

I made many friends among my colleagues and the bosses. They treated my sister and me very well and were always solicitous over our welfare. One strong impression I had was the industriousness of the average Chinese worker. They or their forefathers had crossed the wide ocean to cleave and hew a foreign land, lay the tracks across the face of the earth, wait at tables, serve food and wash dirty clothes for a living. They had suffered persecution and discrimination of all kinds to attain what little they now have. They knew that a new wave of anti-Chinese feelings could wipe out what they had accumulated over generations. Caught in a ghost town that is neither in America nor in China, they quietly went about working, saving, raising their children and sending them to schools.

Soon after, I completed my studies and left for home. My experience with the Chinese in America however continued when I returned to America to pursue my Ph.D. This time it was under different circumstances that I met fellow Chinese. Some were Taiwanese students who were intensely patriotic and staunchly anti-communist. My flat mate was a mainland Chinese scholar, representing the new generation of Chinese youths who go overseas to learn from the West. He was very bright, hardworking and polite and tried his best to accommodate the Taiwanese students.

There were also the Vietnamese Chinese, victims of the anti-Chinese purge in the mid-seventies. Many of them have direct recollections of the flight and the journey they made with their families to the West. Having experienced death at close quarters, they were grateful to America for their new lease of life, though many were sad over the fate of their loved ones back home.

Then, there were the Chinese Americans, young American-born Chinese whose parents had migrated long ago. They are very articulate in English, dress like the typical American youth and invariably score high grades in the examinations. Though some speak Chinese and know something about Chinese culture, many are so assimilated in American society that they are ashamed to admit that they are of Chinese descent.

I came away from my latest sojourn in America with mixed feelings, over this very mixed bag of Chinese. There are many things I admire about Chinese culture, not least of all the Chinese love for family, admiration for scholarship, the Chinese people's perseverance and hardworking nature. There are also some misgivings – their superstitions, conservative nature and family centredness, sometimes excluding everybody else from their care and concern. But if there is anything else I want for my daughter, it is that she will glean the dross from the gold, assimilate what is valuable from the long history and culture of her people and be someone that I, having been educated in both the East and the West, can be proud of.

2
YOUR CHINESE ROOTS

LOOKING back through Chinese history, it is clear that Confucianism provided the Chinese with great cultural resilience and stability, enabling Chinese civilization to continue largely unchanged for thousands of years.

Confucianism, with brief lapses, was the official state ideology for nearly two thousand years of Chinese history. It formed the staple of the imperial examination until its abolition by the reformers in 1905. However, even today, it continues to influence the hearts and minds of Chinese everywhere – whether they are in Hong Kong, Singapore, Malaysia, or the Chinatowns of America and Europe. In Taiwan, the descendants of Confucius are given great respect, and Confucius worship continues to this day. In mainland China, after the excesses of the cultural revolution, Confucianism has been resurrected once again as a subject worthy of study and contemplation.

EARLY HERITAGE

Confucianism

Confucius (551–479 B.C.) was the greatest of the Chinese philosophers. It was said of him that no man did more to impart enduring shape and character to a civilization. His teachings occupy one spectrum of the Chinese philosophical tradition, followed by a whole host of other programmes and thoughts that differ from his philosophical stand in greater or lesser degree, such as Taoism and Buddhism.

Confucianism is characterized by a few key features, among which are conservative values, strong ethical sense, emphasis on the family unit and reverence to elders, social responsibility and a constructive, rational approach to man's immediate problems. These can also be said to characterize the Chinese world view.

The aim of Confucianism was to create an orderly society by regulating the relationships within the most important of human groupings, the family. These tenets relate to filial piety and loyalty to family and lineage. Specifically, all the morality of ancient China seems to concentrate on the parent-child relationship. To be sure, it was an unequal relationship based on the dominance of elders, but it served important functions in the teaching of and inculcating of values in the young, and the care of parents in old age. The latter, filial piety, has been given rhetorical expression in exhortations, proverbs and stories.

The *Confucian Classic of Filial Piety*, which seems to have been written by a confirmed parent, states quite emphatically:

> Now filial piety is the root of all virtue, and that from which all teaching comes . . . Our bodies, in every hair and bit of skin, are received by us from our parents, and we must not venture to injure or scar them. This is the beginning of filial piety. When we have established ourselves in the practice of the Way, so as to make our name famous in the future ages and thereby glorify our parents, this is the goal of filial piety.

Other aphorisms and proverbs found in the *Book of Rites* (礼记) and elsewhere state that 'Of all virtues, filial piety is the first', and, in case this is too general to have any practical value, 'Filiality has three expressions: the greatest is to honour one's parents; the second is to refrain from disgracing them; the third is to support them.' Almost every Chinese is familiar with tales of filial piety – one lovingly recounts how a young woman suckles her aged father in the way a mother cares for her infant.

Filial piety is the basis of ancestor worship. It is filiality beyond the grave. Death does not terminate the interest or involvement of the individual in his family – instead the deceased is worshipped and beseeched for help and assistance from the nether world. Only direct male descendants could partake of the rites of ancestor worship. This in turn gives rise to the importance of male descendants to attend to ancestor-worship and tending of the ancestral graves. Mencius himself was known to have pronounced that the most unfilial act was not to have any descendants.

The dominance of the elders was emphasized in the law, which recognized the head of the family, the father or the grandfather, as having supreme authority over their offspring. Corporal punishment could be used, though in practice, there were often more threats than actual punishment.

The law upheld that a child of whatever age, who scolded, cursed, beat or seriously disobeyed his parents, could be put to death by them

without fear of intervention. If children were guilty of unfilial behaviour, their parents could hand them over to the authorities to be
flogged or imprisoned.

Professor Scharfstein lists such unfilial behaviour as follows: legal
prosecution of parents or grandparents; residence away from parents
or grandparents; failure to support parents or grandparents; separation
of one's property from that of parents or grandparents; marriage,
entertainment, or other neglect before the end of the mourning period
for one's parents, and the incitement of a parent or grandparent to
suicide.

The responsibilities and duties of son to father are however not
one-sided. Confucius placed strict emphasis on 仁 *rén* (benevolence or
goodness); that a man of *rén* must strive for righteousness rather than
immediate profit or benefit. Mencius, his great disciple, elaborated on
this ethical aspect of Confucianism, by his pronouncement that every
man is inherently good and a potential sage. He is born with the
incipient beginnings or 'buds' of benevolence (仁 *rén*), righteousness
(义 *yì*), respect or propriety (礼 *lǐ*), and knowledge, especially the
capacity to distinguish good from bad (智 *zhì*). Parents and officials,
especially because they have charges and subjects under their care and
jurisdiction, should develop these innate qualities to the fullest so that
they become the embodiment of ethical precepts and principles.

Confucius fully accepted the ethics of a family-centred society.
The individual's primary duty is to the family, and the grades of
responsibility lessen as one goes beyond the family to the extended
clan, the village or community, the state, and finally, to the whole
society of man, uniting it harmoniously with heaven or the cosmic
order. The ethical foundation of familism could however be general-
ized to apply to political life as well. As a classic statement put it,
'The efficient ruling of a state necessarily consists in bringing its
families into an ordered harmony.'

A parallel could be drawn between the ethics of submission to elders
in the family (孝 *xiào*), to loyalty to the state and its leaders (忠 *zhōng*),
even though the first loyalty supersedes the second in the Confucian
litany. This leads to the peculiarly Chinese emphasis on the traditional
family and a suppressing of civic responsibility to others outside the
kinship group. It is not unusual for whole clans or villages to march out
in opposition against government forces if these are seen as conflicting
with their primordial loyalty to family and kinsmen. However, in times of
peace and order and strong government, the same loyalty and respect for
family elders should also be given to local officials as representatives of
the central government, all the way up to the emperor himself.

This support of the monarchy is not given unconditionally. The mandate of heaven, which is given to the ruler, is nothing more than the expression of the people's satisfaction with his rule. If he fails to be a kingly ruler, the people have the right, as expressed in Confucian teachings, to resist and rebel. In contrast, neither Confucius or Mencius has anything to say for rebelling against one's parents. Unfortunately one cannot infer that because they keep silent, they will condone rebellion against irresponsible parents.

In the Confucian order, the harmony of family and state are complementary and mutually contagious. Confucius himself probably did not foresee the potential tension between family and state over issues of taxation and conscription. Politics to Confucius was merely the extension of ethics to the larger society. The state exists because there must be a means by which men can associate with other men in an ethical rather than a merely contractual manner.

The chief function of the state therefore, appears to be education – both in getting the best and most able administrators and officials to govern, and in educating the largely illiterate peasants in Confucian virtue.

The first aim is achieved through the Chinese examination system based on the Confucian classics; the second through ensuring that the family system based on Confucian precepts (that is, filial piety, brotherly respect and dominance of elders) continues to survive. This could be seen in the way the imperial government tried to inculcate the villagers with Confucian teaching.

In the mid-seventeenth century, for example, local scholars or suitable elders were required to lecture to the less literate villagers on the Imperial Maxims, these being a list of do's and don'ts based on Confucian principles. They include 'perform your filial duties to your parents', 'instruct and discipline your sons and grandsons', and 'do not commit wrongful deeds'. Once again, the assumption appears to be that the foundation of a stable country is the well-disciplined family.

Taoism

Lao Zi, the reputed founder of Taoism, lived during the time of Confucius. A mythical man, of whom there is little historical veracity, he is credited with the authority of *Daodejing* (道德经), a 5,000-character book that sets out the basic belief of Taoism in highly allusive language.

Compared to Confucianism, Taoism is considered a minor mode

in Chinese civilization. Yet, its fanciful and eccentric teachings have gained some popular appeal among the more imaginative and unbridled Chinese minds.

A classic statement attributed to Lao Zi is 'the Dao which can be named is not the true Dao'. Since the Dao (way) cannot be attained through speech or discussion, it is beyond the associative conventions of human society. It is common to link naturalism with Taoism, which is to say that nature, not man, is the touchstone of Taoist values. In contrast to Confucianism, which sees man and his relationship with other men as central, Taoism sees man as ideally living in harmony with nature, and if necessary, isolated from other men. This streak of naturalism was to find later expression in Zen Buddhism. The saying of Dogen, a thirteenth-century Zen master, for example, immediately comes to mind. 'I came to realize clearly that my Mind is no other than the mountains and rivers and the great wide earth, the sun and the moon and the stars.'

In the Taoist's view, the artificial constructs of society, its government, social conventions and laws are not the concern of the enlightened man. Instead, the intuitive and expressive nature of man is emphasized. It urges a form of natural spontaneity and vitality divorced from the shackles of ritual and propriety and other artificial devices of civilization. This does not verge on egotistic behaviour, for Taoism abhors self-interest and the accumulation of material things. Instead it advocates a release from self to a more natural order of life.

Popular Taoism, from the third or fourth century A.D. onwards, tended to degenerate into a search for the elixir of life, alchemy, the healing arts, exorcism and so on. But in the process, it also gave rise to another current in China's intellectual life, which is more allusive and fanciful poetry, stronger and more expressionistic paintings, and more introspective and intuitive reaches in philosophy.

The great eighth-century poet, Li Bai (known to most as Li Po) and Su Dongpo, who was famous for his 'drinking poems', were both Taoists. They constantly searched for completeness and immortality, training themselves in breathing and meditation exercises, the Dao of poetry being to 'hold the whole universe in your hand'.

Taoism provides for a different intellectual view of the world, and a way of organizing one's life. Its appeal of spontaneity was not just confined to the world of art. The romantic, the credulous and the frustrated all found its teachings congenial. Its effect on Chinese political life, however, is limited as after all the Confucian scholars and mandarins were the ones who dominated the courts and dictated policies.

Buddhism

Buddhism reached China from India in the first century A.D. It is the only foreign creed other than Marxism to have an impact on Chinese life. However, the Buddhism that has taken root in China is probably very different from that found elsewhere.

It is often remarked that the Chinese are a secular people not given to religious speculation and piety. Confucianism, for example, appears to have little need for the spiritual world or the question of ultimate reality. In a now classic reply to a disciple's query of the supernatural, Confucius replied that if we are not able to understand this mundane world, how are we to understand the spiritual? This is taken to mean that what is real and unquestioned is the material world; the socio-ethical issues that confront man, here in this world, are his main concerns.

Buddhism raised the question of ultimate reality to a higher level of intellectual and spiritual quest. It introduces the ideas of trans-migration of the soul and *karma*. Man must purify himself through meditation, good deeds and prayers in order to achieve *nirvana*, the state of eternal bliss without rebirth.

The Buddhist pantheon consists of innumerable gods ranging from Amitabha, the Laughing Buddha, and Guan Yin, the gentle madonna-like Goddess of Mercy, to other lesser deities. Through time, the distinction between these gods and spirits become blurred, as they merge with the deities of other creeds and faiths of Chinese culture. Thus Confucius becomes a *bodhisattva*, and the Buddhists and Taoists freely intermingle their gods and saints. A more popular god like Guan Yin is often worshipped together with spirits of ancestors. A syncretic folk religion is most commonly practised in China and this outcome could be interpreted as a certain lack of earnestness in reli-gious matters as well as a penchant for compromise among the Chinese.

Buddhism initially sparked much resentment and suspicion among the Confucian gentry, who regarded its teaching as heretical, because priests had to renounce their families to live with others in what was seen as sterile and pointless austerity. Also, they were viewed as social parasites as they did not perform any 'productive' labour.

However, through the passage of time, and royal patronage, Buddhism gained wide acceptance by the time of the Tang dynasty. There was a mushrooming of temples and monasteries and works of art were inspired from Buddhist influences and teachings. The ordinary Chinese could find in Buddhism one more avenue for the under-standing of the world, their existence and the afterlife. It provided an emotional outlet in the sense that gods could be beseeched for help to turn away evil and to grant wishes or blessings. An unexpected spin-off is that Buddhism liberated Chinese women from their homes, making their seclusion less complete and more endurable. This is because a legitimate and laudable excuse for going outdoors in ancient China was to visit the local temples on important feast days and festive occasions. Many romantic tales are spun around chance or arranged meetings in the temple grounds.

Buddhism also provided a vocation and a release from earthly cares. Throughout Chinese history, numerous men and women have shaved their heads to enter into a life of seclusion and prayer.

THE TRADITIONAL CHINESE FAMILY

Confucianism is the backbone of the Chinese family, spelling out its organization and relationships – the relationship between father and son, husband and wife, and elder brother and younger siblings. The other relationships, between friends, and between king and subjects, are important too. The relationship between friends is usually interpreted by scholars to mean friends that can be included within the family circle. Only the king-subject relationship relates the Chinese individual with society outside the family. The three relationships between family members spell out the forms of obligations or duties of the elder to the junior members. How the family members are ranked are determined on the basis of age, sex and generation, in descending order of their distance from the senior ancestor, usually denoted as the founder-patriarch of the family.

The male member nearest to the founder-patriarch is considered the most senior in the family. He is also usually the oldest member in the family. In all cases, authority is vested in the males, and inequality among the sexes is an expressed and accepted custom both in Confucian theory and in practice. An ancient saying, for example, maintains that a woman is subordinate to her father before her marriage, to her husband after her marriage, and her son after her husband's death. Women thus have little structural importance in Chinese society. Their activities and functions were important only within the family. Beyond the domestic unit, women had no role, either in the lineage, or the wider society. Their position was defined through their ties with men; they did not feel any solidarity with one another, and did not have the means to act together as a concerted body.

Marriages were usually arranged long in advance by the parents. Generally speaking, these were marriages based not on romantic love, but contracted instead on the basis of familial convenience and interests. A marriage usually meant that the prospective bride and groom had different surnames, and were 'compatible' by the time, date and year of birth.

I remember my grandmother throwing a fit, years ago, when my sister decided to marry someone with the same surname 'Tan'. To make matters worse, they were both born in the Year of the Tiger – not a very congenial prospect for two love-birds. Being young and educated, and having more confidence in their feelings than Chinese convention, they nevertheless went right ahead.

Generally, a wedding would be an elaborate ceremony followed by a feast attended by as many of the groom's *tsu* (*zu*) as his family could afford to invite. The bride would wear red to symbolize her rebirth into a new family. The ideal practice after marriage is for the young man and his wife to live out their married life under the same roof as the husband's parents. Husband and wife are forbidden by social convention to show overt affection for one another. Instead, she has to obey and serve her mother-in-law, do the housework, help out in the farm and produce male offspring for her husband's family.

Patriarchal authority in the Chinese family means that the husband's lineage is preferred over the female. The wife who is able to produce many male children to carry on her husband's lineage is highly prized. She could expect to get along better with her mother-in-law and eventually, both husband and wife could hope to be respectfully served by their own children, as they had once served their own parents.

On the other hand, if some misfortune were to strike her husband and he died young, she would not be allowed to remarry. This is because a virtuous woman must show complete allegiance to her husband's lineage, and is expected even in the event of her own death, to be one of the ancestral spirits in her husband's line.

However, among the males, having more than one wife, and concubines, is freely accepted, especially if there is no heir from a first marriage.

For the Chinese, the family is the centre of human existence, from which all life radiates. In its ideal form, which consists of three or more generations living under one roof, it encompasses both the living and the dead, the latter in the form of tablets commemorating revered ancestors. Its influence reaches down to the children, determining their sources of education, what they should read or do, arranges for marriage, is responsible for their conduct, and claims affiliation with their ghosts or spirits after death. In this way, the generation is perpetuated and the honour of the family kept intact.

The family as a basic human grouping exists in every society. Everywhere it is the institution in which the individual learns the way of life in the society into which he is born, and with which he is identified. Many scholars have pointed out that the family and by extension, the clan, are the most important human groupings among the Chinese.

The Chinese family

The traditional family lays down the basic and general ideas, norms and emotions, folk religions and superstitions that the child will live by. Everything that happens to the child later has to be seen in the context of this first informally organized but very intensive socialization by the family group – parents, elders and siblings. In Chinese society, the family has primary significance. This is in contrast to American society, in which the individual is all-important.

Children born out of wedlock have traditionally no legal or social status. More so than in other cultures, to be without a family is to have no social identity or status at all in traditional China. It is equivalent to being an animal living in the wilds, without parents or kinsmen. The individual inevitably ends up a social outcast, unless he is adopted by a respectable family, or wins a place in an acceptable but socially cloistered institution, like a monastery.

In western and modern societies, the family is but one main source of socialization, the others being schools and peer groups. In contrast, formally organized schools are not important to the Chinese, there being a preference for informal home tutelage and self-study. There are indeed village schools, but these are mainly organized and sponsored by the clans for their own kinsmen. Teaching here could be seen as an extension of the teachings of parents and elders.

The family unit may include a male head of household, his wife, his married sons, their wives and children, and any unmarried sons or daughters. The brothers of the head of the household with their families, the parents of the head of the household, and even great-grandchildren – sometimes up to five generations live in one household! This was the great extended family described in Chinese fiction, like the famous novel of manners variously translated as *Dream of the Red Chamber* or *The Story of the Stone*, or even in Ba Jin's *Trilogy*.

However, in spite of the Confucian ideal of a large household and many descendants, the average household size in China probably numbered five or six, except among the rich city gentry. Among the masses living in the countryside, family property was seldom big enough to support a large household. Moreover, the high mortality rate and lower life expectancy in the countryside would preclude somewhat the probability of three or more generations.

The principle which traditionally governs inheritance could mean that upon the death of the father, the property could be divided among the sons, leading to the setting up of separate households. It is true that the eldest son has superior status, and if he is sufficiently strong or decisive, the married sons could continue to live together under one roof, a wish often expressed by the father. The Chinese abhor the idea of splitting homes or *fen jia* (分家), which is often a very disruptive move, creating much animosity and trauma among those involved.

Even if separate households were set up by the married sons after the father's death, familial obligations or relationships need not automatically cease. The brothers who lived nearby could still co-operate in work, pooling their resources, and deferring to the eldest for major decisions.

CLANS

Clans or *zu* (族) are the normal extensions expected of relatives through five or more generations. The whole system of *zu* formation could be explained by unilineal common ancestry. This means an unbroken line of male descendants with common surnames and tracing their blood ties back to a common ancestor. Wives and daughters are considered part of the clan, though in the case of the daughters, this connection is terminated upon their marriage.

In a patrilineal society like the Chinese, the wives take on the patrilineage of their husbands, while the daughters would eventually be 'lost' to another family or *zu*. Thus the maternal relatives are not part of the *zu*, and there are few prescribed relationships with them. As the maternal group is likely to live in a different village, distance further prevents the development of close ties.

This brings us to another characteristic of the clan, that is, exogamy. Exogamy could be defined as marrying outside one's group. As practised in Chinese society, it means marriage is prohibited between relatives within eight degrees of kinship on the father's side, and within five degrees on the mother's side, as well as between people of different generations. This usually meant that the prospective bride and groom have different surnames and are living in different villages.

Studies have shown that each village is normally inhabited by one clan. Even if there is more than one clan, each clan usually occupies a distinct section of the village. However, there are exceptions to this rule, as there are instances in which a clan could be located in more than one village. This could come about when a clan has grown large enough to form many branches and subgroups to locate in different areas. Some clans have, in the past, also split and moved away, as a result of political upheaval, or poverty, famine, and the need for fresh economic opportunities. Nevertheless, though geographical distance may be extreme, clan members are supposed to adhere strictly to the exogamy injunction. The injunction was upheld by the comparison of surnames. Transgressors were traditionally ostracized by fellow clansmen which often meant that they had to leave their villages.

The *zu* is not just a genealogical group. It is organized to support itself economically and also hold religious ceremonies. The security of the family, and ultimately, the clan, depended on the land it owned. It has been said of the Chinese that to buy land was like holding a wedding, with its promise of fruitfulness and strength; but to sell land was like participating in a fraction of the family's death. Southeast China generally has the most developed clans. This is because the rich, fertile land and the high yields of rice there facilitated the growth of large *zus*.

The *zu* usually owns some common property, such as land or clan temples, schools and graveyards held in trust by the *zu* leaders. Much of the land is usually leased out at subsidized rates to eligible clan members. The *zu* leaders are usually members of the gentry, who legitimize their status on the basis of age, seniority in the lineage, and scholarship.

Zu leaders have been criticized for exploiting clan members – using *zu* resources for personal profit. On the other hand, it is not unusual for poor *zu* families to eke out a living based on *zu* land, and for *zu* schools to educate their talented children. Much appears to depend on the individual group of clan leaders, and the availability of *zu* resources.

The principle of joint responsibility in the clan ensures discipline and mutual help among *zu* members. This is because the peculiar Chinese custom of making family and by extension, *zu*, responsible for their members, meant that punishment for serious crimes such as treason, could visit members of the entire clan. Inversely, an honour attained by one person, especially a great honour like that of passing the imperial examinations, glorified all members of the clan, especially the lineal ancestors and descendants.

The *zu* is also a ceremonial group in the sense that the members come together on occasions like weddings, feasts or funerals. Death, especially of a parent, is a central preoccupation, as it is closely related to the concept of filial piety. When one's parents are alive, they must be cared for in a material way, and shown due respect. Upon their demise, one's duties as filial sons and descendants are expected to continue. The bodies of the dead are kept in the house for as long as it is financially possible, to await the arrival of distant kinsmen. A costly funeral is arranged, as a normal and expected show of grief and commiseration.

Ancestral graveyards are often elaborate structures, tended regularly throughout the years, as if they were part of the family compound. The memory of the dead is enshrined in the form of ancestral tablets, in homes or temples where their spirits are invoked on special occasions. The ancestral souls are worshipped regularly, and representations made to them for supernatural guidance and help. At Ching Ming, during the third lunar month, ancestral and clan graveyards are visited for a cook-out reunion with the dead.

The origin of ancestor worship can be traced to the *Bamboo Chronology* which recorded the event of the death of the Yellow Emperor, Huang Di. His faithful minister, Tzuo Cheh, took the headgear, sceptre and clothings of the emperor and placed them in the temple for the subjects' worship. By the time of the Xia dynasty, worship of ancestors had become popular and the practice came to be regarded as important as the rite of worshipping the Heaven.

Ancestor worship had several facets, as it was practised in traditional China. At the level of the domestic ancestral cult, each household would have tablets to their father or grandfather and perhaps a single tablet for all the ancestors, as well as a shrine to the kitchen god and perhaps, other idols. At the level of the *zu*, however, the clans could afford elaborate ancestral halls where *zu* feasts and ceremonies are held. They could afford the luxury of keeping track of their ancestors through written records and tablets recording the deeds of prominent *zu* members.

The whole clan will first worship at the hall, then split up into smaller lineages to worship at the graves of each ancestor. Worship at the domestic cult level is normally attended by individual families and their close relatives. The order of worship and the centrality of the clan ancestral halls reflect the superlative importance of the clan over the individual lineages and households.

The *zu* monopoly of the collective rituals of worship could be seen as mechanisms to tie the different lineages together as a common unit, and is expressive of the unity of the *zu*. It could be seen as symbolic of *zu* organization, reaffirming through the rituals and ceremonies, the solidarity of the clan.

For the individual, the clan serves both these functions: religious and socio-economic. In the words of an eminent scholar, Hsu Hsien Chin:

> The security offered is twofold: religious, in that the *zu* (clan) assures the individual that the rites in his honour will be continued indefinitely; and socio-economic, by assuring each member of assistance in case of need, both from the group and from individual fellow members. The poor look to it for protection, while the wealthy and prominent expect from it a safeguard against the loss of social and economic position. The former are glad to depend on their group, and the latter find it useful for building up a following and for extending their influence. The larger, the more prosperous and cohesive the *zu*, the more beneficial it proves to all its members.

The *zu* relationship with the central government is a complicated one. Scholars have argued that Chinese dynastic governments are often too weak to exercise control over the entire nation. Since the strength of the government is likely to be stronger nearer the national capital – which happened to have been situated in the north most of the time – the Chinese *zu* tended to be strongest in the south.

There is probably some merit in this thesis, but irrespective of geographical distance, the *zu* relationship with the central government probably fluctuated with the dynastic cycle. Powerful *zu*, which had intrinsic political power in proportion to their size and corporate wealth, could threaten a weak government, as has happened in China in the past. Whole villages had been known to refuse to pay their taxes and get into clashes with troops sent out to impose the imperial will. This decentralization of power was what prompted the communist leadership to break up the clans by seizing clan property and forcibly relocating their members when they took over China in 1949.

However, in imperial times, the interests of the *zu* were protected by a strong government. The state recognises that it cannot totally control the clans – it therefore invests *zu* with the responsibility of keeping peace among their members and generally holding them responsible for the members' behaviour. Once sanctioned by the state, the *zu* then takes on administrative functions and the responsibility for the control of their members for the imperial government.

THE CHINESE CHARACTER

There are many Chinese stereotypes, ranging from inscrutability to villainy, as portrayed in such films as *Fu Manchu*. This lack of understanding of the Chinese people stemmed from the Chinese clannishness, as well as the discriminatory practices of the members of the host society.

A popular stereotype of the Chinese is their oriental inscrutability, that is, the notion that it is difficult to understand what the Chinese are really thinking or doing. This inscrutability could perhaps be traced to a certain lack of self-assertion in the Chinese individual. The Chinese extended family system adjures obedience to parents and elders, and one should bring honour to them, just as one would expect the same treatment from descendants. The Chinese individual learns early to defer to his seniors, bridling his own passions and interests.

According to the author Lin Yutang, one of the most notable Chinese attributes is mellowness, which is the result of a long civilization and a superior culture. The Chinese are apt to laugh at youthful enthusiasm, and hold a certain contempt for brashness and vulgarity. Instead, the superior man is a man of equanimity, of refined ways and polite speech, slow to anger and condemn. He does not easily show his feelings, and learns early to keep his own counsel.

A part of this mellowness is patience and tolerance. Chinese stories and fables abound of the rewards accruing from such virtues. One story recounts the tribulation of Che Yin, a famous scholar, whose family was so poor that they could not even afford to buy oil to light the lamps. In the summer nights, Che Yin would catch many fireflies and put them in a bag so that he could study under the light of the insects. His persistence and hard work paid off. Che Yin was finally made a marquis.

Another famous story told of an eccentric old man who harboured an ambition to level two mountains to open a road from his village southward to the bank of the Han River. He was laughed and scoffed at by his neighbours and fellow villagers. 'How can you dispose of so much earth and stones,' they asked. His reply was simply, 'Though I shall die, I shall leave behind me my son, and my son's son, and so on from generation to generation. Since these mountains can't grow any larger, why shouldn't we be able to level them?' After five generations, the mountains were finally levelled.

The development of such virtue is easily traced to the background of the Chinese individual who has had to grow up amidst continual or frequent contact with a number of relatives, besides his own parents and siblings. In a big family, with little elbow room for the individual, one learns by necessity and parental instruction to be tolerant and patient with the failings of others, and the need for adjustment in human relationships. Patience and tolerance are extolled as great moral virtues, ennobled in sayings such as, 'A man who cannot tolerate small ills can never accomplish great things.'

Unlike American children who are taught to be independent and self-reliant, this is quite unknown in traditional China. Instead, a Chinese knows his proper place and how to deal with the multiplicity of authorities, principally kinsmen. There is less tension between parents and children as the gulf between them is narrow – children are not expected to pursue their own interests and doings. This integration into the parents' world and their expectations renders Chinese children more sensitive to the wishes of the elders. This does not mean that parents and children share an intimate relationship. In fact, parents are often remote figures, expecting only their wishes to be followed but unmindful of the opinions or desires of their charges.

Maturity is another related characteristic which comes with responsibility. Usually married early, with wife (sometimes more than one) and children to think about, parents and elders to care for, associated siblings and cousins to assist, and the honour of the lineage to uphold, the Chinese man quickly learns sobriety and restraint. In fact, scholars like Lin Yutang and Hsu have noted that by adolescence, most Chinese have already entered the adult world with a good understanding of human realities.

Reason or moderation (中和 *zhōnghé*), which in Chinese means 'moderate and harmonious', is also highly prized, one of the cardinal Confucian virtues. In fact, the aim of the Chinese classical education has always been the cultivation of the reasonable man. It is related to restraint (节 *jié*) which means 'control to a proper degree'. This moderation is embodied in the Confucian doctrine of the Golden Mean, which admonishes man to listen to different counsels and to 'hold the mean', that is, to take the middle, and not the extreme course of action. This Golden Mean meant that in an imperfect world, caution is required in all things. Moderation, if not total abstinence should be exercised with regard to man's seven passions of pride, covetousness, lust, envy, gluttony, anger and sloth.

All these traits would perhaps suggest that the Chinese people have no sense of humour or fun. Life appears to be a serious business of responsibility and self-cultivation. This view is not true in reality. Humour comes from a philosophical and deep understanding of life and tolerance of all kinds of possible upsets in human affairs. The

Chinese civilization is perhaps great enough to go beyond the form to see that life is merely a farce, and that we are all bit players in a theatrical show.

This farcical view of life is embodied in the teachings of Taoism, principally in the thoughts of Zhuang Zi, the great Chinese humorist, who helps us perceive man's futility, his own smallness, follies and inconsistencies. When, for example, his disciples were making arrangements for his funeral while Zhuang Zi was on his deathbed, he confronted them in his typical quizzical fashion: 'Why can't you leave my body in the open air? Yes, if you leave me in the open air, birds would come to eat my body. But if you bury me, the ants would still do the same. Why are all of you so much in favour of the ants?'

Taoism acts like a morphia to the Chinese people, with its dose of romanticism, poetry, worship of nature and disdain for all human institutions. It is commonly written that all Chinese are Confucianists when successful, and Taoists when failures.

The Chinese character is not without its flaws. In fact, the extreme emphasis on the collective good needs to be re-examined. The family system, if it is too self-centred and autocratic, tends to hold back the individual, often robbing him of enterprise and initiative. It does take a person of strong conviction and character to stand up against the system and right what he considers wrongs and abuses. But there are such Chinese individuals in history, like those immortalized in Ba Jin's novel *Family* (家), or in Shi Nai'an's *Water Margin*, also known as *Outlaws of the Marshes* (水浒传). The latter, one of the best-known and much loved ancient Chinese classics, tells how and why some 100-odd men and women banded together on a marsh-girt mountain in what is present-day Shandong province, to wage famous battles against corrupt officials and tyrants.

Another related trait is indifference, which often manifests itself as a lack of social consciousness. Man's social obligations to the stranger, or what is called 'samaritan virtue', is not unknown, but practically discouraged because one's duty is first and foremost to the family and fellow kinsmen.

This indifference to strangers is in part shaped by the practical implications of Confucianism, though to be fair to Confucius, he had in more than one instance mentioned that recognition of others was important to one's self-development. He has for example said of the gentleman: 'Wanting to be successful himself, he helps others to be succesful; wanting to stand on his own feet, he helps others stand on their feet.' He sees the family as providing the pattern for the State so that the good son would also become a good citizen. Thus he said,

'Those who love their parents dare not show hatred to others.' However, Chinese history has shown that the family has proven so strong that the individual is more often a filial son than a good citizen.

The other factor accounting for indifference is the absence of protection of personal rights in traditional China. The lack of such rights impedes the free expression of speech and criticism – so that the Chinese individual would rather look askance than get embroiled in public controversy. This is especially so when the principle of joint responsibility decrees that a wrong deed could betray his family and bring shame and disgrace to his ancestors as well.

The Chinese individual is a composite of many traits; some good, others not too positive. It would be impossible to determine which particular characteristic defines the Chinese personality as it would vary from individual to individual and perhaps even within the individual in different circumstances. But one point is certain – the Chinese belong to a very old civilization which has bequeathed to them a rich and varied culture honed through time and experience. The best of men are those who are willing to learn from the past, and in this the Chinese are not lacking in both the depth and dimension of their historical and cultural heritage.

3
HISTORICAL BACKGROUND
AND EMIGRATION

More than a thousand years before the birth of Christ, China had developed an advanced civilization. Her long written history recorded the rise and fall of mighty dynasties. Her populous and hardworking people have had an affinity with the land for thousands of years. Perhaps in no other civilization has there been a more mature adjustment between man and his environment. The geographer George B. Cressey wrote:

> More people have lived in China than anywhere else. Upwards of 10 billion human beings have moved across her good earth; nowhere else have so many people lived so intricately with nature. A thousand generations have left their indelible impress on soil and topography, so that scarcely a square foot of earth remains unmodified by man.

Although China remained an essentially agrarian country, great cities were established from the surplus generated by the vast countryside of China. Literature and painting flourished and attained the height of brilliance in the Tang dynasty (A.D. 618–907). The scholar-gentry class devoted time and marshalled resources to the arts, education and government.

In the hierarchy of Chinese life, three social classes predominated – firstly the officials, most of whom had passed the state examinations to earn the right to rule, but these also included the relations of emperors and those of royal blood. Next came the commoners, the ordinary, legally respectable people. Chief among these commoners were the peasants, since they worked to support everyone else. Occupying a lower rank in this commoner class were the soldiers, artisans and merchants, as they were not productive like the peasants. The lowest class included those who were slaves, prostitutes, entertainers and beggars. These people were held in contempt and barred by law from the government examinations, which was the only established path to a higher social status in traditional China. This prohibition however ceased to apply after the third generation; allowing the great-grandsons of the individual in question to enter into the competition and eventually move up in society.

In the fourth century B.C., China was made up of several independent states, each constantly at odds with the other. Each state was a polity based on the relationship between the vassal and the ruling class. Land was owned exclusively by the feudal lords and nobles, and it was leased out to the commoners, who tilled the land and contributed a large proportion of the crops, time and labour to the service of their masters. Eventually the king of Qin, one of the bigger outskirt states, was able to win the decisive battles and exercise complete domination over the rest. By 221 B.C., the king of Qin had become the first emperor of all China, having conquered the rest as 'a silkworm devours a mulberry leaf.'

CHINA'S FIRST EMPEROR

The first emperor – or Shi Huang Di as he was called, was viewed as a tyrant by many; not only was he responsible for the murder of hapless prisoners-of-war, and conscripting millions in the building of the Great Wall, he also committed the atrocious act of burning almost the entire body of Chinese literature at that time, saving only fragments on agriculture, medicine and divination. Thus it was that the precious heritage of the golden age of Chinese philosophy, which had so strikingly coincided with that of Greece, in the sixth century B.C., went up in flames.

The philosophical underpinnings of his empire were based on Legalism, a harsh doctrine for manipulating human behaviour so that people would forego their natural individual interests in the service of man. Its prime concern was how to achieve stability in an age of turmoil; this was usually managed through methods of enticement and intimidation, ethics having no relevance. Thus Shi Huang Di's regime was marked by trickery, brute force and harsh law. Yet it was this efficient system that made possible the ascendancy of the Qin state, a province-sized kingdom, with the first organically centralized administration that China had known.

In spite of Shi Huang Di's notoriety, his achievements were not meagre. He was the first great unifier of China, abolishing the different competing fragments and dividing the country into districts administered by the Imperial officials of his centralized government. He standardized the laws, the customs and the written language of the country so that a common shared culture would provide the ingredients of a great civilization. Weights and measures, the agricultural tools and even the lengths of cart axles were standardized. Great strategic high-ways 280 feet wide were built to link up the different parts of the empire. These were meant to regulate and improve communication and transportation among his people.

The first reforms of Shi Huang Di together with others after him form the main administrative and cultural framework of Chinese civilization. As the prominent Chinese historian Ma Tuan-lin has noted, the laws and institutions of China cannot be easily divided into dynasties.

> Thus from the Ch'in and the Han down to the T'ang and the Sung, the regulations concerning rites, music, warfare, and punishments, the system for taxation and selection of officials, even the changes and elaborations in bureaucratic title or the developments and alternations in geography, did not suddenly spring into being as something unique for each period. Thus the court etiquette and governmental system of the Han was based upon regulations of the Ch'in; the military and tax systems of the T'ang were based upon Chou statutes.

FOREIGN INCURSIONS

Chinese civilization remained more or less intact until the foreign incursions in the early nineteenth century. By this time, Chinese civilization had lasted for almost 3,000 years. China, written in Chinese ideogram, means Middle Kingdom, the centre of the known world. Kings and princes from surrounding countries visited the capital regularly to pay their respects to the Emperor and to acknowledge Chinese rule.

The Chinese considered themselves superior to others, and be-lieved that they were self-sufficient, both materially and culturally. As such, they did not feel the need to open their doors to trade and social intercourse with the outside world. If China were to engage in some limited relations, it was only because others could benefit from Chinese culture and civilization. She herself had nothing to gain or learn from the West. Such a view is best expressed by Emperor Qianlong's declaration to King George III of England in 1790.

> Our Celestial Empire possesses all things in abundance and lacks no products within its borders. There is therefore no need to import the manufactures of outside barbarians in exchange for our own produce. But as the tea, silk and porcelain which the Celestial Empire produces, are absolute necessities to European nations and to yourselves, we have permitted, as a signal mark of favour, foreign *hongs* (business establishments) to be established at Canton.

In the mid-nineteenth century, China in the Qing dynasty was a land of upheaval. She was in one of her recurrent cycles of decay, where officialdom was corrupt to the core. Funds for the repair of dykes and dams were regularly embezzled so that the very basis of the country's economic life, irrigation farming, was undermined. With an increase in taxes and levies, the hapless peasants, who formed the masses, found they had little left over for their own needs.

Lawlessness was rife. Bandits roamed freely in the mountains, and villages were indiscriminately looted. Even the feeble attempts of the local constabulary to drive out the outlaws were usually also accompanied by rape, looting and slaughter.

The incursions of the foreign powers only exacerbated tension and threw open the traditional social order. The age of Imperialism for China began in the humid waterways of Guangdong (Kwangtung), when 28,283 chests of opium belonging to the British were burned by Chinese authorities in 1839. War followed and China was quickly subjugated by the fire power of the western gun. Economically, China was laid prostrate.

Politically, a series of unequal treaties were imposed by the foreign powers which opened China's coastal cities to trade at a nominal 5 per cent tariff for imported goods. Furthermore, different nations were granted territorial footholds which later developed into foreign spheres of influence with their own system of laws and jurisdiction. This system of extra-territoriality exempted foreigners from the jurisdiction of Chinese law and the payment of Chinese taxes.

The British brought opium and its corrupting influences into China. Chinese officials were bribed and along the coast piracy was rampant, running the opium trade. Using Guangzhou (Canton) as a base, opium was distributed throughout the empire. By the 1830s, the balance of trade was heavily stacked against the Chinese empire. The resultant outflow of silver, the monetary standard of the country, caused an inflationary spiral in land, pricing it beyond the reach of the common peasants. Indeed the cost of living became too high to bear. Foreign cotton goods and other commodities drove Chinese handicrafts to the wall, especially in the southern provinces.

While the peasant and artisan classes were undergoing massive disruption, the Chinese ruling class was finding resources for self-renewal by participating directly and indirectly in profits of the foreign trade. Among the Chinese merchants and officials, a new class took shape from amongst the old ruling class – the class of compradores, brokers for foreign capital in the Chinese markets. These compradores were contractual employees of the foreign trading firms, who handled the Chinese side of the business and the inter-port trade.

The commanding economic position held by the foreigners block-
ed the channel of indigenous, independent capitalist development.
Thus there existed no significant local industry based on Chinese
capital. This was also because the wealth accumulated by these compradores was not channelled into capitalist enterprises, but back into
increasing their family holdings and into usury at high interest rates to
the peasants. Most of the officials also participated in the highly
lucrative opium smuggling, and thus allied with the foreign traders in
exploiting their own people.

The Imperialists, having battered the Manchu court into submission, and adapted the upper strata of Chinese society to their own
uses, protected the Chinese rulers against the wrath of the people.
This was to become the basic formula of foreign control in semi-colonial
China.

Exploitation, together with floods and famines during the mid-
decades of the nineteenth century, resulted in mass pauperization and the
creation of a large floating population. The dissolute peasants began to
join forces with bandits, and many rebellions occurred, the most famous
of which was the Taiping Rebellion (1850–1865), which was the last
attempt to respond to the need for change in the traditional manner –
that is, by peasant rebellion and the change to a new dynasty.

The Taiping Rebellion originated in South China, and came close to
toppling the Qing dynasty. Started in 1850 by an unsuccessful Hakka
scholar, Hong Xiuquan, he and his army captured Nanjing
(Nanking); controlled half of China and created panic in Beijing
(Peking) all within nine years. It was estimated that six hundred cities
and towns were destroyed in the course of their crusade and all the
central provinces of China were ruined in thirteen years of vicious
fighting. Twenty-five million people perished and the very foundation
of the Qing dynasty was shaken to its core by a rebellion that burned
Buddhist and Taoist temples and substituted Christ for Chinese deities
everywhere. The rebellion was finally quelled with the aid of the
western powers, who feared the Chinese people more than they did the
inept Manchu emperor.

There were several reasons for the failure. Firstly, the rebel
peasants' seizure of land placed the rebellion in confrontation with the
aristocratic and compradore-merchant classes, which had heavily in-
vested in land. The decisive factor was however the opposition to the
opium trade, which was still the most lucrative feature of the China
trade. This then led to the armed intervention of the British and
French forces.

The Taiping Rebellion was followed by the Nien and other revolts. In 1900, the Boxer Rebellion and its attendant humiliation of the Qing dynasty by the foreign powers caused the dynasty's prestige and authority to plummet further.

The sorry state of the government spawned numerous indigenous movements to modernize China. They fell broadly into two main camps – the reformers who attempted to revive China within the political and cultural context of Chinese society; and the revolutionaries who wished to promulgate a new China based upon Western parliamentary democracy.

These reformers were mainly provincial officials who had longer and closer contacts with the West in the treaty port provinces. Their programme for China was grounded in the axiom, 'Chinese ethics was for living, while Western learning was for use.' It did not withstand the test of time. For example, attempts to integrate the modern school with the old civil service examination met with failure.

At the head of the reformist movement was Kang Youwei, a distinguished classical scholar-official. He was able to influence Emperor Guangxu in 1898, to issue forty or more reform edicts dealing with almost every conceivable subject, from the setting up of modern schools, revision of Chinese laws, promotion of agriculture and industry, to sending students abroad for western education.

This so-called 'Hundred Days Reform' failed, its leaders were executed or imprisoned. Kang Youwei himself was lucky to escape. The reactionary forces under the Empress Dowager promptly restored the status quo. The victory of the conservative forces led to the Boxer Rebellion of 1900, which was essentially an anti-foreigner and anti-imperialist movement. The rebellion was however quickly crushed and even Beijing was occupied and burned. After this defeat, the ultra-conservative Empress Dowager finally recognized the need to reform and strengthen China.

The most far-reaching reforms promulgated by the Manchu dynasty were in education. Promising youths were selected and sent for studies overseas. In 1905, the classical civil service examination was abolished, more modern schools were built to teach 'western' forms of education, and Confucianism was greatly de-emphasized. Since Confucianism was the political and moral prop of Chinese society, these reforms meant that the foundation not only of the state but of Chinese culture was being undermined.

The political structure of China was to be transformed into a constitutional monarchy. In 1909, provincial assemblies were inaugurated and a national assembly convened in 1910. Although membership in these bodies was largely by election, this was only of a very limited franchise. A parliament was promised but before this could be convened, the revolution took place and the centuries-old monarchial government came to an end.

The revolution of 1911 was the direct result of Imperialism. Renewed imperialist pressure by one power after another during the closing years of the century resulted in predatory exactions from China of territorial, trade and other concessions.

Totally defenceless against these predators, the timely Japanese victory over Russia in 1905 showed China the positive effects of modernization, that an Occidental power could be just as easily defeated by an Oriental nation. New movements quite different in character and class originated from the peasant rebellion and the reform movement quickly arose to plot a new course for China.

These new agencies of change developed in the upper strata of Chinese society. Foreign political and economic pressures had moulded the Chinese ruling class into a shape fitting the foreigners' requirements, and foreign privileges closed most doors to native capitalist development. Nevertheless, the accumulation of wealth by this class did not fail to stimulate efforts to compete with the foreigners on their own ground.

Chinese merchants and capitalists began to assert themselves more boldly. This was never proven more clearly than in 1905, when boycotts were staged against the United States for its abusive attitudes towards Chinese immigrants, and against Japan in 1908 over a shipping incident. Yet class consciousness had not developed fully to the extent of concerted action.

Ironically, the non-indigenous bourgeois elements, namely the overseas Chinese business communities, played a more significant role in the revolution than the indigenous middle class. These overseas Chinese communities, having grown up outside the traditional mainland society with non-conformist commercial values, and who were nationalistic but frustrated in their political loyalties, provided decisive financial support for the revolutionary forces.

The 1911 revolution had a strong leadership in the group of Westernised patriotic youths, the scions of Chinese upper and middle classes who had studied overseas. Sun Yat-sen, father of the revolution, studied in Hawaii and Hong Kong, and travelled widely in England, Europe and America. Because of their paradoxical position of being a product of modernization before modernization had reached or become widespread in their own country, their beliefs of democracy, equality and social justice, which arose out of the industrial environment of the countries they had studied in, this group was subversive to the existing government. In China as in other underdeveloped countries, the intellectuals were to play a leading role in the modernizing and revolutionary movements of their own countries.

In 1911, the whole basis of the ancient monarchial bureaucratic rule in China came to a halt, and with it the prestige of the scholar-literati class based on Confucianism. With the end of the monarchy, the first crucial step towards modernization had begun paving the way for the 'complete revolution' of 1949.

CHINESE EMIGRATION
Official Attitude to Emigration

During the Qing dynasty, China generally forbade emigration. This prohibition applied not only to persons wishing to settle permanently abroad but to itinerant merchants as well. It seemed to have stemmed at least in part from the Chinese attitude of superiority over other peoples. The Chinese who preferred to live among barbarians were likewise considered inferior.

There was however another side to this self-imposed insularity. The Manchu (Qing) dynasty, which came to power in 1644 was a foreign dynasty, and was therefore unpopular with the Chinese people. Open revolts against the Manchu were not uncommon even at the heyday of the empire. The Manchu autocracy did not wish their subjects to engage in extensive contacts and trade with the West as it feared the importation of alien ideas inimical to their rule and the setting up of rebel bases outside China that were beyond their policing and control.

The criminal law of the Qing dynasty not only prohibited Chinese from emigrating, but also imposed an extremely severe penalty on the overseas Chinese who tried to come back on the hush. According to that law, 'any Chinese, who lives abroad and does not return to China by making excuses, yet comes back secretly, should be executed immediately after he is arrested.'

This law was only repealed after 1898, and the Chinese diplomatic and consular officers overseas were instructed for the first time to protect Chinese residents abroad. The authorities gradually realized that the flood of emigrants to the Nanyang and elsewhere could not be stemmed. China was suffering from widespread impoverishment, and tremendous new commercial opportunities were opening up elsewhere. Furthermore, China stood to gain from the emigrant Chinese through foreign exchange earnings and the illegal 'squeeze' put on them when they returned from abroad.

Reasons for Emigration

In spite of the combined restraints of law, religion and family ties, millions of Chinese have migrated overseas since the 1880s. Much of this emigration could be traced to the tumultuous events in eighteenth- and nineteenth-century China, when neither life nor property was safe. Nature added to the destruction with floods and famines, rampant in the mid-nineteenth century. As late as 1929, more than 3 million Chinese people starved to death when the Yellow River, aptly called 'China's Sorrow', overflowed its banks.

Overpopulation was also putting tremendous pressure on available land in South China in the late nineteenth century. Along the coastal areas of East Guangdong and South Fujian, the original home of most overseas Chinese, a population of a little over 4 million people occupied a land area of 4,492 square miles, a density of about 890 persons per square mile. Some parts of South China were even more crowded. In the Shih-ming district of South Fujian, for example, 519 persons subsisted on an acre of cultivated land. (The national average in 1812 was about 219 *mou* per person or roughly 3 persons to 1 acre.) Thus land, the ultimate desire of all peasants, became scarce and more expensive due to population increase. Many parts of South China became an agrarian hell of rack-rent and hopeless sharecropping. To keep their families alive, many were forced to migrate. Confronted by the harsh facts of political turmoil and natural calamities, the attraction of a decent livelihood elsewhere proved irresistible to many.

The late nineteenth and early twentieth centuries was a period of western mercantile expansion into the Far East. Japan had been opened to western commerce, as had the treaty ports of China. India had long been a colonial possession and was in fact a base for British imperialist and commercial activities in the East.

In Southeast Asia, the British established the Straits Settlement States of Penang, Singapore and Malacca by 1824. Singapore especially proved very valuable to the British. Situated off the southern tip of the Malay peninsula, Singapore was strategically located astride both the north-south seaway between China and the Indian Ocean/Cape of Good Hope route to Europe, and the east-west seaway between India and China or the Dutch East Indies. Thus it provided the British with a valuable entrepôt port as well as a strategic location to capture a share of the rich East Indies trade. Its location also enabled the British to extend their rule over the Malayan states and the nearby North Borneo coast which was not under Dutch rule.

Singapore's potential was soon realized with the rapid increase in the volume and value of its trade. Its trading partners included not only the East Indies and Malaya, but also Siam, Cochin China, China and the countries of Western Europe. Immigrants from China and India, attracted by this island city, came to engage in trading activities; there was plenty of work for labourers, artisans, shopkeepers, farmers and domestic servants. From the last quarter of the nineteenth century onwards, tin was discovered in large deposits in the Malayan states. Rubber was found to be commercially viable and was quickly discovered to grow well in Malayan soil. The tremendous expansion of the world market for both commodities encouraged both European and Chinese entrepreneurs to undertake vast mining and plantation enterprises in Malaya. This in turn attracted Chinese migration to British Malaya and Singapore, the largest compared to other parts of the Nanyang. The hardworking and opportunistic Chinese were naturally drawn to these areas of burgeoning economic activity and growth, where a quick profit could be made.

The British establishment of law and order in the Malayan States and the Straits Settlements, their respect for private property and their policy of free trade, also made the area safe and profitable for a mass influx of Chinese immigrants. These factors were abetted by the emergence of the initially unrestricted British immigration policy and the policy of non-interference in the affairs of the migrant population. It is also no secret that the British favoured the immigration of the Chinese, who were described by one source as 'a hardworking and money-loving people'.

The Chinese also migrated to other parts of the Nanyang. For example, Chinese merchants were actively involved in rice milling in Cholon and rice distribution in Java. Chinese labourers could be found in the tin mines of Banka and Billiton in the Dutch East Indies, and in rubber and tobacco plantations throughout the area. They also performed unskilled labour as longshoremen, rickshaw or pedicab drivers, dock and warehouse labourers and factory workers in the big cities such as Phnom Penh, Bangkok and Manila.

However, Singapore, and to a lesser extent Hong Kong, provided the pivotal role in the Chinese economic incursion into the Nanyang. They served as major ports through which the flow of indentured labour from China was distributed to other parts of the area. Many Chinese also returned to these two ports to reside, or on transit to their homelands after the completion of their terms of contract.

Whereas the colonial presence and the opening of economic opportunities were responsible for the Chinese immigration to the Nanyang, it was the lure of gold that initially attracted Chinese immigration to America, Australia and New Zealand. When gold was first discovered in California in 1848, the wide dissemination of this news quickly rocked the Guangzhou Delta. Tens of thousands of Cantonese flocked to the goldfields of California. Stories were told of gold which was found in great abundance and in a short time with a minimum of effort.

A few years later gold was also discovered in the Bathurst, Bendigo and Ballaret regions of the Australian continent. This discovery coincided with the decline of the gold fever in California when the gold ran out or did not pay enough. Many gold miners from California who did not turn to other occupations or were free from ensnaring debts quickly left for the Victoria goldfields so that by 1859 there were some 42,000 Chinese in Australia compared to only 25,000 Chinese in 1854.

From time to time a few groups of miners drifted across the Tasman Sea to New Zealand in search of new opportunities or purely out of adventure. However when gold was discovered in large quantities in Otago in the early 1860s, larger groups of Chinese began to leave their claims in Australia for New Zealand. These Chinese joined the earlier arrival of white men from the goldfields of California and Victoria, who were no more true colonizers than the Chinese. They however had the advantage of the colour of their skin and soon the Chinese found that they were no more welcome in New Zealand than in Australia or California.

However, throughout the nineteenth century, as the economic situation in the Guangdong province continued to deteriorate, a steady stream of Chinese migrated to these three countries, paralleling the migration of others to the Nanyang, in the hope of an economic livelihood away from certain starvation and death. The courage and tenacity of purpose of these Chinese pioneers can never be overrated.

Sources of Immigration

The Hokkiens had for centuries been known for their active Junk Trade in the Philippines, Indonesia, and Siam. Their emigration to the Nanyang was a natural consequence of physical proximity and their familiarity with the trading routes. From the mid-seventeenth century onwards, their departure began in earnest with the Manchu's clearing of the coastal region of Fujian in order to deny food and shelter to the seafaring supporters of Koxinga. (Koxinga was a Ming loyalist who fled with his army to Taiwan and there defied the recently triumphant Manchus on the Mainland.) Many Hokkiens fled across the Straits of Taiwan to Taiwan or to countries further south.

During this time, the Cantonese had not emigrated in significant numbers. By the time they realized that profit and fortune could be forged in the Nanyang, which was now under European influence, it was too late for many of them. The principal group of Hokkiens had arrived first and was now actively monopolizing trade, retail business and work in the tin mines and plantations. The organization of Chinese migration along family lines – fathers or uncles sending for their sons and nephews, or older brother bringing in a younger brother – further strengthened the Hokkien position and helped stave off other dialect groups from the more lucrative businesses. To be sure, some Cantonese did go to the Nanyang, but they were a rather late appearance in the drama as artisans and labourers.

Among the different dialect groups, Cantonese women were the most liberated. An anti-marriage movement originated in the last century in Shunde, right in the heart of the Cantonese emigrant areas in Guangdong province. As a result a great number of Cantonese females entered pacts and sisterhoods directed against marriage, and left home for different pastures. Many ended up as earth-carriers and labourers in Singapore's construction industry. Known popularly as Samsui women, having originated from Sanshui district, they were a common sight in the 1950s and 1960s.

Most Cantonese had to go further afield to make their fortunes. Fortunately they were a hardy and enterprising people. Like the Hokkiens, many Cantonese were traders and seafarers in the Junk Trade covering the countries of the Nanyang with Africa and the Near East as trading outposts. The more adventurous of them have in fact traded across the Pacific to the Americas from around the sixteenth century. With the participation of the Chinese in the Philippines, they manned or chartered Chinese junks bringing silks and other luxury goods from China to Manila for shipment on the Manila Galleons to Mexico. Some of these Chinese engaged in this trade had visited California long before there were official reports of their arrival in America. The pioneers of the early gold rush in California were those who were either directly involved or related to those who had taken part in the Manila Galleon trade.

From the 1840s until past the turn of the century, the main sources of emigration were the Cantonese from the Sam Yup (Three Districts) area of Nanhai, Panyu and Shunde and the Sze Yup (Four Districts) area of Xinhui, Taishan, Kaiping and Enping in the Pearl River delta south of Guangzhou.

As a people, the Cantonese have had more contacts with westerners than any other Chinese. Until 1842, Guangzhou was the only port in China open to foreign trade. More than other Chinese, the Cantonese were familiar with life in the big port cities of Guangzhou, and later Hong Kong. Some authors have speculated that the early Cantonese exposure to Western culture has made them more open to external influence and change. This perhaps helps to explain their readiness to migrate far away, especially in the face of political and social turmoil.

The Nature of the Chinese Emigrant

The Chinese emigrant was unique because he saw his departure as only a temporary solution to pressuring poverty and deprivation at home. Whether he found himself in the tin mines and plantations of Malaya or panning for gold in the rivers of California, his first thoughts were for his family and kinsmen in the village where he grew up, and to which he hoped eventually to return.

His hope and that of his immigrant brothers was to earn enough to return to China with some capital, if not as a wealthy man. Most saved just enough for a passage home, while others were more fortunate – tales of rags-to-riches being not uncommon among the overseas Chinese.

In the early years few stayed on in the host societies. It was estimated that about 4,850,000 emigrants left the principal ports of Xiamen (Amoy), Shantou (Swatow), Guangzhou and Hong Kong in the years 1876 to 1901; the majority bound for Southeast Asia. About 4 million returned through these ports in the same period, part of the difference being accounted for by death abroad.

In America, much of the same situation prevailed. 65,758 Chinese arrived between 1850 and 1859, but even with the 775 Chinese already in California, the total number of Chinese in America in 1860 was only 34,933. This showed that nearly half of the immigrants returned to China within this period even though conditions had not improved.

Comparable statistics among the other ethnic emigration groups were not easily available. Millions of Europeans moved into North America in the nineteenth century. For example, the Irish and Germans came after their countries were ravaged by crop failures, famines and political unrest. It was estimated that the 1845 to 1847 potato blight killed half a million Irish and drove a million and a half to seek succour in America, especially in the areas of Boston and New York. Most appeared to have stayed and assimilated easily into American society.

In contrast, the Chinese mental orientation to their homeland produced the typical sojourner. He clung on to his cultural heritage, and sought to finish his term abroad in the shortest possible time. Because he did not have any long-term commitment to the host society, he saw no need to learn or adjust to the values, norms or behaviour patterns of the society he found himself in; preferring instead to live among fellow Chinese. He did not judge himself by the standards of the society but by the standards and values of his homeland.

The Chinese sojourner lived in a nether world – suspended between a social system that is physically inaccessible and the present society which he is either unable or unwilling to fully participate in. The solution to his difficulty was, of course, to find the earliest opportunity to return to China where he could function as a social being.

However while he was overseas, even for a limited time, the sojourner and his fellow countrymen banded together to replicate miniaturized Chinese worlds. These were the famed Chinatowns, common throughout the world wherever a sizeable Chinese population congregated.

In this regard, the Chinese appear to be unique among the other ethnic groups. They seem to have a penchant for grouping together and transplanting certain features of their culture, institutions and social organizations of their homeland to societies which have never before experienced an Asian habitation. Although there are Japan towns, Korean towns or Little Italies in the history of American settlements, these are however not as pervasive as the Chinatowns which are present in every major city – Los Angeles, San Francisco, New York City, Chicago, the north American cities of Vancouver and Toronto, Philadelphia and Honolulu, even if Chinatown in these last two cities only constitutes one narrow street with a few Chinese restaurants. There are a whole spectrum of Chinatowns across the continent; and the bigger ones in San Francisco and New York have indeed become familiar and permanent fixtures of America's ethnic landscape.

Part II
OUT OF CHINA

Emigration requires powerful motivation. Creatures of habit and tradition, men are inclined to stay where they are and endure what they must, rather than strike out for uncertainty and the unknown.

Betty Lee Sung
Mountain of Gold

DECK OF A CHINESE JUNK

4

ACROSS TO THE NANYANG

THE story of the Chinese in Singapore is inextricably interwoven with the history of Chinese immigration in the surrounding countries. A brief description of the Chinese in the countries of Thailand, Malaysia, Indonesia and the colony of Hong Kong will form an essential backdrop for an understanding of the historic movement of people from an overburdened economy to lands of new opportunities in the Nanyang; of which Singapore was a major transit point or destination for the immigrants.

HONG KONG

The Crown Colony of Hong Kong has an overwhelming Chinese majority. Out of its population of 5.5 million people, 98 per cent are Chinese, mostly Cantonese from Guangdong province. It was ceded to Britain under the terms of the Opium War in 1842, as part compensation for the loss of British life and property. Some years later, the territory was enlarged with the lease of adjoining areas.

Hong Kong's role as a gateway for British trade with China and the Far East was soon fulfilled as its harbour was handling a large proportion of foreign trade with China. The island, initially sparsely populated and barren, quickly grew into an international trading port and a beacon of business and economic opportunities. Hong Kong was also a centre for emigration from the Chinese mainland to the Nanyang and elsewhere. Refugees from the mainland were attracted by its bright lights and success story. The population in Hong Kong grew by leaps and bounds as a result of which cultivable land and jobs became scarce and housing an intractable problem.

Of all the countries mentioned so far, Hong Kong is closest geographically and culturally to mainland China. Historically it is part of China and will revert to Chinese suzerainty in 1997.

Its historical and cultural links to China are sustained by the fact that illegal immigrants from China reached approximately half a million persons in the ten-year period from 1971 to 1981. After this date, the Hong Kong government, in collaboration with China, pursued a more rigorous immigration policy which required most if not all illegal immigrants to be repatriated back to China.

Those who arrived in Hong Kong before this policy was implemented still maintain ties with numerous close relatives living in Guangdong or the surrounding provinces. Visits to these relatives are very common, especially during holidays and festival periods like the Lunar New Year when tens of thousands pour across the colony into China.

Entry into China for Hong Kong residents is made easy by the 'visit the homeland' scheme which allows Hong Kong residents to visit China as frequently as they wish for ten years at a time. China also has a very liberal policy towards maintaining contacts with Hong Kong. It allows about 70 legal immigrants to leave China daily to join their relatives in Hong Kong. It also has a scheme which brings Chinese tourists from China to visit the colony and meet with relatives. These tours to Hong Kong are organized three times a day with about 50 people per tour, and are generally paid for by the relatives of the mainland Chinese.

Because transportation and communication links with China are excellent this further strengthens ties with the motherland, deepening the sense of Chinese identity among Hong Kong residents. There are four direct trains daily to Guangzhou with numerous regular trains running from the early hours to past midnight. Guangzhou is but 3 hours away by rail while Shenzhen, an important, officially designated special economic zone, is even nearer – only an half-hour or so from Kowloon. There is also an assortment of water transport including jet foil and cruise ships which ply to Xiamen, Shanghai and county towns on the estuary of the Pearl River. For cities and regions further afield, air transport made them easily accessible.

By all standards, Hong Kong is truly a democratic country. The press is not muzzled and most newspapers are openly sympathetic to mainland China's ideology even if they are not communist in orientation. Freedom of speech extends to the individual as long as he does not cause a traffic holdup while having his say. Most residents in Hong Kong appear to be proud of China's achievement under communism, and contemptuous of the Kuomintang record, even if they are not totally committed to the communist ideology.

The mainland's omnipresence in Hong Kong is evidenced by the large number of delegates and traders, business firms and corporations, mainland Chinese movies and artistes. Given the coming reunion with China, there is an urgency in integrating Hong Kong economy with China. Hong Kong businessmen recognized early the potentially huge market for Hong Kong's goods and services. As one Hong Kong official said, 'Hong Kong is China's gateway and China is Hong Kong's future.' Already Hong Kong businessmen are tapping China's vast resources and market potential. Under the more laissez-faire policy of Deng Xiaoping, Hong Kong businessmen are setting up branches and houses in the capital cities and provincial towns, duplicating those they have established in Hong Kong.

There is little likelihood that the Hong Kong Chinese will lose their Chinese roots – given the constant trading with China or the many visits to relatives in nearby provinces. In fact there is renewed interest in China's achievements, her modernizing attempts, in learning Mandarin and doing things the Chinese way – especially in business, with the Chinese disdain for documentation, relying more on patient negotiation, circumlocution and trust. In fact Hong Kong middlemen are likely to emphasize their cultural affinity with the mainlanders, especially their Cantonese-speaking cousins in Guangdong – despite the totally different socio-economic systems – as this could give them a decisive edge over foreign businessmen in winning China contracts.

Although the average Hong Kong youths seem wholly western in outlook and orientation, yet they are probably more Chinese than the Chinese youths from the Nanyang. Deep down they are clannish, speak principally Cantonese, and are disdainful of other languages and cultures. They are conscious and proud of the long history of Chinese culture while being, at the same time, committed to the capitalist system of 'free-for-all' commercial enterprise.

THAILAND

The Chinese came very early to Thailand. The first published European accounts in the seventeenth century mentioned the presence of several thousand Chinese artisans and merchants at the capital at Ayuthia. In the eighteenth century, more Chinese flocked to Thailand as a result of the generally benign policy towards Chinese immigration. For example, King Taksin (1767–82), who was himself said to be the son of a Chinese immigrant, actively encouraged their immigration.

Periods of anti-Chinese feelings were not absent. When King Wachirawut ascended the throne in 1910, he authored a pamphlet on the Chinese entitled 'The Jews of the East'. However, except for brief repressive periods the Chinese were appointed to official posts; some even became governors and chief justices.

After the middle of the nineteenth century, immigration to Thailand as to the other countries of the Nanyang began in earnest. This was the result of several factors, mainly the relaxation of the Chinese government's attitude towards immigration of its people, the problems of overpopulation and natural disasters in the southern provinces of China, and the economic activities of western powers which opened up tremendous new commercial opportunities.

Thailand felt the impact of this commercial revolution when the Bowring Treaty was signed between Thailand and Great Britain in 1855. The treaty negotiated for the end of seclusion and threw open the doors to virtually unrestricted trade with the West. More Chinese quickly moved into the new economic niche as middlemen between Western importers and exporters on the one hand and the mass of the peasant population on the other. Manufactured goods found their way to Chinese shopkeepers and itinerant traders who also acted as collection agencies for local products such as tin, rubber and shellane. Later the Chinese supplied both unskilled labour and craftsmen for the opening up of the country, in the building of infrastructure like roads, railways and canal construction. As Thailand developed and industrialized, the Chinese found new inroads in careers as rice traders, moneylenders and barge operators.

Among all other countries in the Nanyang, Thailand has been most successful in assimilating the approximately 3.5 million Chinese. Given favourable political and social conditions, assimilation normally takes place within two to three generations. This is what happened in Thailand and this fast pace could be attributed to the open access Chinese has to Thai education and the rewards that come for those who assume Thai culture and identity.

The absence of a colonial ruler in Thailand makes the upward climb of the Chinese with the ruling class a real possibility. The considerable degree of affinity between the Chinese and Thai cultures – sharing the Buddhist religion, for example – also renders assimilation more palatable to the Chinese.

It was not uncommon, therefore, for the grandsons of Chinese immigrants to sever ties with China, adopt Thai names, marry Thai women and conform to Thai norms and culture. Chinese businessmen often enter into partnership with prominent Thais. Communication between the partners is not a problem as the Chinese invariably speak good Thai.

MALAYSIA

The Chinese began entering the Malay peninsula in large numbers from the middle of the nineteenth century. Very similar to the situation in Singapore, the Chinese came to partake of the increasing opportunities under the British. They followed the British flag not only into the Malay peninsula but into Sarawak in 1841 and North Borneo in 1881.

Recruited directly by contractors or coming on their own, the hordes of Chinese coolies worked in the tin mines and rubber estates of the Malay peninsula. Some settled into market-gardening while others who could, entered into small rubber production, industries and retail shops. Their success in the retail trade is everywhere evident in Malaysian towns, where one can see long rows of Chinese shops.

Like the Chinese in Thailand and Singapore, the principal Chinese success is in trading. The spur to their role as middlemen came after the arrival of the British in Penang from 1785 to 1786, and the opening up of Province Wellesley (1800), Singapore (1819), and Malacca (1825). Many Chinese in Malaya became rich towkays, their firms rivalling the big western companies in volume of business and profit. These towkays were able to set themselves up in big bungalow houses, have many wives and mistresses and send their children to the best English schools.

For every success story, there are scores of failures. Indeed there were many Chinese who could not save enough to return home as wealthy men. A famous saying of Fujian province puts it this way: 'Of every ten who go abroad, three die, six stay and one returns.' Whether apocryphal or not, it is nevertheless true that the majority of the Chinese immigrants were ordinary workmen who had to slave hard to keep their families from starvation.

In Malaysia, the Chinese number 4.4 million or 32 per cent of the population. The problem of assimilation is therefore more intractable as historically, the majority of the Chinese marry their own women, send their children to Chinese language schools and organize themselves in their own traditional associations.

Even then, the Chinese are not impervious to indigenous cultural influences. A distinct group, the Babas have adopted many Malay customs and manners. They are generally the descendants of Chinese men who married Malay women though technically anyone who adopts the Baba way of life and considers himself or herself a Baba should be considered as one by others.

Baba or nonya cooking makes use of Chinese ingredients as well as Malay condiments and spices. Their language and dressing is also different. They speak a form of *patois* Malay with many words borrowed from Hokkien. Their dressing is principally the *sarung* (a wrap-around long skirt) and the *kebaya* (a long-sleeved blouse), both of Malay origin.

The majority of the Chinese, however, keep apart from the Malays, though recent years have seen a marked change. The government has 'nationalized' Chinese schools to provide a more locally-oriented curriculum. Malay is the national language and the medium of instruction.in most schools and universities.

In recent years, the government has also discouraged the formation of new Chinese associations, preferring to encourage the growth of Malay or mixed voluntary associations. The official policy is to favour a situation in which the Chinese would not congregate in their own numerous associations as these serve to perpetuate their own distinctive culture and community at the expense of national unity and a truly Malaysian society.

Today most young Chinese in Malaysia can speak Malay. However it is not as easy for the Chinese to join the national culture as it is for the Thai. To marry a Malay woman requires conversion to Islam. Even then, such converts are often viewed with suspicion by both ethnic groups as having 'ulterior motives'.

INDONESIA

In contrast to Malaya which came under British control, Indonesia fell under the Dutch sphere of influence. In the first thirty years of the seventeenth century, they established their key controls in the Moluccas, Java and Sumatra. The Dutch encouraged the Chinese to settle in the environs of Batavia to grow and process sugar and other crops. Their descendants stayed on, despite the laws which have since been repealed which required the Chinese to live only in the urban areas.

Most of the Chinese in Indonesia today who are living in the cities are principally those who migrated later in the nineteenth century. This later wave of immigration was encouraged by the opening up of Java and Sumatra by the Dutch when they colonized the East Indies.

Like their fellow Chinese in other Nanyang cities, the Chinese have been very successful economically. They dominated the small businesses like factories and retail shops. Not a few were wealthy individuals, like Oei Tiong Ham, who took advantage of new opportunities in export of smallholder products and inter-island trade. These businesses were not only owned by the Chinese but employed Chinese workers as well. It is estimated that out of Java's 508 rice mills, about 400 were owned by Indonesian citizens of Chinese descent in 1954.

Compared to Thailand and Malaysia, the history of the Chinese emigration and settlement in Indonesia was a turbulent one. Forming only 3.5 per cent of the population or about 3.5 million Chinese, they went through long periods of discrimination and violence.

The Chinese in Indonesia could be divided into two categories – the Peranakan and the Totok. The Peranakan have a long history of settlement and like the Babas in Malaysia, have adopted many features of Indonesian culture. They are likely to be of Chinese-Indonesian descent. Totok, on the other hand, still cling on to their Chinese culture, speaking Chinese, wearing Chinese or western clothing and eating traditional Chinese food. They also generally mix with members of their own community and avoid intermarriage with the local people.

The Baperki, a conservative body for Indonesian citizenship, is the leading organization representing Indonesian citizens, mostly of Chinese descent. Its emphasis on educational and cultural activities marked it as an 'exclusive' Chinese organization. Moreover, its friendly relations with the PKI (the Indonesian Communist Party) tainted the Baperki as a left-wing organization.

In October 1965, the attempted coup by the PKI brought a backlash that resulted in the eclipse of the Baperki. The Baperki's Res Peblica University was burned down, most of its branches were forcibly closed and many of its leaders jailed or killed.

The years that followed were dangerous ones for the ordinary Chinese. Their property was looted and burned and persons of Chinese descent attacked. All Chinese schools were closed, and the Chinese banned from living in certain areas. Indonesian citizenship of persons of Chinese origin were reviewed and applications for naturalization were stopped. The call went out for the closure of all exclusive Chinese organizations like the traditional associations. Even the Chinese Embassy was not spared – it was attacked and the diplomats' quarters searched and plundered.

Conditions improved somewhat for the Chinese after 1968. A Cabinet decree enabled the Chinese to change their names to Indonesian-sounding ones more easily. It was estimated that nearly a quarter million Chinese changed their names to enable them to move more freely in Indonesian society. Today the political climate is more temperate but the pressure is definitely on the Chinese to assimilate as fast as they can into Indonesian society.

SINGAPORE

Singapore is the hub of overseas Chinese commerce in the Nanyang – it is the most important entrepôt port for the handling, storing, sorting, processing and financing of raw materials such as rubber, tin, tobacco, rice, copra and pepper. Hundreds of thousands of Chinese descended on this thriving seaport, so that today it has the largest overseas Chinese community outside of China and Taiwan.

The migration of Chinese to Singapore, as well as to other parts of Southeast Asia, has a long history. The Chinese settled in the Nanyang long before the British established themselves in Singapore. By the fourteenth century, Chinese merchants had traded southward from Guangzhou and other South China ports, particularly along the coast of Vietnam, on the routes that had been opened before by the Indians, the Persians and the Arabs. A system of state trading with the Nanyang was established through the famous voyages of Admiral Cheng-ho between 1405 and 1433. By the seventeenth century, substantial numbers of Chinese traders and farmers were resident throughout the region; in fact a few were already living on Singapore island when the British established their trading post. An authoritative source mentioned that there were about thirty Chinese planters of gambier, together with 120 Malay fishermen, on this tiny island even before Sir Stamford Raffles arrived.

The first immigrants to Singapore were chiefly Malays and Chinese from Malacca or Rhio, who were attracted by the excitement and greater opportunities of the British free port. The majority, however, originated from the overburdened peasant communities of South China. Raffles himself claimed that within four months of its founding, Singapore had 'received an accession of population exceeding 5,000 – principally Chinese, and their number is daily increasing.' A more guarded estimate indicated that of a total population of 10,683 in 1823, the Chinese immigrants constituted 3,317 or 31 per cent.

Estimates of population continued to vary considerably throughout the first half century of the city's existence, but the available data indicate that during the first twenty-one years the number of inhabitants had increased to approximately 35,000 of which one-half were of Chinese birth or origin and slightly less than one-tenth were immigrants from India. It is difficult to estimate at which stage the Chinese began to predominate numerically. One source has it that the Chinese formed a majority of the city's population of nearly 53,000 by 1849. In 1901, they were nearly three-quarters of the population, a proportion they maintain to this day.

During the first fifty years of Singapore's existence, the immigrants from overseas were largely ordinary workmen engaged in the trading activities of the port. Others were mainly labourers on the agricultural enterprises on the island or nearby Johore, while a sizeable number were able to establish themselves as independent tradesmen. The discovery of large deposits of tin and the industrial uses of rubber, from the last quarter of the nineteenth century onwards, together with the tremendous expansion of the world market for these two commodities, encouraged both European and Chinese entrepreneurs to undertake vast mining and plantation enterprises in Malaya. This in turn attracted a large number of immigrants seeking jobs and economic security. Singapore became one of the major ports through which the flow of indentured labour from China or India was distributed to these operations in Malaya and other parts of Southeast Asia, and to which many returned after they had completed their terms of contract.

Characteristics of Chinese Society in Singapore

The fluidity of the Chinese population can be attested to by the phenomenal increase in population over the years, in particular from 1823 to 1891. Such an increase was due to the emigration and the comings and goings of a largely transient population.

A boom of arrivals from China was experienced in the years immediately before the First World War when 200,000 Chinese arrived in 1910 and another 270,000 in 1911. After falling off sharply during the war, gross immigration from China peaked again from 1926 to 1927. After these years, the decline in raw material prices on the world market led to a reduced demand for coolie labour. The Depression, followed by the Sino-Japanese war and the Second World War disrupted the coolie trade which, fortunately, was never to peak again. The next wave of immigrants was in the years before 1949, but these were mainly white collar workers, bureaucrats and literati fleeing from the Chinese communists.

The highly imbalanced sex ratio meant that there were very few independent Chinese households. It reached its lowest point in 1827, when there were 5,847 males to only 363 females, or about one woman to every sixteen men. In addition, unlike the Chinese in Malacca, who had a long history of settlement and intermarriage with the local Malays, Chinese immigrants tended to keep close together in their own community. There were thus few chances for inter-ethnic contacts and few inter-ethnic marriages. Even marriages into the Straits-born Chinese (or Baba) society in Singapore were few.

Fortunately, the British authorities were interested in encouraging females to emigrate to the Straits Settlements. It was felt that women would exercise a calming influence on the male population, and, with their families around them, the Chinese in the Straits Settlements would settle permanently in the country. This helped pave the way for the Convention of Peking in 1866 in which the Qing government allowed women to emigrate from China, but only as wives and dependents of male emigrants. And with the establishment of the Chinese Protectorate in 1877 there was an increase in immigration of females from the respectable classes. It also prevented many of the abuses – like prostitution and servitude as bondmaids – to which female immigrants to the colony were previously subjected. In the meantime more and more rich and successful Chinese were bringing their families out as they began to have vested interests in the colony. Available statistics indicate that in 1878, 1,327 women immigrants landed and stayed on permanently. In 1888, 3,164 arrived, and by 1898 the figure had risen to 6,192.

In 1930, the British implemented the Immigration Restriction Ordinance which limited the number of male immigrants while allowing for unrestricted women immigrants to land in Singapore. Its aims were to achieve a better sex ratio and to recreate a more stable population. In these, the Ordinance was largely successful; the number of immigrants fell, and the sex ratio was corrected. It was estimated that about 200,000 women migrated to Singapore and Malaya from 1934 to 1938.

In addition to the unsettled nature of nineteenth-century Chinese society in Singapore, another significant characteristic was the divisive and fragmentary nature of the Chinese community. From various parts of the south-eastern provinces of China came Hokkiens, Teochews, Cantonese, Hainanese, Hakkas, and other dialect groups – with their own distinctive tongues and temperaments. Each dialect group had its own customs and mores, and was organized into a different occupational and class hierarchy.

Speech was the main barrier keeping the various dialect groups apart. Teochew is very close to the southern Fujian dialect (Hokkien). A Hokkien and a Teochew individual would be able to understand more than half of each other's dialects, conversing slowly. However, among the Hainanese, Hakkas and Cantonese, and between them and the other dialect groups, the possibility of being understood was much lower. They might as well have been speaking in different languages.

In customs and religious matters, the dialect groups also exhibited some differences. The Hainanese, for example, had their own tradi-

Chinese Dialect Population in Singapore, 1881

GROUP	MALE	FEMALE	TOTAL	PERCENTAGE
Hokkien	23,327	1,654	24,981	28.8
Teochew	20,946	1,698	22,644	26.1
Cantonese	9,699	5,154	14,853	17.1
Hainanese	8,266	53	8,319	9.6
Hakka	5,561	609	6,170	7.1
Foochow and Others	259	13	272	0.3
Straits* Chinese	4,513	5,014	9,527	11.0
Total	72,571	14,195	86,766	100.0

* denotes those Chinese born in the Straits Settlements, otherwise known as 'Babas'.

Source: M. Freedman, Immigrants and Associations: Chinese in Nineteenth Century Singapore. In G. W. Skinner (ed.), *The Study of Chinese Society: Essays of M. Freedman*, California, Stanford University Press, 1979.

tional theatrical shows and as a seafaring people, worshipped the Goddess Tian Hou Sheng Mu or Matsu (Taoist Queen of Heaven). The popular Hokkien gods were Guan Gong (God of War and God of Justice) and Da Bo Gong or Tua Pek Kong (the Household God of the Earth). Other than the Hokkiens, the dialect groups do not observe the ninth day of the first moon, as the principal Chinese New Year Day. Legend has it that many centuries ago, the Hokkiens were forced to go into hiding in the sugar-cane plantations and were able to come out from hiding on that day, which was henceforth celebrated as the dawn of the Chinese New Year. To this day, sugar-cane stems are symbols of reverence and good fortune to the Hokkiens.

Among nineteenth-century Singapore Chinese, occupational specialization tended to follow dialect-based divisions. In 1822, Raffles implied in a letter to European officials on the island that the more respectable traders were found among the Hokkiens. In 1876, Pickering, the knowledgeable British official who became the first Protector of the Chinese, wrote that the miners and artisans in the Straits Settlements were mainly Cantonese and Hakkas, while the agriculturists, boatmen and small shopkeepers were Teochews and Hokkiens. Another British observer noted the strong preponderance of Cantonese in the crafts, of Hokkiens among the most wealthy merchants, and of Teochews in gambier and pepper agriculture. The Hainanese, as latecomers, tended to have limited economic opportunities and were found at the lower end of the economic ladder as domestic servants, seamen and shop assistants.

Unlike the social structure in China, the Chinese community in Singapore was not clearly stratified. There were two rough divisions of *Shang* (merchants, traders, planters and tin-miners) and *Gong* (artisans, craftsmen, shop-assistants, clerks, school teachers, tin-mining workers, gardeners and employees in plantations).

According to scholars this division was a result of several factors. Firstly, the growth of the Chinese population in Singapore and Malaya was not entirely spontaneous, but was mainly created by the British administrators to meet the demands of rapid economic development. Secondly, the structure was largely determined by the nature of Chinese immigration – the early settlers being merchants and political refugees, whilst those coming later were poverty-stricken peasants. Members of the scholar-gentry in China did not migrate to Singapore and Malaya. In short, Singapore was a society that lacked a class of literati, unlike the richer agricultural areas of south-eastern China and urban centres where the great clans clustered.

What was most distinctive about the social hierarchy was that from the beginning wealth was the chief measurement of status. This was contrary to the traditional Chinese social order, which had lasted for at least twelve centuries in China, in which literary qualifications based on the Imperial examination system were the criteria for status.

The key reason for this phenomenon was that when the Chinese migrated overseas, they moved into the commercial and business sectors in which such Chinese institutions, like the traditional examination system, had little or no bearing. Little attention was paid to education in the early years, the Chinese being interested in quick monetary returns in commercial pursuits. In addition, except for a small number of Babas (Straits Chinese), who were Straits-born and English-educated and whose occupations were concentrated in clerical and administrative work, the main Chinese population was barred by the British from entering the British government service. Therefore, channels for upward mobility were available to the Chinese only in commercial undertakings.

The various occupational and class differences tended to exacerbate existing divisions based on dialect, social customs and mores. These differences were further accentuated by the traditional voluntary associations, which were the institutionalized means by which cooperation outside the family sphere was established. Overt conflicts between dialect groups occasionally broke out. In 1854, a ten-day riot killed some six hundred people. Vaughan, a noted British observer, asserted that it was a fight between natives of Fujian and Guangdong provinces and had nothing to do with the secret societies. In 1889, there was also another serious clash between the Hakkas and the Teochews in Singapore's Chinatown.

If there were few contacts between members of different dialect groups, there were even fewer relations with members of different ethnic groups, like the Malays and the Indians. These ethnic groups were similarly organized in distinct residential and cultural communities.

The British colonialists made no attempt to close the cultural gap between the ethnic groups. On the contrary, its divide-and-rule policy often had the opposite effect of causing further division and a feeling of separateness. One of the more pernicious legacies of British colonialism in Singapore was the development of a multi-racial society comprising the indigenous Malays, Chinese and Indians who often regarded one another with suspicion and distrust.

Historical Development after the War

The collapse of British colonialism in Singapore and Malaya began with their invasion and capture by the Japanese in the Second World War. At a stroke, the myth of British invincibility was shattered. Many politically conscious locals were convinced that the old colonial order could not be re-established. Fortunately the aspirations of the independence movement after the war were met by the post-war British policy which advocated the gradual transfer of power into local hands.

The indigenous movement for independence was a tumultuous one. Political parties of all ideological shades arose to compete for power. The political life of Singapore in the 1950s was dominated by numerous riots and industrial unrest in the struggle for self-governance. Chinese students and workers were then extremely receptive to communist influence. To a great extent this stemmed from the impressive success of the Chinese communist revolution and the rise of China as a major world power. Suddenly the old tradition-bound socio-political system in China was discredited by a new ideology. A new activism took the Chinese students into the streets. Their grievances against the prevailing colonial system were further augmented by their feelings that the Chinese-educated and China-born were politically and socially ostracized by the British colonialists.

The anti-colonial student-worker movement was, according to the Prime Minister Lee Kuan Yew, 'a world teeming with vitality, dynamicism and revolutions.' It was inevitable that any party which wanted to carry the Chinese-speaking votes could not afford to be anti-communist. The PAP was far-sighted enough to harness the groundswell of the student-worker movement. Originally led by Lim Chin Siong and Fong Swee Suan, two of the fourteen leaders who inaugurated the PAP in November 1954, the PAP-controlled student-labour movement unleashed a wave of strikes to discredit the ruling LF-Alliance government and to hasten the process of self-government.

The PAP eventually captured power in the 1959 election. However, the communists' hope that the PAP rule would bring about a more liberal constitution, which would facilitate communist subversion and eventual takeover of the island, was shattered when over a hundred leading left-wing politicians and trade unionists including Lim and Fong were arrested just prior to the 1963 election. Earlier on, continued differences between the left wing and the moderates had led to the split in the PAP. In 1961 a new party, the Barisan Sosialis with Lim Chin Siong as Secretary-General, was formed. After the arrest of the prominent left-wingers in 1963, the Barisan was left leaderless, and henceforth with relentless government supervision and periodic arrests the Barisan floundered and began a slow decline to its present almost defunct status.

The ruling People's Action Party's first term of office from 1959 to 1963 was marked by a turbulent movement towards merger with the Federation of Malaya and rapid social and economic progress, especially in public housing. The government fought for Malaysia (the merger with Malaya) so that Singapore could free itself entirely from the remnant shackles of colonialism. Another reason was the close historical, cultural and geographical ties with Malaya. The merger also offered all the territories involved a chance to develop a common market of some ten million people. When a nation-wide referendum was held, 71 per cent of the electorate voted in favour of merger. And so it was that on 16 September 1963, Singapore became a part of the

Kingdom of Malaysia. Meanwhile, in a snap election called five days later, the PAP won 46.9 per cent of the popular vote, amounting to 37 seats in the 51-member Assembly. The communist faction which had by that time split with the PAP to form the rival Barisan Sosialis managed to win thirteen seats. Lee Kuan Yew remained Prime Minister of the state of Singapore after the merger and Singapore continued to handle its own labour and education. Police matters, finance and communications came under the Federal Government in Kuala Lumpur.

Singapore's merger with the Federation of Malaya was rocky from the very start. The Malayan Communist Party (MCP) denounced Malaysia as a British ploy to preserve their colonial interests and Indonesia proclaimed a policy of confrontation – an economic, social and military offensive against Malaysia. Internally there was a leadership tussle between the PAP and the Malayan Chinese Association (MCA) in Malaysia for the representation of the Chinese in the Alliance, the ruling coalition of three communal parties under the leadership of Tunku Abdul Rahman, the prime minister of Malaysia. There was also a problem because of the PAP's persistent call for a multi-racial Malaysian Malaysia with equal rights for all communal groups, while the dominant United Malays National Organisation (UMNO) felt that Malaysia was for the Malays and should not therefore be governed by a mixture of races.

The uneasy merger had to come to an end. On 9 August 1965 Singapore was separated from Malaysia and became an independent and sovereign nation. A month later, Singapore became the 116th member of the United Nations, and in October 1965, the 22nd member of the British Commonwealth of Nations.

The twenty-one years after independence saw rapid economic growth. There was a marked shift from commerce to manufacturing and recently to high-technology industries with high value-added advantage. The standard of living of the people have been raised with the provision of low-cost housing and the encouragement of foreign investments. Wages have gone up, there was full employment for many years until recently, and its political stability is the envy of many developing Third World countries.

Singapore society has undergone a radical restructuring. From a historical perspective, Singapore first started as a migrant society. The bachelor society was transformed into stable families with the arrival of single women, wives and children. After one or two generations, the family began to build up its own kinship network locally. With the implementation of the family planning programmes, and the general effect of modernization, future families will tend towards the two-children norm.

In time to come the aged (those 60 years and above) will form 10 per cent of the population in 2000. However, presently, it is a young, youthful society with 39.9 per cent of its population under twenty years of age.

The Chinese. Identity

From about 1970 English has been progressively emphasized as the main language in Singapore. As English becomes the language of greatest economic value and job opportunities, the enrolment in English-medium schools increased while those in Chinese and the other streams declined. In 1975, 69.4 per cent of the primary and secondary students were enrolled in English-stream schools compared to 28.2 per cent in Chinese-stream schools. In 1981, the enrolment in English-stream schools had increased to 84.7 per cent while the Chinese-stream school enrolment had declined to only 15 per cent.

The declining enrolment in Chinese schools, plus the difficulty of competing with the English-educated on an equal footing for jobs and remuneration, became the primary basis for the government's decision to close down the Chinese-medium Nanyang University in 1980.

Round about the same time, the government showed a renewed interest in the Chinese language and in instilling traditional Chinese values in Singapore society. From 1979, overseas Confucian scholars visited Singapore to give public lectures and workshops. Books were published and work started on a new curriculum to prepare for the introduction of Confucianism as an optional subject in schools under the compulsory religious knowledge programme. Confucianism, Buddhist studies and other forms of 'religious' knowledge are seen as a foil to protect impressionistic young minds from the more pernicious aspects of western culture, materialistic values and a 'hippie' lifestyle.

A 'Speak Mandarin' campaign was launched in 1979. As the majority of Singaporeans are Chinese, the government felt that there was a need to be unified by a common spoken language, Mandarin, rather than the divisive dialects. In tandem with the Mandarin campaign is the Hanyu Pinyin system (a standardized phonetic tool to romanize Chinese characters) for the spelling of Chinese names.

There were also fears that the family, the traditional bastion of Confucian values, was breaking down in Singapore society. Government officials pointed frequently to the breakdown of the Asian extended family and the predominance of the small nuclear family of parents and children living in HDB flats. The kinship linkages with older parents would weaken or disappear, the argument goes. In the process, grandchildren will miss out on the transmission of well-tried values of the past. This, coupled with the 'two-is-enough' phenomenon, could mean overprotected and self-centred children used to having their own way. By the early 1990s, one would expect the first generation of these children to come into maturity, and the consequences to society of a self-centred and individualistic generation could only be conjectured.

In many ways the fears of a society becoming unglued from traditional Chinese values are oversimplified. The doomsayers tend to ignore or gloss over the adaptability of family forms, the persistence of Asian values and the strength of emotional bonds between close relatives.

Many studies including those by the Ministry of Social Affairs (1983), Report of the Committee on the Problems of the Aged (1984) and Eddie Kuo and Aline Wong's book on the contemporary family of Singapore (1979) will testify to the high frequency of visits to parents, who played an important linkage role between siblings and other relatives. The majority of the elderly receive financial and other material support from the immediate family members and other relatives. Singapore couples tended to linger as part members of one or another parental household. The parents, in turn, help children when there is an illness in the family, provide child care and gifts, and, to a lesser extent, give advice about child-rearing and major family decisions.

The family will probably never degenerate to an isolated unit cut off from all close kinship ties. Relationship with parents and close relatives would remain strong enough though the same cannot be said of relatives further removed. Conscious government policies like the multi-tier family scheme and joint balloting for flats scheme will also shore up the weakening foundation by getting parents and children to live together or near one another.

The fears expressed over a more individualistic generation coming of age is probably justified, though individualism does not necessarily connote selfishness or an uncaring attitude. In Singapore this individualism has manifested itself in preferences among certain young Singaporeans for single status, flatting out and career fulfilment. Such preferences, however, do not mean cutting off all commitment to parents, children or the wider community. What it does mean is that there will be a greater degree of personal selectivity in terms of persons, organizations, or causes one would espouse or commit oneself to.

The teaching of Confucianism and different ethical-religious systems in schools can perhaps slow the growth of individualism though the change of lifestyle as a result of affluence and western education and values cannot be arrested. On a more positive note, however, recent years have seen an increased awareness of our cultural past among Singaporeans. There are widespread sentiments to preserve the old, whether these are buildings, monuments or values.

The opening up of China has kindled interest not only among businessmen but also ordinary people. During the last five to six years, many old and young people have been returning to their respective villages and ancestral homes in China. The renewal of ties with the mainland, no matter how tenuous, and the newfound interest in China's cultural past and values, will probably ensure in the years to come, a consciousness of Chinese roots among our young in Singapore.

Singapore Pioneers

The lives of Tan Kah Kee and his son-in-law Lee Kong Chian, spanned the major economic transformation and political events of Singapore from the late nineteenth century to the modern era.

Tan Kah Kee was born in Jimei village in Dongan district of Fujian province in 1874. His father was a well-known merchant in Singapore's Hokkien community. In 1890, after receiving some education, Tan made his first trip to Singapore to join his father's rice business at the age of seventeen. In 1893 he returned to Fujian to get married, and upon his return he diversified his father's failing rice business to the more lucrative pineapple and rubber trade.

By the end of 1900 his firm of Jit Sin had secured about 70 per cent of the export trade in pineapple packing and his 'Sultan' brand of preserved pineapple was in great demand.

Using his keen business acumen, he was quick to see the good trade prospect in the industrial use of rubber. He was one of the pioneers in the cultivation of rubber in Singapore and Johore. The firm of Tan Kah Kee and Company owned the largest factory for cleaning and treating rubber and later for the manufacture of rubber goods.

His interests in business were matched only by his devotion to China. During the revolutionary period in Singapore history, he became a mentor of the T'ung Meng-hui (TMH), Sun Yat-sen's political party first formed in Japan in 1905. Using this party, he supported the nationalist cause against the ruling Qing regime in China.

Although Tan's contributions to the Chinese nationalist cause were notable during the 1920s and 1930s, it was during the Sino-

Japanese war that he emerged as the most outstanding leader of the Nanyang Chinese. His closest rival was Aw Boon Haw and their dislike for one another was legendary in the Chinese community in Singapore.

This dislike stemmed from a mixture of business rivalry, challenges for leadership of the National Salvation Movement (the campaign for overseas Chinese support against imperialist Japan) in Singapore and the fact that both belonged to different groups. Tan was Hokkien, while Aw was a Hakka. Though Tan was undoubtedly the best-known overseas Chinese leader, Aw was very famous in his own right. Known as the Tiger Balm King because his companies manufactured and sold Tiger Balm ointment, he owned newspapers (including the *Sin Chew Jit Poh*) in Singapore and Hong Kong and was very generous and active in his personal fund-raising drive.

Tan was at the time president of the Hokkien Huay Kuan, the biggest Chinese association in Singapore and an executive committee member of the Chinese Chamber of Commerce (SCCC). Through these organizations, he was pivotal in organizing the overseas Chinese National Salvation Movement during the 1937–41 period. His headquarters was at the Ee Hoe Hean (Joy and Memory Club) which he founded in the 1920s. From the very beginning, the Ee Hoe Hean was a centre of nationalistic activities. Many of its past and present members are leading luminaries of the Chinese community, holding high positions in the traditional Chinese associations and the SCCC. It is still in existence and from its location at Bukit Pasoh Road, serves as the leading social and recreational club for Singapore Hokkiens.

Tan maintained polite if distant ties with the colonial authorities in Singapore. In fact, Tan disclosed in his autobiography that he was the colonial appointee to head the Chinese relief organization. At that time, before war actually broke out, the British were ambivalent in their attitude towards the anti-Japanese activists. On the one hand, they were interested in maintaining friendly ties with Japan. On the other hand, they were deeply suspicious of the Japanese especially after the Japanese-German friendship pact of 1936. The British were however willing to accept the co-operation offered by the more responsible anti-Japanese activists like Tan Kah Kee.

As leader of the overseas Chinese, Tan also had the initial backing of the Kuomintang government in China. However, after a tour of 15 provinces (including the communists' base in Yenan) in 1939, he came back disillusioned with the corruption and inefficiency he found in the Chinese government. He then no longer took an active role in the National Salvation Movement. The Kuomintang then switched

A rare photograph showing Singapore's Tan Kah Kee with Chinese leaders in Beijing in 1949. Tan Kah Kee is in the front row, second from right, Mao Tse-tung in the centre, with Chou En-lai, last row, extreme left. Other famous personalities include General Chu Teh, standing to Mao's left, and contemporary writers Mao Dun (front row, extreme right), and Guo Moruo (second row, fourth from right).

their support to Aw and began a concerted effort to discredit Tan as a communist sympathizer.

When war broke out, Tan managed to escape from Singapore. The actual evacuation was carried out on the morning of 3rd February 1942 in a small motor-boat provided by a friend, Tan Kwee-chian, who had a sawmill at Beach Road. Two other friends, Ng Aik-huan and Lau Boh-tan, also helped make arrangements for the escape.

Tan returned to Singapore after the war and openly declared his support for the Chinese Communist Party under Mao Tse-tung. He returned to China in 1949 and subsequently participated in the Central People's Government Council and the Oversea Chinese Affairs Commission. Apart from a brief visit to Singapore in 1950 he stayed the rest of his life in his motherland, and was laid to rest in 1961 at the age of 87.

The life of Lee Kong Chian takes us into Singapore's post-independence era. Kong Chian was born in Nanan in Fujian province and came to Singapore to join his trader father in 1903 at the age of ten. Like Tan Kah Kee, he was a great philanthropist, using his wealth to spread education and help the poor.

He was one of the few businessmen who could speak English. He also studied civil engineering in Shanghai on an imperial Qing government scholarship.

When he returned to Singapore from Shanghai, he was, in turn, a translator for a Chinese newspaper, teacher and surveyor. He then joined rubber tycoon Tan Kah Kee's company and, being a promising young man, the boss was happy to have him marry his eldest daughter, Ai Lay, in 1920.

In 1931, Kong Chian founded his own group of companies. His business expanded from processing rubber to canning pineapples. Lee Pineapple was one of the first manufacturing companies in this part of the world. He also helped to reorganize the Chinese banks in the 1930s and was chairman of the Oversea-Chinese Banking Corporation for many years.

In addition, he was the chairman of a property company, Eastern Realty, long before many businessmen dealt in property.

Kong Chian was a very successful businessman because he was able to see the business potential of new ideas. For many years he was the president and a management committee member of the Chinese Chamber of Commerce. He drew plans for the construction of the present Singapore Chinese Chamber of Commerce Building in Hill Street.

In 1952, he set up Lee Foundation with a capital of $3.5 million, to help schools and charitable organizations. An ardent supporter of education, many schools like Chinese High School, Tao Nan School and Anglo-Chinese School benefited from him. He was the first Chancellor of the former University of Singapore, from 1962 to 1965. He was also one of its principal benefactors.

In recognition of his public service, he was conferred an honorary degree of Doctor of Laws in 1958 by the then University of Malaya in Singapore. Later, in 1965, he also received an honorary degree of Doctor of Letters from the university, whose name had been changed to the University of Singapore.

When he died at the age of 74 after an operation for liver cancer, thousands showed up to pay their last respects, including many prominent and ordinary Singaporeans whose lives he had touched.

5
THE CHINESE IN AMERICA

In 1848, gold was discovered in Californian streams some 35 miles north-east of present-day Sacramento. This news electrified enterprising young men in North America and many parts of the world and triggered off the Gold Rush and the immigration of hundreds of thousands to California. The news quickly reached remote villages of the Sam Yup (Three Districts) area of Guangdong province through couriers sent out by merchants who had 'struck it rich'.

Thousands of Chinese began to flood Portuguese Macao and later to Hong Kong after it was ceded to Britain in 1842, hoping to catch a ship to the Golden Mountain (*Gum Shan* in Cantonese). The method of their coming was barbaric by today's standards. Cramped into sweltering holds in leaky vessels without proper navigation and provisions, many braved the long journey that often lasted 30 to 60 days. Many Chinese came independently on their own savings or through loans from families and relatives. Others came on the labour contract system. Fares were paid for in return for a contract that enforced high interest rates of repayment and brutal working conditions.

We have a first-hand account of an early emigrant, Huie Kin, who was to establish the first Protestian Mission in New York. Reminiscing about the time he set sail for California in 1868, he wrote:

> Finally, the day was set for the ship to sail. We were two full months or more on our way. I do not know what route we took; but it was warm all the time, and we stopped at no intermediate port. When the wind was good and strong, we made much headway. But for days there would be no wind, the sails and ropes would hang lifeless from the masts, and the ship would drift idly on the smooth sea, while the sailors amused themselves by fishing. Occasionally, head winds became so strong as to force us back. Once we thought we were surely lost, for it was whispered around that the officers had lost their bearings. There was plenty of foodstuff on board, but fresh water was scarce and was carefully rationed. Not a drop was allowed to be wasted for washing our faces; and so, when rain came, we eagerly caught the rain water and did our washing.

On a clear, crisp, September morning in 1868, or the seventh year of our Emperor Tung Chih, the mists lifted, and we sighted land for the first time since we left the shores of Kwangtung (Guangdong) over sixty days before. To be actually at the 'Golden Gate' of the land of our dreams! The feeling that welled up in us was indescribable. I wonder whether the ecstasy before the Pearly Gates of the Celestial City above could surpass what we felt at the moment we realized that we had reached our destination. We rolled up our bedding, packed our baskets, straightened our clothes, and waited.

Prior to 1870, most of the Chinese were working as miners in California. In 1850, they numbered about 500 of the 57,787 miners. In 1852, this went up to several thousands and by 1860 to 35,000 Chinese miners, forming the largest non-White minority. They were however still a fraction of the hordes of White Americans, native Indians, Irish, German, Englishmen and blacks that had invaded California. This 35,000 in 1860 represented a mere 0.1 per cent of the total United States population of 31,500,000.

The largest contingent, almost a quarter of a million Chinese, arrived between 1871 and 1880. As in the previous decade, many were recruited by agents of mining and railroad companies, the latter for the development of the trans-Mississippi frontier, especially the Western and the Rocky Mountain States.

At first, the Chinese miners were objects of curiosity. However their skill and diligence soon proved a threat to the other miners. It was said that once a Chinese combed a digging you wouldn't find enough gold left 'to fill the tooth of a bug.' Their obvious difference in colour, their clannishness, and the fact that they did not speak 'proper' English also created resentment and suspicion. As early as 1849, a rampaging group of white miners drove out sixty Chinese working for a British mining company. This uprising spurred more than a half-century of violence against the Chinese.

By 1870, the gold mines of California were worked over and on the decline, especially for the Chinese who were forced to confine their labours to claims already abandoned by Whites. The more hardy Chinese followed new gold discoveries in the Pacific Northwest, the Rocky Mountain States, British Columbia and Alaska. There they encountered widespread hostility based on allegations that they were robbing the states of their mineral wealth and shipping gold to China. Their increasing numbers fuelled fears that the Chinese hordes were swarming over America. Nativist movements sprang up to oppose them so that, as one observer noted, the Chinese miners were 'moving from one mining locality to the next, fleeing from the kicks of one to *ere cutto* of another with no fixed abiding place.' Everywhere they went they were greeted by severe miners' tax and other harassing revenues.

Fortunately during this time, there was a demand for Chinese labour on the railroads. The contribution of Chinese labour to the building of America's railway system has long gone unacknowledged. The first transcontinental line was to link California and Oregon with the industrialized eastern states. In the 1850s it took six months to travel by wagon train from the Missouri River to San Francisco. It was actually faster and cheaper to reach Frisco from Guangzhou in China, which was a 60-day sea voyage. The Chinese set upon this task with great enthusiasm, building 1,800 miles of track through the Sierra Nevada and Rocky Mountains over sage-brush, desert and plains to link it with the shorter eastern line being built by the Irish. The two lines were officially joined at Promontory, north of Ogden in Utah, in 1869. Among the old-timers it was common to attribute the building of the eastern end of the transcontinental railway to 'whisky' (Irishmen) and the western end to 'tea' (Chinese).

This heroic effort was described by one noted transportation engineer as 'without doubt the greatest engineering feat of the nineteenth century.' Most of the work was done with pick and shovel, hammer and crowbar, with baskets for earth slung from shoulder poles and put on one-horse carts. Working in extreme heat and freezing cold, sometimes working on sheet granite buttresses and steep shale embankments without any footholds, it was one of the mightiest feats of Chinese labour, besides the Great Wall.

No one knew how many men gave their lives to this stupendous task. It was rumoured that a few thousand sets of bones were sent back to China and that 'there's an Irishman buried under every tie of railway track.'

Tributes to the Chinese were slow in coming. This particular tribute was from Charles Crocker, who was in charge of construction for the Central Pacific Railway Company. Upon completion of the first transcontinental line, he said: 'I wish to call to your minds that the early completion of this railway we have built has been in large measure due to that poor, despised class of labourers called the Chinese, to the fidelity and industry that they have shown.'

In the next twenty-four years from 1869, four more transcontinental lines were built which together, more than any other factor, helped make the United States a united nation. The railways were to provide the infrastructure of American industrial might in the twentieth century. In all these efforts, as in the building of the smaller lines, the skills of the Chinese as railroad builders were much sought after. In almost every railway team, there were Chinese men. Many years later, in one of the finest epitaphs to Chinese labour, Oswald Garison Villard wrote in the *Christian Century* (1943) :

> [The Chinese] stormed the forest fastness, endured cold and heat and risk of death at hands of hostile Indians to aid in the opening up of our northwestern empire. I have a despatch from the chief engineer of the Northwestern Pacific telling how Chinese labourers went out into eight feet of snow with the temperature far below zero to carry on the work when no American dared face the conditions.

After the first transcontinental line was completed, many took their hard-earned savings and went back to China. Some, like the protagonists in Satyajit Ray's *Apu Trilogy*, ferried themselves on the trains of hope to places further east and south in search of their fortunes. Yet others settled in the towns that had sprung up along the railway line. Most of them however made their way back to California and took what jobs they could find in that state's growing industries.

One of these was in the agriculture industry working as farmers growing cabbages, pumpkins, celery and asparagus, and as pickers of fruits such as grapes and apples. Here Chinese labour was respected for their availability and skill in the tending, harvesting and packing of crops. An alliance of unemployed White workers and small farmers joined forces to prise the Chinese employees of the big growers off the land.

Beginning in Fresno in August 1893, organized mobs attacked Chinese field and factory workers in Compton, Tulare, Visalia and as far north as Ukiah. Terrified Chinese fled from the small rural China-towns to San Francisco or back across the ocean to China. This mass exodus of Chinese from the fields resulted, according to one estimate, in half a million acres of land temporarily going out of production.

The expulsion of the Chinese from the rural fields was repeated elsewhere – in the canneries and fisheries, in mines and in factories all over America. The Chinese had pioneered the Californian fisheries, having first begun to fish in the West Coast waters since 1849. Harsh revenue law was enacted against Chinese fishermen and in 1876 a law that regulated the size of the mesh in shrimp and drag outs, followed by one prohibiting the use of special nets employed by Chinese fisher-men, did much to eliminate the Chinese engaged in that industry.

The Chinese miners, who formed an important part of the miner-al extraction industry, were in many cases forcibly removed. In a particularly noxious incident in 1885, twenty-eight Chinese were mas-sacred and fifteen wounded in the Wyoming coal-mining town of Rock Springs over an argument between a Chinese and a White employee.

By 1940, only fifty-five Chinese remained in the vicinity of Rock Springs, a town that in 1890 had nearly 500 Chinese.

They were systematically thrown out state after state. Imported to work picked-over gold mines in Alaska, they were confronted by angry, demoralized and unemployed White and Indian mine labourers who attacked them with dynamite. One year later they were incarcerated and then expelled from the territory. After 1886 no more Chinese were employed in Alaskan mines. In the same year, Tacoma expelled their entire Chinese population, Seattle having expelled theirs one year earlier.

Labour's campaign against Chinese workers in the industrialized cities forced many Chinese out of their jobs where they were employed in making bags, brooms, soaps, bottles and other products. Many unemployed Chinese began to drift to the bigger Chinatowns like those in San Francisco and New York to become part of the isolated, overworked and underpaid labour forces.

The dispersion of the Chinese towards the north-eastern, north-central and the southern regions was coming to an end. Because of the hostility against Chinese workers, more and more of them were concentrated in the bigger cities. By 1920, 66 per cent of the Chinese were in cities of over 25,000 inhabitants, with an even greater concentration in cities with over 100,000 inhabitants, such as San Francisco, Los Angeles, Philadelphia, Boston, Chicago and New York. Here in the large cities, inhabited by various ethnic and racial groups, the Chinese were more readily accepted.

The nature of their occupations reflected this urban trend. Systematically excluded by state and federal laws and the concerted efforts of labour unions from participation in mining, agriculture, manufacturing, civil service, teaching, medicine and others, the Chinese managed to find a 'soft spot' or two in the country's labour force. Two of these 'soft spots' are in the laundry and restaurant businesses. Rose Hum Lee, a Chinese American sociologist, found that of the 669 business enterprises operated by the Chinese in Chicago in 1950, 430 were laundries, 167 were restaurants and 72 were groceries and general merchandising stores. Many of these businesses were probably financed by monies from the *hui*.

Laundry work developed out of the early Chinese immigrant performance of essentially domestic duties like washing, ironing and cooking in the frontier lands. As the Chinese were closed out of trade after trade they naturally drifted to the urban centres where laundry and restaurants provided alternative economic options. Laundries did not need much capital to operate; only a small outlay was necessary to go into business as it was labour-intensive. All that was needed was a scrub board, iron, ironing board and some soap, and a laundry business was launched. The advent of the steam laundry and the automatic washing machines in the 1960s, however, spelt the end of the independent hand-operated laundry business.

Though opening up a restaurant in terms of capital investment is much more substantial, there is greater business stability. What is needed is not just good location, but most important of all, good food to titillate the palates of a jaded eating public. Working on a restaurant is more lucrative and creative than ironing shirts day after day. It is also a less lonely business as there is invariably someone to talk to compared to laundry work, some of which are one-man operations in side alleys off the main thoroughfare.

Other Chinese opened and operated tailor shops, truck-farm produce stores, curio shops and other tourist-attracting enterprises. Most found employment within Chinese owned and operated establishments especially in the restaurants and garment factories. A few worked as domestics in wealthier homes, a carry-over from the days when they performed 'women work' in the lumbering and mining camps of the north-west frontier. These were occupations either disdained or avoided by the White Americans. To this day, many first- and second-generation immigrants are still confined to these occupations in America.

ANTI-CHINESE LEGISLATION

Between 1840 and 1870, 40 million emigrants of all nationalities flooded into the United States which in turn caused industrial and social problems in the major entry cities like New York and Boston. Elsewhere wages were on the decline as unscrupulous employers used immigrant labourers as strike breakers and as cheap sources of labour.

The public outcry for the restriction of immigration was picked up by politicians, for extra votes. In 1882, the Exclusion Act was the first federal attempt to limit immigration by nationality. The Chinese were selected as the main target even though the percentage of the Chinese arriving in America was very small compared to other nationalities from the European countries.

The Exclusion Act specifically prohibited the entrance of Chinese labourers on the premise that free immigration from China led to the creation of a race problem. It provided that no skilled or unskilled Chinese labourer or miner could enter the United States for ten years, but it exempted certified merchants, students and itinerants from this prohibition. A special provision of the Chinese Exclusion Act stipulated that 'no state court shall admit Chinese to citizenship.' The original provisions of the Act were later extended to 1902, after the expiry period. This meant that, in practice, the enforcement of the provisions led to the permanent exclusion of Chinese labour.

The legal exemption of those not classified to enter encouraged would-be-immigrants to assume one of these privileged identities in order to enter the United States. Hundreds of Chinese were held in detention at any one time on the infamous Angel Island in San Francisco Bay, where they were subjected to long and harsh examinations and interrogations. In the end only about one in four immigrants were allowed to land. Some immigrants actually languished on Angel Island as long as two years before their cases were settled. To this day, poems embroider the barrack walls, lyrical testimonies to the longings and sufferings of the incarcerated Chinese.

With the passing of the Exclusion Act, the composition of the Chinese immigrants changed. From then on until the repeal of the Act only merchants, students and visitors were allowed into the United States. In spite of this, the appellation of Chinese as coolies and laundrymen persists to this day.

In 1924, the Immigration Act further tightened the definition of student, limiting it only to those pursuing Masters degrees, so that it became even more difficult for Chinese males to enter under this category. Previously Chinese males could enter the United States to study English as long as their financial or personal conditions permitted.

In 1921 another law was enacted specifying that an alien-born woman marrying a citizen could no longer automatically assume his citizenship. This meant that a common practice for American males of Chinese descent to marry mates in China, and then effect their admission to the United States, was no longer feasible. These alien-born women could no longer enter to join their husbands even though their minor children could gain admission.

In the early days, the vast majority of Chinese in America were here without their families. The sex ratio was very uneven, numbering hundreds of males to one female. Even as late as 1890, it was dozens of males to one female. This phenomenon was in no small way attributed to the effect of the Act which curtailed the immigration of women, thereby impeding the formation of natural family units.

The implementation of the Exclusion Act drastically cut down Chinese immigration.

CHINESE ARRIVING AND RECORDED IN THE UNITED STATES
BY DECADES, FROM 1820 TO 1957

Year	Total Admitted	Total Recorded	Per cent Increase or Decrease
1820 to 1830	3	—	—
1831 to 1840	8	—	—
1841 to 1850	35	758	—
1851 to 1860	61,397	34,933	—
1861 to 1870	64,301	63,199	80.9
1871 to 1880	123,201	105,465	66.9
1881 to 1890	61,711	107,488	1.9
1891 to 1900	14,799	88,869	− 16.4
1901 to 1910	20,605	71,531	− 20.4
1911 to 1920	21,907	61,639	− 13.8
1921 to 1930	29,907	74,594	21.6
1931 to 1940	4,928	77,504	3.4
1941 to 1950	8,947	117,140	51.8
1951 to 1957	9,110	135,000	13.2
Total	441,727		

Source: Rose Hum Lee, *The Chinese in the United States*.
Hong Kong: Hong Kong University Press, 1960.

Between 1881 and 1890 admission to the United States was halved, compared to the previous decade. The total number of Chinese recorded (i.e. those in the United States), actually shows a decrease from 1890, which was not to pick up until the 1920s.

The enforcement of the Exclusion Act also caught some 30,000 sojourners visiting China, whose return was denied because of their status as labourers. They were not part of the ten exempted classes.

Anti-Chinese agitation did not cease with the passing of the Exclusion Act. In fact it made matters worse for the Chinese because the Act and the passage of subsequent discriminatory laws gave a stamp of congressional approval to anti-Chinese violence. The massacre of the Chinese miners in Rock Springs was an example of the inflammatory repercussions of the Exclusion Act.

The exclusion of Chinese labourers after 1882 also meant that the existing labour force would age without the possibility of replacement by young workers. At least one industry, the cannery industry of the north-west, declined after 1900 because of the aging of the Chinese labourers. Many of them retired to the urban Chinatowns, which also physically decayed and festered during the exclusion years. There were many old labourers living alone in dilapidated tenements. Independent family units were few, and it was rare to find young men and women. It was not until the movement started for the 1943 repeal of the Exclusion Act that the slow process of rejuvenation began for Chinatown and the Chinese.

The repeal of the Exclusion Act came about through the vicissitudes of history. The 1930s and 1940s were the years of the Sino-Japanese War, Pearl Harbour and the emergence of the Chinese as America's heroic allies. As violently as the Chinese had been maligned in the past, they were now glorified and mounted on pedestals.

A new class of villains took over from the Chinese; these were the Japanese, the more unfortunate of whom were incarcerated in America's prison camp during the war.

In the 1943 repeal, a quota of 105 was established for 'persons of Chinese ancestry'. 1946 saw new laws passed for the first time which gave the Chinese the right to become naturalized citizens. The same act provided for the admission of alien wives of citizens on a non-quota basis, while the alien wives and alien children of resident aliens were given preferential treatment within the quota limitations.

In 1948 and 1949 other Acts were passed allowing for the entry of husbands of United States citizens and war brides of approximately 6,000 Chinese women. Taken together these acts and amendments resolved the question of legal inequality, although to this day, prejudices and acts of racial discrimination still remain.

STEREOTYPES OF THE CHINESE

It is one of the ironies of history that the presence of so few Chinese (about 107,000 persons of Chinese ancestry during the 1880s), brought about such a national and local furore in America. This could be partially explained by the fact that the Chinese became convenient scapegoats during the times of unrest and unemployment, attendant upon the reconstruction period following the Civil War. Much of this discrimination however has to do with the notion of racial inferiority imputed to the Chinese.

In the eighteenth and nineteenth centuries, the western nations were in the ascendancy and carried with them assumptions of racial superiority wherever they went. Whether they went to China to make money or to save souls, a great many of the western White men were convicted of the superiority of their own race, religion and civilization over the puny, ignorant and heathen people with whom they came into contact.

The Chinese were rumoured to be overrunning the United States even though in actuality numbers were too few to pose a threat. Because of this fear and their imputed inferior status, they had to be kept out of America at all costs. The Chinese were felt as 'bringing filth, vice and disease', and that 'every incoming coolie means . . . so much more vice and immorality injected into our [America's] social life.'

In a speech before the Joint Congressional Committee to investigate Chinese immigration in 1876, a witness described the Chinese in the following terms: '[The Chinese] are inferior to any race god ever made. There are none so low. I believe that the Chinese have no souls, and if they have, they are not worth the saving.'

One Chinese student compiled for various periodicals and newspapers, the stereotypes held by the Americans of the Chinese. Funnily enough, some of these were contradictory:

> The favourite delicacies of the Chinese are rats and snakes.
> The Chinese say yes for no and vice versa . . .
> They eat soup with chopsticks.
> Chop suey and chow mein are their national dishes and that besides these dishes they eat nothing but rice.
> Chinese men wear skirts and women pants.
> A Chinaman never gets drunk.
> A Chinese is properly a Chinaman and that the word 'Chinee' is singular for 'Chinese'.
> The Chinese are a nation of laundrymen yet have a highly developed civilization . . .
> All Chinese are cunning and crafty.
> All Chinese are honest and absolutely trustworthy.
> The Chinese never lose their tempers.
> The United States is the friend and protector of China.
> All Chinese look alike.
> The Chinese have no nerves and can sleep anywhere . . .
> They have no souls because they are not Christians.
> They never say what they mean and abhor straight lines.
> The Chinese invented pretty nearly everything that was ever invented.
> The Chinese all hate water and never bathe.

Perhaps the most sinister and evil portrayal of the Chinese is best remembered in Dr Fu Manchu, the creation of Sax Rohmer, the pseudonym of an English writer. The *Fu Manchu* film series, starting from the first in 1929, catered unabashedly to the lovers of Melodrama, serving a diet of double-cross, magic, torture and bedlam. One viewer stated her reaction to the machinations of the slant-eyed villain in the following extract: 'I hate to admit it but I grew up with a fear of the Chinese that emanated from movies I saw as a child, and I still can't walk through Chinatown in New York or San Francisco without an uneasy feeling, even though I know it is stupid and ridiculous. These old pigtailed villains of my childhood made a lasting impression, slinking around in their opium dens, thinking up unspeakable tortures for kidnapped white girls.'

The advent of Charlie Chan, the famous Chinese detective, masked a subtle change in the nation's mood. Introduced to the public by Earl Derr Biggers in 1925, he graduated from the columns of the *Saturday Evening Post*, a raft of books, and no fewer than 48 feature films, to the status of a national institution. Instead of an evil genius as in *Fu Manchu*, Charlie Chan was portrayed as a 'damned clever Chinese'.

Intelligent, wise and cool-headed, he was always depicted as having his hands folded over his fat belly, standing pigeon-toed and raising a forefinger in the air while speaking. Most of his statements are prefaced with 'Confucius says . . .' One could instantly contrast this cerebral, almost effeminate image of the Chinese with the depiction of the American detective type – like those in 'Hawaii Five-O'. These film heroes do use their brains but are more often portrayed in situations where they use their muscles – in breaking down doors and grappling with the villains. The effeminate portrayals of the Chinese aside, the bits of Confucian sayings come across as a lot of double talk.

All these films in one way or another and in varying degrees, portrayed the Chinese as inscrutable, sly, with intelligent but unfathomable minds. People who may know a lot but are unable to communicate in everyday situations. This notion of inscrutability imputed to the Chinese is further reinforced by the lack of contact between the Chinese and the Americans. Both by choice and the result of prejudices and hostilities, the Chinese have always, until recently, tried to disappear by withdrawing as far as possible into their tiny little communities and an unreacting expressionlessness. They sought safety and comfort in numbers concentrating in trades where they might remain undisturbed. These factors of cultural preference and external discrimination led directly to the rise of Chinatowns, that sprang up in various cities around the country.

The Second World War brought a softening of the Chinese image. The Chinese were portrayed in American mass media as heroic defenders of their land. The character of the Chinese peasant was built up by books and films like *The Good Earth* and *Dragon Seed*, where Chinese were dramatized as being hardworking, strong and persevering personalities able to withstand the most severe adversities, kind towards children and respectful towards elders. Pearl S. Buck's greatest achievement, especially in the film *The Good Earth*, whose debut coincided with Japan's invasion of China in 1937, was providing a face for the faceless mass of the Chinese peasantry. When America entered the war after Pearl Harbour, and China became her ally, the Chinese image grew significantly. The traditional associations and the *tongs* were glorified as mutual help agencies that helped the Chinese to keep off the relief rolls, and the dark and dangerous alleys of the rat-infested Chinatowns became the quaint, fascinating and sentimentally attractive homes of the Chinese.

Rose Hum Lee, a prominent Chinese American scholar writing about the 1940s, warned of this new tendency to glorify the Chinese and put them on a pedestal compared to the previous trend of violence. She wondered how long this trend would last, grounded as it was on the sandy loam of sentimentality.

She did not have long to wait. The loss of China to the communists in 1949, severely jolted the Americans out of their complacent relationship with China. The corrupt Kuomintang government and the swift collapse of its army projected the image of a hopeless Chinese leadership rendered impotent by its own internal weakness.

In America, there was much self-introspection and a feeling of guilt amongst a whole generation. This great loss was magnified shortly after by the staggeringly new spectacle of Americans suffering defeats at the hands of the Chinese. The 1950s produced McCarthyism, the relentless pursuit of public officials who helped 'sell China down the river to the Communists', and which abated only after many innocent lives and public careers had been ripped or destroyed.

In the 1960s, at the height of the cold war with communist China, the Chinese began increasingly to take on the role of the bad guys. Mort Fine, co-director of the 'I Spy' series, was in fact quoted as saying, 'The Russians aren't acceptable as villains any more.' Presumably that left only the insidious machinations of the Red Chinese in films such as *Goldfinger*, where Mr Ling is identified as a Red Chinese official behind the plot to contaminate America's gold reserve. Similarly in the 1962 *Manchurian Candidate* the diabolical Yen Lo had malevolent intentions against the free world, as did many of the Oriental villains in the 'Man from U.N.C.L.E.' series.

However in 1972, President Nixon's rapprochement with China and his visit to Beijing sparked off an intense exploration which broke many Asian stereotypes and brought to an end the genre of 'bad guy' stereotypes in films. A CBS-TV documentary, 'Misunderstanding China', addressed itself directly to the development of the Chinese stereotypes. The relaxation of political tensions with China aroused a new public interest in Chinese culture. An interesting aspect of this was the introduction of Chinese Kung Fu, as a carrier of Chinese culture into mainstream American culture.

The 1970s saw the debut of the famous television series 'Kung-Fu' starring David Carradine as the wandering Chinese, Kwai Chang Caine. The series was quite positive in its portrayal of the Chinese and highlighted the role of the Chinese in the building of America. However it was not able to escape stereotyping especially in its pseudo-religious slants in which Carradine and his martial arts teachers (the monks of Shaolin temple in China) mouthed more. Charlie Chan sayings. The 'Kung-Fu' series quickly became a popular subject for satire, complete with bald heads, 'phony sayings and hand to hand combat.

Fortunately the opening of China and the subsequent cultural exchanges impressed many Americans with the cultural attainments of China. Today, programmes in Asian-American studies have appeared in every important West Coast college or university, and courses teaching Chinese civilization are offered across the nation.

THE CHINESE MIDDLE CLASS

The beginnings of the Chinese middle class closely follows the pattern of Chinese emigration. There are roughly 3 stages – the first wave is before the 1882 passing of the Exclusion Act. The Chinese who came during this period were largely illiterate and impoverished peasants – the coolies with their conical hats and pigtails that came to stigmatize all Chinese long after they had passed from the scene. The second wave is the post-Exclusion period from 1882 to 1943. In contrast to the first period, there were much fewer Chinese immigrants. Instead of coolie gangs, most came as individuals engaged in trade or as students who came to study in American schools and colleges. The third wave corresponded with the repeal of the Exclusion Act. From this date onwards, there came a great influx of women, wives and children. Soon after, with the communist takeover in China in 1949, a large contingent of professionals, scholars and students also arrived in America.

Immigrants from the first and second waves had much in common. Most of them shared the view that their forced exile was a temporary one. They came principally to eke out a livelihood for their families back home in the villages of China. Once they had made a little money, most packed their bags and left. There was little motivation to assimilate into the host society, so the majority invariably ended up living in or near Chinatowns, with their own kind, until the time came for their return.

The second wave of immigrants were however of a higher socio-economic class. Most came under the category of merchants, traders and students. Some of the richer merchants actually had their own houses in the suburbs, and came into town in their own automobiles, but these belonged to the minority. Many of the students who arrived came under the Chinese government's sponsorship for technical training and were obliged to serve the government upon their return to China.

The third wave from 1943 saw the appearance in America of many Chinese women, wives and children – a large proportion being families of earlier immigrants who were not permanently domiciled in America. In the entire period between 1943 and 1965, there were 37,228 women immigrants, or 70 per cent of the total 53,044 immigrants admitted. Increasingly there were more and more students and professionals, not only from China but also Hong Kong and Taiwan, especially after 1949. Enrolment of Chinese students in colleges and universities rose from 823 in the 1944–45 period to a high of 3,916 in the 1948–49 period.

These students and professionals, both those who came to America before 1949 and after, boosted the Chinese image considerably. The United States Census shows that in 1940 only 2.4 per cent of Chinese males were employed in professional, technical and kindred occupations. By 1950 the decennial census recorded a rise of 4 per cent to 6.4 per cent.

More important than the accretion of new immigrants of higher socio-economic status was the new phenomenon of more stable families and an increasing birth rate among the Chinese in America. The increasing influx of women from 1945 onwards helped offset the highly imbalanced sex ratio that condemned many a Chinese man to enforced bachelorhood and a lonely existence in old age. This more balanced sex ratio was soon reflected in the increasing proportion of persons who had ever married compared to singles. In the 1960 census, for example, about 65 per cent of the Chinese males were in this first

Habitués of Portsmouth Square in San Francisco Chinatown
indulging in a game of Chinese chess.

category, which compared favourably with the total United States
average of 75 per cent.

The birth rate soon shot up from only 14.5 births per 1,000
Chinese in 1940, the lowest of all the ethnic groups in America at that
time, to an all-time high of 43.9 in 1950. This birth rate slowly tapered
off to a more moderate growth from 1951 onwards.

THE *ABC'S*

A new group of young Chinese began to make inroads into the demographic face of America from the 1940s onwards. This group of
American-born Chinese (hence the ABC's) was, by the rights of the *jus
soli* principle granted to the Chinese in 1898, entitled to American citizenship. It was a painfully slow process for the Chinese in America; it took
them almost one century after the first Chinese arrived in America before
the native-born finally outnumbered the foreign-born in 1940. According
to the 1960 United States Census, almost 61 per cent of the Chinese in
America belonged to this category of Chinese Americans. This group of

Second- and third-generation American-born Chinese.
As discrimination abates, a bright future awaits them in America.

native-born of Chinese ancestry is neither fully Chinese nor American in culture and values. Yet their political aspirations appear to be closely identified with America – they want to be called citizens and to be entitled therefore to all the rights and privileges of true-blue Americans.

With the increasing predominance of the native-born, the Chinese are veering more and more into mainstream American life. Correspondingly the socio-economic characteristics of the Chinese population have changed, pointing to a period of accelerated social mobility.

The proportion of Chinese males in professional occupations increased from 6.4 per cent in 1950 to 20.1 per cent in 1960. This change in only a decade was due partly to the immigration of Chinese students and professionals between 1945 and 1955, and the increasing numbers of native-born Chinese.

The Second World War which had just ended had also helped in the demand and absorption of Chinese professionals, both native and foreign-born, due to the expansion of the American war industry. This figure of 20.1 per cent was relatively high compared to the 10.3 per cent average for the total employed male population in the United States. And in fact, by 1970, one source listed that of all the Chinese males employed, an impressive 40 per cent were in professional and related fields. (The same source gave Chinese women a rating of 23 per cent.)

The increase in occupational status was matched by the educational sector, which sees the Chinese males ahead in the proportion of those with college education (18.9 per cent as against 18.4 per cent for the Japanese and 10.3 per cent for the Whites). By 1970, 24 per cent of Chinese American men had college degrees – double the United States average and higher than any other ethnic groups in America. Figures from the 1980 census also show that the median household income for the Chinese in America (US $22,550) exceeded not only that of American families in general (US $19,900) but also the level reported by Whites (US $20,800).

Chinese Americans form the largest Asian subgroup in America (806,000). This group has made a visible impact in American society by their contributions in the fields of science, technology and the arts.

One of the most famous is Dr M. C. Chang, who discovered the birth control pill. Equally well-known are the China-born physicists, Yang Chen-ming and Lee Tsung Dat, the first Chinese to win the Nobel Prize in 1957. Both came to America in the 1945–46 period and for a long time were unable to get permanent residence status because of discriminatory immigration and naturalization laws.

I. M. Pei is probably the world's most famous architect. The son of a Cantonese banker, he is the designer and architect of notable landmarks like the Kennedy Memorial Library, the new wing of the National Art Gallery in Washington, and the Oversea-Chinese Banking Corporation (OCBC) Centre and Raffles City in Singapore.

Other big names include March Fong Eu, who is the first Asian-American to be elected California's secretary of state. She is a second-generation Chinese born in America of parents who operated a hand laundry. There is also An Wang, creator of the 'memory chip' and a multi-million dollar electronics business. The son of a Shanghai teacher, with a Ph.D. in physics from Harvard University, he is today one of the five richest men in America.

In the field of letters we have notables like Francis K. L. Hsu, an anthropologist who has written widely on studies in China, the United States, Europe and India, and prolific author of Chinese culture and customs, Lin Yutang.

The Chinese have produced skilled men and women in every field of human endeavour. Beginning as coolies and miners, they have within a short time reached the highest ranks of American society.

6
THE CHINESE IN AUSTRALIA, NEW ZEALAND AND BRITAIN

AUSTRALIA

SOON after gold was discovered in California in 1848, Australia also experienced a mini-gold rush when gold deposits were found in the Bathurst, Bendigo and Ballaret regions of the continent. To the Chinese who flocked to Australia, it was the Xin Jin Shan (新金山 , the New Goldfields) in contrast to California which was 'old' (旧金山 , Jiu Jin Shan).

These later immigrants were mostly from the Sze Yup districts located on the fertile delta of the Pearl River. They were all uniformly Cantonese though loyalty to village, county and district asserted itself in the form of various traditional associations.

The discovery in Australia coincided with the decline of the gold fever in California. Many gold miners from California who did not turn to other occupations or were free from ensnaring debts quickly left for the Victoria goldfields so that by 1859 there were some 42,000 Chinese compared to only 25,000 Chinese in 1854. In one camp alone, north of Ballaret there were 8,000 Chinese miners. Today the Chinese presence could be found in several spots like Campbells Creek in Victoria where Chinese graves lie in desolation. In Hill End, tours are being conducted to New South Wales' richest goldfield. There amidst the mine-pocked landscape, heaps of spoil, overgrown mine shafts and rusted machinery, stands a museum which has two Chinese tombstones, temple panels with motifs, candle stands and other artefacts.

Life in the goldfields of New South Wales and Victoria was hard and brutish. Panning for gold and repairing equipment the whole day and into the night was back-breaking labour. Opportunities for recreation were few, gambling and opium smoking being the most common. These recreational 'vices' were to bankrupt many immigrants – with their savings gone, they had to take out loans at high interests; most ended up working in servitude for others. The Chinese miners generally kept to themselves. They worked in their own valleys and maintained their old-world style of life.

A move was made by the Victorian legislature early in the gold rush to have all Chinese repatriated. Though this was fortunately unsuccessful, a poll tax of £10 was subsequently levied against all Chinese landing in Victoria. The ingenuity of the Chinese was put to the test – they quickly got around this levy by landing at Guichen Bay in South Australia, from which point they trudged overland into Victoria by various routes. Today a memorial stands in Robe, South Australia, showing a line of Chinese carrying their own load slung at each end of a pole and carried on the shoulder, in loose jackets and trousers with hats of basket-weave on their heads and strong rope sandals on their feet moving forward in single file. The following words are inscribed on the plaque: 'During the years 1856 to 1858 16,500 Chinese landed near this spot and walked 200 miles to Ballaret and Bendigo in search of gold.'

The pressure on Victoria eased somewhat as gold was discovered in New South Wales and Queensland. The hostility against the Chinese mounted with each subsequent wave of immigrants.

The Australians ridiculed the Chinese for their stingy, timid and retiring mannerisms. Their physical characteristics, traditional apparel and inability to speak English segregated them from the Whites. Their rice-eating, tea consuming habits and their supposed fondness for opium and gambling made them the objects of jibes and ridicule. They were allegedly addicted to unnatural practices like sodomy which was called the 'Chinese vice'. Their congested living conditions led to widespread disease. As a result the Chinese were accused of bringing all sorts of epidemics, like smallpox, into Australia.

A miners' paper in Lambing Flat, New South Wales, has this to say of the Chinese miners:

> . . . the incursions of a swarm of Mongolian locusts who have forced us to fly with our wives and families from all other diggings in the country until we are obliged to turn at bay upon this our last resting place – our only hope of establishing a homestead – and drive the moonfaced barbarians away.

In Queensland, the Chinese had not only to face the hostility of the Whites but also of the aborigines who killed and devoured them. These aborigines appeared to fancy Chinese flesh (called Yellow Fella long pork), finding them more delicate and succulent than the Whites. Frederick Folkard, in his book *The Remarkable Australians*, wrote of Chinese stragglers being rounded up and hung by their pigtails, awaiting their turn to be cut down and roasted. Conditions were so alarming that around Cannibal Creek of north Queensland, the Chinese lived in perpetual fear of their lives and could only leave their diggings in groups.

As in California, the Chinese were seen as an inferior race, a source of possible contamination of the ideal of a White Australia. Their hardworking nature and cheap wages posed a threat to White working men. The Intercolonial Trade Union Congress, for example, passed a resolution in 1888 to exclude all coloured labour from Australia. Racial riots against Chinese goldminers broke out in the 1850s and 1860s, and the most infamous of these was unquestionably the Lambing Flat riot of 1881.

A mob of 2,000 to 3,000 Whites rounded up the Chinese as they would a bunch of cattle. They were struck with bludgeons and whips and their swags were cut down. A big bonfire was made of their tents, stores, rice, blankets and boots. Their windlasses and tools were thrown down the shafts. Men with picks and axes destroyed everything they could not burn.

According to newspaper accounts of that time, the Chinese did not put up any resistance. All those who were able to, risked hiding their gold, and many indeed lost their lives for refusing to disclose their hoards. Others who were not quick enough in getting out of the holes and drives were burned alive in them.

Riots like. the Lambing Flat were directly responsible for the passing of various state bills to restrict Chinese diggers. These anti-Chinese legislations culminated in the Immigration Restriction Act which was passed with the formation of the Commonwealth of Australia in 1901. The most onerous aspect of the Act was the dictation test in English which was meant to exclude all coloured immigrants so that the ideal of a White Australia may be preserved. The Naturalization Bill in 1903 further prevented locally domiciled Chinese from taking up root in Australia. Without the benefit of naturalization, all Chinese were not allowed to vote, to hold Crown lands and to seek redress from injustices. The restrictive policy of limiting the entry of wives and dependents, except for those of merchants and well-established families, reduced drastically the number of women. Even then, these wives were admitted only for short periods of usually six months.

This kind of policy led to a lot of hardship for *bona fide* Chinese families. The controversy over the case of Poon Gooey illustrated the seeming injustice of upholding the notion of a White Australia over humanitarian considerations. Poon Gooey, a Chinese greengrocer, managed to secure permission for the entry of his wife for 6 months in 1910. Following the chaotic conditions in China after the revolution, an extension of her stay was granted by the Department of External Affairs.

During this time, Mrs Poon Gooey gave birth to two children. When her case came up for review, the whole family was booted out of Australia in 1913 despite general widespread public support for the family to continue to stay in Australia.

A direct consequence of the tough immigration law, then enforced, was the ingenious response of many Chinese to smuggle their way into Australia. These illegal immigrants suffered unimaginable hardship, going for long periods without food and water and seeing daylight, hiding under cargo, in bunkers or rice bins. Many died, a few were caught and deported, while some others were successful in smuggling their way into Australia.

In 1908, the Federal government made an attempt to register all Chinese residents in Australia for the purpose of checking the trickle of Chinese stowaways. The leader of the Chinese in Australia at this time was one Quong Tart, a wealthy tea merchant who was honoured by the Qing dynasty while at the same time moved easily in the elite White society of Sydney. An unconventional man (he married a young English girl and was a spirited singer of highland ballads), Quong Tart was able to marshal enough support to stop the proposal. Registration was not required for aliens until 1916, when under the War Precaution Act, all aliens, both Chinese and others, were required to register.

Though there was widespread interstate agitation by the Chinese and some local clergymen and politicians, the Immigration Restriction Act stayed largely intact in spite of some union concessions. The net effect of the Act was the breakup of Chinese families, in cases where the admission of wives and relatives were prohibited. The highly uneven sex ratio led to the unnatural retardation of the domiciled Chinese population. Therefore the anti-Chinese legislation checked the inflow of fresh immigrants, bringing about a decline in Australia's Chinese population in the twentieth century.

At the peak of the gold rush, there were an estimated 45,000 to 50,000 Chinese. By 1911, there were only about 23,000 Chinese, and this was to drop further to under 10,000 in 1947. During the period 1901 to 1947, Chinese departures generally exceeded arrivals. An exception occurred during the war years when about 9,000 non-Europeans were evacuated to Australia. There were Chinese among them, mostly seamen in the merchant navy recruited in Shanghai or workers working in the Pacific areas. Eventually a handful of them were naturalized and became permanent residents and citizens of Australia.

The Chinese community has its early beginnings in large settlements like Sydney where they operated retail stores and market gardens.

However, as we now know, it was gold that opened up the floodgates. Chinese camps could be found wherever there were goldfields in Victoria and New South Wales. Here there was a concentration of the Chinese population until the 1870s when the alluvial gold mining petered out. After this date, the Chinese returned to or started afresh in market gardening in the small settlements and towns that had sprung up. The Chinese market gardener was a familiar sight in the Australian landscape from Sydney to remote outposts of the continent. In most cases, the Chinese not only grew the vegetables but hawked them as well, around the streets of the village, town or city nearest to his garden. They thus rendered a vital service, providing the nation with fresh, cheap vegetables.

The move to the urban areas accelerated so that by 1901, the Chinese population in Melbourne and Sydney had increased to approximately 3,000 each in the two major cities. As the Chinese communities in the goldfields disintegrated these urban centres became more populated, and by the early twentieth century Chinatowns thrived in both Sydney and Melbourne. In 1911 only 32 per cent of the Chinese resided in metropolitan areas. This increased rapidly to 59 per cent in 1947, exceeding that of the general Australian population.

Compared with the large and developed Chinatowns of San Francisco and New York of 50,000 or more, these Chinatowns are small. However, they serve roughly the same purpose as bases for Chinese economic and social life away from the hostility of White Australians. Some gold diggers who were engaged in making boxes for the despatch of gold bullion to China, stayed on after the gold rush to become cabinet makers. There also sprouted laundries, import and export firms, fruit shops, grocery and retail stores.

As competition in the furniture-making business and laundries was keen, discriminatory laws were soon passed against Chinese businesses. The Factories and Shops Act put the Chinese in a disadvantageous position. Because Chinese in those industries were not allowed to sponsor assistants or workers from China, businesses suffered from the natural processes of aging and death. When the Second World War drew to a close, Chinese furniture and laundry shops were almost extinct.

The market gardening and vegetable and fruits distribution business continued into the post-war period. In the sixties, there was a marked shift away from primary industry. The Chinese began to feature prominently in the restaurant industry. Chinese restaurants which had previously been found in a few inner urban sites were now located in many suburban areas.

The period after the war saw a general relaxation of immigration laws. With the relaxation of entry criteria came an increase in arrivals of workmen, substitute workers, cooks and dependents to help out in businesses run by the Chinese. There was a continuous increase in the number of Chinese in Australia since 1947 so that by 1969 they numbered about 23,000. In 1956 naturalization was granted to the Chinese but only after 15 years of residence. This was subsequently reduced to 5 years in 1966.

Most of the new arrivals came from stopping places like Hong Kong, where they could have stayed for anything from a few months to several years. The overwhelming majority were Cantonese coming from the same migratory areas in the Guangzhou Delta who seemed to have some family connection with the Chinese in Australia. Another group that came after the war consisted of private students, many of whom enrolled independently in Australian colleges and universities. Unlike the previous group, they were predominantly not China-born nor from the traditional areas of emigration like Guangdong or Fujian. In fact most were from Hong Kong, and Southeast Asian countries like Singapore and Malaysia. They remained to become permanent residents or naturalized citizens. The last group consisted of professional and highly skilled persons who entered Australia under the special admission category of 'Distinguished and Highly Qualified Persons'.

With the post-war immigration, the Chinese population underwent a transition. The sex ratio improved to a more balanced one with its salutary effect on stable family life. A faster rate of natural increase is expected as new family units are formed. The median age for males fell to about 26 years as a crop of new immigrants and Australian-born Chinese replaced the older foreign-born immigrants.

The post-war immigrant Chinese were generally better educated and occupationally mobile Chinese from China, Taiwan, Hong Kong and other parts of Southeast Asia. At the same time, a new generation of Australian-born Chinese is coming into maturity with access to education, proper nutrition and stable family life. These groups of Chinese would be found at many professional levels of Australian society, especially in medicine and business.

Prominent Chinese Australians include Tchan Yao-Tseng, Professor of Microbiology at a prominent university, and an active member of the Chinese Academics Association. Professor Tchan had an interesting story to tell. When he was a boy he was asked by his teacher what he wished to be when he grew up. His reply was that he would like to go to university. His teacher was surprised by his answer and queried why he did not wish to follow his father's footsteps and become a market gardener.

There is also Alice Erh-Soon Tay, Professor of Jurisprudence at the Faculty of Law at Sydney University. Born in 1934 in Singapore, Professor Tay is an Australian citizen married to Professor Eugene Kamenka, a historian.

Other prominent Chinese Australians are David Nang Hwang, prominent businessman and politician who arrived from Shanghai to Australia in 1948, and Dr Victor Chang, pioneering heart surgeon who was recently voted Australian Man of the Year in a poll conducted by an Australian paper.

NEW ZEALAND

New Zealand's Chinese population of 20,000 is minuscule and, like the Chinese in America and Australia, most (over 60 per cent) are concentrated in the big urban centres of Auckland and Wellington. The principal reason for the Chinese arrival was similar to that of the Chinese in America and Australia – the lure of gold and wealth. The migration in Australia began with gold discoveries in Victoria and New South Wales. In New Zealand, the discovery of vast quantities of gold in Otago attracted a small number of Chinese who crossed the Tasman Sea and landed in Dunedin and across the harbour in Port Chalmers. Later-day immigrants came mostly from Panyu and Sze Yup.

Here, too, the same pattern of discrimination repeated itself. Taking their cues from California and Australia, the New Zealanders raised the spectre of the yellow bogeymen, the contamination of race and culture, the threat to ordinary citizens and workmen in terms of the loss of jobs and the depletion of the country's wealth through the export of gold. The measures adopted by the various colonial governments to exclude the Chinese included poll-taxes and literacy tests.

The 1881 bill calling for a poll-tax of £10 and the limitation of one Chinese passenger per ten tons of burden on any ship travelling to New Zealand effectively prevented the possibility of any coolie trade in New Zealand as had occurred in California and Peru. Anti-Chinese discrimination reached its peak under the stewardship of the Prime Minister Richard Setton who pressed for a bill to bar Chinese and all other Asiatics from New Zealand entirely. The British Colonial Office however would not hear of discrimination on the basis of race, and an ingenious substitute was therefore devised in the form of literacy tests, to allegedly measure the quality of the prospective immigrant. Further

legislations stiffened the literacy tests and increased the poll tax to
£100 for each Chinese immigrant. The culmination of these discriminatory practices was in 1920 when a bill was passed to limit Asiatic
immigration on an 'application basis'. Thus each application would be
judged on its 'merits' and no reasons were offered for refusal. The only
exceptions to this were the wives and children of permanent residents
in New Zealand, but even this category was slammed with a heavy
poll-tax.

Up until 1900, the Chinese in New Zealand were mainly miners.
As the mines became depleted and discrimination increased in the
goldfields, goldmining camps became depopulated. A few diehards
stayed behind, too old or sick to move. The tragedy of the miners was
best summed up by Alexander Don (1843–1934), the best loved White
missionary who worked among the Chinese in Otago and in their
native Guangdong. ' . . . the heads of more than half our Chinese
white with the snows of 20 to 40 Otago winters, and with the sorrow
of the rugged path they have trodden for gold.'

The Chinese began drifting to cities in search of jobs. These they
found mainly in market-gardening and in the wholesale and retail fruit
and vegetable business, mainly in the North Island centres of Auckland
and Wellington. The Chinese quickly set up permanent product shops
selling directly to Chinese and European clientele. Some others opened
laundries and restaurants which have traditionally been the mainstay of
Chinese economic enterprise in America.

As in America, the stereotypes of the Chinese in New Zealand
improved almost overnight with the outbreak of the Sino-Japanese War
and the resultant show of Chinese resistance and heroism. As the war
waged on, the Japanese army began to close in on the immigrant
province of Guangdong. Guangzhou fell in 1938 and Hong Kong 3 years
later. The urgency of the Chinese in New Zealand to have their
immediate relatives moved across to join them was swiftly approved by
the New Zealand government. Thus in 1939, 249 wives and 244 children
entered the Dominion on special and temporary visas. In 1947 they were
all granted permanent residence status instead of being forced to leave
New Zealand.

The war with Japan ended, but only for a short respite before the
Civil War erupted in China. The overseas Chinese found themselves in a
painful predicament. Almost in a twinkle, the political situation had
changed so drastically that returning home to their relatives and
ancestral villages was an impossibility. Reconciled to their fate in the
overseas communities, the Chinese petitioned for improved treatment
and naturalization.

In 1952, after a halt lasting over forty years, the Chinese were permitted to take out New Zealand citizenship. By this time, most of those under thirty would have been New Zealand-born. There were many Chinese children and youths in public schools and universities in the Dominion. In the years to come, those who knew Guangdong personally or through close association with parents and kinsmen would have died and with their passing a new generation would come into maturity.

This generation was educated in public schools where English is the medium of instruction and the *lingua franca*. Literacy in Chinese therefore is slowly vanishing. Within a generation, the Chinese have risen from their lot as goldminers, market gardeners, small shop-owners and laundrymen to professional occupations such as lawyers, doctors, architects and businessmen. The good life appeared to seduce the average Chinese in a welfare state like New Zealand. Here in a sparsely populated country richly endowed with natural resources, the Chinese can be credited with having made the best use of the opportunities that are readily available.

Strangely, though, no Chinatown exists in New Zealand. Its small number of Chinese did not gather significantly in any particular area. New York or San Francisco Chinatowns alone contained more Chinese than the whole Chinese population of New Zealand. Whereas in these settlements, the concentration of Chinese was made possible by multiple dwelling cubicles in tenement buildings, in New Zealand almost its entire population live in single dwelling units or private houses.

The fact that there is no Chinatown or wide concentration of Chinese in New Zealand has made the task of assimilation and acculturation an easier one. Scattered throughout cities with no fixed point of cultural focus, the Chinese are susceptible to the process of intermingling and intermarriages. Even the ubiquitous Chinese shops cater to a mixed clientele with rare displays of Chinese signs. Just like these Chinese shops, which attempt to create the impression that they are no different from the other establishments, many young Chinese appear to choose their friends and eventually their spouses not on the basis of race but on the basis of assimilation into mainstream New Zealand life.

BRITAIN

The earliest Chinese immigrants were sailors who lived in the dock areas of Liverpool and London. At one time the Chinese population of Liverpool rivalled that of London but today there are more Chinese in London than in Liverpool. Organized into little wards that do not amount to ghettos, the main Chinese settlements are in these two cities.

The history of Chinese settlement began as early as the 1870s after the opening of the Suez Canal had stimulated British trade with the Far East. The increasing number of cargo ships brought Chinese immigrants who originally came as seamen. Before the First World War, there was virtually no control over the movement of aliens in and out of Great Britain. By 1911, therefore, there were about 1,490 China-born foreigners living in Britain. Many of those were sailors who conveniently jumped ship after their ships had docked in Liverpool or London. Subsequently the majority left Britain after failing to make their fortunes though some did stay on to become proprietors of small laundries and chop-suey shops.

With the war and the tighter economic situation, British Parliament passed the Alien Restriction Act which allowed aliens to land on British soil on condition that the aliens were economically self-supporting. This legislation – compounded by the economic difficulties of the inter-war period – tended to reduce Chinese immigration. The outbreak of the Second World War reversed the trend momentarily with the influx of about 10,000 Chinese seamen who fled from enemy-occupied countries to join the British merchant navy in Liverpool. The Chinese settlement in Liverpool was given a hefty boost with this influx. Unfortunately the blitz in Britain destroyed the original Liverpool Chinatown. After the war, most of these Chinese seamen were repatriated; some 500 seamen who had married British women during the war years were however granted conditional permission by the Home Office to remain in the United Kingdom.

Most of the early immigrants before the war were single young men as was true of Chinese immigrants elsewhere. The proportion of unmarried persons amongst the overseas Chinese in Britain was therefore very high – about 70 per cent in 1911. However, this steadily declined to about 36 per cent in 1951 indicating a trend towards inter-marriage with the local women. The majority of these immigrants were engaged in seafaring and in personal service jobs – predominantly as servants in British homes or as independent laundrymen.

The 1950s and 1960s however witnessed a big increase in the proportion of Chinese engaged in the catering trade. These were the years of the economic boom which saw a rise in living standards and intense explorations in areas of food, fashion and various fads. After the austerity of the war years, the British appetite for good and reasonably-priced food was insatiable. The Chinese, mostly from Hong Kong but also from Malaysia and Singapore, never slow from exploiting an economic opportunity, quickly flocked to Britain to set up restaurants and cafés to cater to the newly-acquired British taste for foreign cuisine. Not surprisingly, it was the Chinese from Hong Kong who migrated in droves. Capitalizing on Hong Kong's status as a British colony, the Hong Kongnese, as British subjects or stateless aliens, found it easier than others to immigrate to Britain.

Most of these Hong Kong immigrants were Cantonese speaking Punti (native settlers), whose forefathers had emigrated a long time ago from Guangdong province. The Hakkas, who lived in small hamlets scattered throughout the hills and islands of Hong Kong, also migrated, albeit in smaller numbers. The Punti were generally thought to be descendants of northern Chinese pioneers who gained control of South China by the tenth century. The majority of present-day Hong Kong Chinese are descendants of immigrants from China, especially Guangdong province.

The familiar story of poverty at home and economic opportunity abroad soon lured young men from Hong Kong to try their luck in the booming catering trade in Britain. Before the Second World War, there were hardly any Chinese restaurants in Britain, except for the few that catered primarily to students and members of the Chinese community. Few Englishmen ever ventured into Chinatown, let alone ate at a Chinese restaurant. Today there are an astounding 4,000 Chinese restaurants and take-away shops. In every city or town with a population of 5,000 or more, there would usually be at least one Chinese restaurant or shop. In London alone, it is estimated that there are at least 150 to 200 restaurants.

Most of the villages that sent their menfolk to Britain were located in the New Territories. The New Territories is a 365-square mile stake of the Chinese mainland and associated islands ceded to Britain for 99 years in 1898. There are over 600 villages in this small area organized into 5 dominant lineages.

One of these is the Man lineage residing in the biggest emigrant village of San Tin (新田, New Fields), in the New Territories. San Tin is typical of the numerous rural villages that dotted South China before the 1949 revolution. Located in the north-west corner of the colony, it comprised 8 sub-villages surrounding a central market plaza and the ancestral temples. There were approximately 4,000 occupants (including 1,000 who were working in Britain and Europe), almost all of whom belonged to the Man lineage, which claimed to trace its ancestry to the brother of a famous Chinese general.

James Watson's intensive study of the San Tin immigrants traces the history of the lineage settlement in Hong Kong, its forms of social organization and the emigration of lineage members to Britain. He followed up his field research in San Tin with a study on its emigrants working in London.

Some of his more interesting observations relate to the nature of emigration and its impact on social organization and cohesion in the native village. One of the most striking features of San Tin is the absence of men between the ages of 18 and 50, as almost all work abroad as restaurant workers or owners in Britain or Europe. According to Watson, the Mans own and operate nearly one hundred restaurants in England.

Like the villages of Guangdong that sent their men to the goldmines of America, Australia and New Zealand, the Man lineage organized and financed the great proportion of San Tin emigrants to Britain and Continental Europe. In the 1950s and 60s, Britain, and London in particular, was the main hub of the lineage's activity. After consolidating their catering bases in Britain, the Man expanded their holdings into Continental Europe – especially to countries like Holland, Belgium and West Germany. Holland has at least 10,000 Hong Kong Chinese vying with the Indonesian immigrants in the restaurant trade. There are fewer Chinese immigrants in Germany and Belgium due to the immigration restrictions placed on non-European sources.

Restaurant owners and operators in Britain and Europe belonging to the Man lineage would prefer to employ fellow Mans as employees because they are believed to be more trustworthy. This form of preferential employment, which was the norm in Chinese immigration to other parts of the world, has the chain effect of cornering a large slice of the overseas catering business for a particular lineage as well as expediting the immigration of other members of the lineage.

Kinship bonds play a crucial role in the organization of emigration from San Tin. The most common way of financing the cost of air passage to Britain is through a variant of the 'credit ticket' system – which simply means that the initial payment is treated as an advance on the employee's wages. The employee, normally also a close kinsman, would then be able to pay his cost of passage through monthly deductions from his wage. Other forms of financing include borrowing from relatives and using the funds (earnings from the common property, usually land), held in trust by sub-branches of the lineage. In recent years, the commercial banks have also got into the act – giving out loans to would-be emigrants based on land as corollary asset, though this was not a popular means of financing the emigration loans.

The following case-study taken from Ng Kwee Choo's 1968 study

of the Chinese in London gave a vivid account of a Hong Kong
Chinese immigrant's life in Britain.

> Cheung, a 28-year-old waiter, emigrated to England in 1959 by sea. He
> was born in Lok Ma Chau, a village north-east of San Tin in the
> district of Yuen Long in the New Territories; the inhabitants of the
> village, numbering about 150, have the same surname Cheung and are
> all Cantonese. Cheung has three brothers and a sister; his father is
> dead. Neither he nor any of his brothers is married. Cheung graduated
> from a Chinese secondary school in 1958 and found it very difficult to
> get a job at home. One of his brothers, a waiter in a Chinese restaurant
> in London, wrote to Cheung asking him to join him here; Cheung's
> brother managed to persuade his employer to give Cheung a letter
> offering him a job in the restaurant though in actuality there was no
> vacancy, a device apparently to outsmart the immigration authorities
> concerned. Within a week of his arrival he got a job as a pantry boy in
> a Chinese restaurant in Rathbone Place; however, he worked there for
> only four days and then left.
>
> Cheung was then offered a job as a waiter in a restaurant at Tot-
> tenham Court Road; the proprietor told the writer in a separate inter-
> view that he employed Cheung because "we are t'ung heung hing'tai"
> (fellow villagers). Thus Cheung launched out in his catering career as a
> commis waiter. When his employer opened another restaurant in Gol-
> ders Green, Cheung was transferred there; as he became more experi-
> enced and efficient his employer began to trust him more, and Cheung
> was given more responsibilities. This reliance of the employer upon his
> clansman Cheung was perhaps understandable in view of the fact that
> the former, though he came here as a seaman in 1939, could speak only
> a few words of English whereas Cheung was quite fluent in the lan-
> guage. The restaurant in Golders Green was small and the employer
> wanted to open a bigger one in the West End. With Cheung's help in
> the negotiation, he managed to get a suitable place in Old Compton
> Street and so set up a Chinese restaurant there; Cheung was promoted
> to the grade of maitre d'hotel.
>
> As among waiters everywhere in England, Cheung's fixed wage was
> not very high, being 6 pound 4 shillings a week, but with "tips" he
> could easily get 16 pounds a week. It may be of some interest to know
> how gratuities are shared among the waiters in Chinese restaurants. The
> method adopted by Cheung and his fellow waiters is also found in other
> restaurants and is commonly known as the "tronc" method, but in this
> case, the method of dividing the "tips" according to seniority is an
> ingenious one. There are five waiters in the restaurant, including
> Cheung. Gratuities collected by all waiters are put in a common box
> and at the end of every week are divided among them according to
> seniority in length of service. The total amount is divided into six
> shares, each waiter being entitled to only one share. The sixth share is
> subdivided into fifteen portions and the most senior waiter is entitled to
> five portions; second in seniority, four; third in seniority, three; fourth in
> seniority, two; and last in seniority, one.

In 1960 Cheung and his brother in London helped to pay to bring another brother over; the latter is now working in a Chinese restaurant in West Ham. Cheung's remaining elder brother in the New Territories has pestered Cheung to obtain a work voucher from the Ministry of Labour for him, but Cheung has been persistent in discouraging him from emigrating, for he feels that someone must stay at home to look after their elderly widowed mother. Cheung admitted that he was more fortunate than others because he need not remit money home regularly, but he will readily do so whenever money is needed; he once remitted 100 pounds to his elder brother when the latter was hard up for money. His brother-in-law, according to Cheung, sent 20 to 25 pounds home every month.

At the time of interview Cheung was thinking of setting up his own restaurant soon. Cheung considers jobs in Chinese restaurants more lucrative than white-collared jobs. Admitting that most New Territories emigrants have little education, Cheung maintained that in spite of this they earn more than highly educated English workers.

The Chinese population in Britain today is estimated to be about 60,000. This figure excluded approximately 6,000 full-time students and 2,000-odd nurses on temporary visas in Britain. London has the largest concentration, about 14,000 and distributed in its 28 metropolitan boroughs. Next comes Liverpool with approximately 1,500 Chinese. Most of the 60,000 Chinese are employed in the catering trade, though recent years had seen the emigration of professional Chinese to Britain. Some of the students and nurses already in Britain would also have stayed on to work and take up permanent residency.

The dispersed nature of the Chinese catering trade precludes the establishment of large Chinatowns. In almost every small British town, there is a Chinese restaurant or take-out shop. The craving for Chinese food among the local population resulted in the Chinese being spread out over the country. Expensive West End rentals also preclude the establishment of a residential core. The Chinese in Britain as in Australia and New Zealand could be labelled as forming a non-residentially-based community of shared or mutual interests.

Part III

A COMMUNITY TRANSPLANTED

The Chinese . . . are immensely and intricately organized – by family, by class, by dialect, by commercial grouping; in literary, religious, economic, regional, political, occupational, and secret societies. This facility, if not passion, for organization is noted by every writer for every country. In terms of good relations with a national majority, it is both a useful and a dangerous quality.

Guy Hunter
Southeast Asia: Race, Culture & Nation

A joss house in Hong Kong.

7
CHINESE TRADITIONAL ASSOCIATIONS

When the Chinese migrated overseas, they took along with them their cultural baggage, which included not only their speech, customs and mores but also the forms of social organization that had ordered and governed their lives for centuries. There are, broadly, four types of traditional associations; these are the clans, *hui-kuans*, dialect associations and guilds.

Clans

Clans (in reality, they are clan associations rather than clans) are voluntary associations formed on the basis of consanguinity or blood ties. In overseas Chinese communities, this is often judged on the criterion of all those having common surnames. It is a well-known fact among the Chinese themselves that common surnames do not necessarily mean common ancestry. However, for an overseas Chinese a common surname is enough ground for him to claim kinship ties and to address even total strangers as if they are his kinsmen. This phenomenon attests to the strength of the kinship mystique. It also underlines the fact that due to the very heterogeneous overseas Chinese population, and the low incidence of large numbers of biologically related kin, the relationship implied by like surnames logically becomes the common and more general basis of organization.

Hui-kuans

Hui-kuans refer to associations organized on the basis of places of origin in China – anything, in fact, from a small village to a large province. In overseas communities, the Chinese typically group themselves on the basis of much smaller territorial units than in China. Organization on a *sheng* (provincial level), would have yielded only two provincial associations, as most overseas Chinese migrated from many discrete villages and towns from the two southern provinces of Fujian and Guangdong. This would definitely have been insufficient to cater to the pressing needs of so many immigrants at the grassroots.

Dialect Associations

These 'speech' associations are organized not on the basis of surnames or places but according to spoken dialects. Speech-based groups are in a way a natural formation among the Chinese because their spoken dialects are distinctive and effectively divided the Chinese community into different groupings. The many dialect groups in Singapore gave rise to Hokkien, Teochew, Cantonese, Hakka and Hainanese associations, and others, which all serve broadly similar functions.

Guilds

In Chinese history, the origins of guilds are veiled in the legends of mythical figures. Their origins were however dependent on the development of commerce and crafts and the organization of individuals with similar interests or skills in China. It is important to distinguish between modern trade unions, trade and professional associations and the guilds.

- The guilds practise traditional skills and use 'old-fashioned' techniques. Their functions are typically multi-faceted, covering not only occupational interests but mutual benefits, educational and burial aids to the workmen and their families.
- They are typically 'closed' associations; membership is limited to those from the same dialect group.
- They worship patron gods, and have a paternalistic organization based on kinship.

In contrast, modern trade unions and trade and professional associations are secular in nature, possess a 'rational-based' structure, are more specific in function and readily admit members of other dialect and ethnic groups as members.

PRIMARY FUNCTIONS

In the midst of discrimination, the Chinese must create their own institutions for social control, worship, recreation, and the management of external relations. The many traditional Chinese associations established reflect the Chinese emphasis on kinship and the principle of collective responsibility which in traditional China were very extensive.

The average migrant arrived in Singapore without funds or family. He needed a wide range of social and economic services in order to survive. Transported to a new land, the Chinese immigrant looked to his or her clan – or, in its absence or lack of effectiveness, to other villagers – for mutual aid, protection, leadership, and representation to strangers.

The associations' functions encompassed the building and management of temples, cemeteries, schools, medical institutions, and transit houses for members. On a more personal level, they housed and fed new immigrants, helped them find jobs, provided them with short-term loans through the associations' funds or through the informal *hui* (rotating credit circle), arranged for deaths, funerals and the worship of their souls, and represented them in their relations with the wider community. Mediating of internal disputes and those between members of different dialect groups was another function. In short, the traditional Chinese voluntary associations fulfilled many physical and social needs of new immigrants and allowed them to find a niche in an otherwise unfamiliar society.

The traditional associations offer an alternative structure of social control that is familiar to the Chinese. The system of social control that the British had set up by ordinance, for example the law against bigamy, was often at variance with traditional Chinese customs, and was aggravated by cultural barriers and the inability of each to speak the other's language. The plethora of Chinese associations could be seen as a natural development that arose to police and govern the Chinese community against outside interferences.

The overseas Chinese traditional voluntary associations were also cultural organizations, in the sense that some of their aims were to perpetuate descent lines, to promote clan (and fellow countrymen) solidarity, and to foster traditional values which in turn upheld the idea of kinship. These traditional values showed a strong Confucian influence – filial piety, loyalty, virtue, harmony, reverence for elders, and exaltation of educational achievement.

The voluntary associations offered those who are ambitious leadership positions within the Chinese community. The topmost leaders represented the Chinese community in their external relations with the British colonial government. Some were even co-opted by the British to sit on their Legislative and other Committees. The conferment of such an honour was only possible for those Chinese leaders holding top positions in the most important Chinese associations.

COMMUNITY ORGANIZATION IN SINGAPORE

In nineteenth-century Singapore, the organization of the traditional voluntary associations was neither formalized nor well regulated. Vaughan in 1879, gave us a picturesque idea of the running of these associations or 'kongsi' as they were locally called:

> One member is elected annually as chief or chairman of the society to whom the trustees account for the money collected by them; he is called the Loo-choo. On that day of election the members of the kongsi meet at their house and each man's name is written on a separate piece of paper, which is rolled up tightly and placed in a box. A pair of lots is thrown up before the idol, if they fall with one flat side and one convex side uppermost three times successively, one of the papers is unrolled and the man whose name is written on it becomes the Loo-choo for the ensuing year. In the same manner are the trustees chosen. On the election closing, the image of the guardian deity of the kongsi is removed from the ex-Loo-choo's house to that of the new chief, where it remains for twelve months.

Such traditional associations frequently incurred the wrath of the colonial authorities. They were often accused of behaving like secret societies with powers to try their own members. The Protector of Chinese had, for instance, this to say of the Gambier and Pepper Society in 1896:

> It arrogated itself the combined powers of a ruling sovereign and the Supreme Court in that it collected revenue on imports by means of custom officers, imposed fines and ordered confiscations after enquiry.

However, in spite of these detractions, the so-called 'friendly societies' were tolerated, if not encouraged by the colonial authorities. Given the British policy of indirect rule, these traditional voluntary associations were at least an improvement over the overtly criminal secret societies. Moreover, in 1890, after the secret societies had been suppressed, there existed a social vacuum which the traditional associations helped to fill, serving as an intervening buffer between the British authority and the Chinese masses.

The most significant part of an association's organization is the mutual benefit section which after 1960 had to be separately registered with the Department of Social Welfare so that the government could exercise proper control over their accounts and memberships. The mutual benefit section normally covers death benefits like the provision of a sum of money for burial, the loan of buses and transport, mourning clothes, and the use of the association's brass band. Another significant part of the benefits is the night-visit paid by the association's members as a mark of respect and condolence to the deceased and his family.

Leadership Patterns

In the nineteenth century, Singapore's Chinese community drew most of its leaders from the merchant class. Most of them were self-made men, wealthy but not formally educated. Due to the reversed social order prevailing in the Nanyang, wealth became the hallmark of social standing, in lieu of education and academic achievements. Nevertheless the three main criteria determining the choice of the clan head remained the same as in traditional China. These criteria were seniority in generation or age, social standing and integrity. Seniority in generation or age was important because it grew out of the kinship principle. Social standing was important because it was connected with the clan's standing, influence and power in the community. And as for personal integrity, it assured the clan that its leaders would not abuse their powers.

In the overseas Chinese communities, the principle of social standing seems to have played a greater role than seniority or personal integrity in the choice of a leader. The most important component of social standing was wealth. A 1968 study by Yong of Chinese leadership in Singapore showed that the leaders of the Singapore Chinese Chamber of Commerce (the premier Chinese association in which traditional associations' leaders hold membership), were overwhelmingly drawn from the merchant class. Though this study focused on the period 1900 to 1941, wealth as the key indicator of social standing was already a social phenomenon in the mid-nineteenth century when the Chinese immigrated in sufficient numbers to form a community and began to stratify themselves according to how successful they were economically. Wealth facilitated social mobility and enabled people to acquire titles and political influence as a means of legitimatizing their status, principally through close ties with the ruling Qing dynasty in China.

Later studies of the traditional Chinese association leadership have shown that most association leaders were males, forty to sixty years old, born in mainland China, and with little formal education. They were in the main self-made, hardworking and enterprising individuals, many of whom had amassed great wealth through business and commercial connections.

EVOLUTION

The evolution of traditional Chinese associations could be divided into 3 distinct periods. During the first period, from 1819 to 1900, the associations were predominantly concerned with social welfare and community work among the Chinese immigrants. The associations entered its second phase from about 1900 when they were caught up in political events in China. This phase lasted until 1949 when the communists captured power in China. The third phase began after 1949 and spans the post-independence years where the associations assume an increasing cultural role. This phase, which continues until today, also saw the gradual displacement of these associations by government-sponsored organizations and modern associations like trade and professional associations based on open membership and specific functions.

First Phase, 1819–1900 : *Social Welfare Concerns*

Under the direct rule of the British colonial government in nineteenth-century Singapore, the traditional voluntary associations were essentially social and community welfare agencies. Their main concerns were the management of temples and cemeteries, transit houses for members, sick houses and medical institutions for dependents, and the fostering of friendship and mutual aid among men of their particular groups. Of primary interest to the newly arrived and destitute migrants was the provision of material aid and mutual benefits to help them find economic security and enjoy fellowship with their own kinsmen and dialect groups. Sometimes small loans were extended to destitute immigrants who needed ready cash to tide them over.

The first clan was probably set up as early as 1819, the year Singapore was founded, by one Ts'ao Ah Chih, according to an authoritative source. Ts'ao Ah Chih, alias Chow Ah Chi, was said to be one of the Chinese who accompanied Raffles to the island of Singapore. According to the same source, the first *hui-kuan* was the Ning Yeung Wui Kun, a Cantonese territorial association established in 1822. The first dialect association, the Yin Foh Fui Kun, was organized in 1823 as the centre of the Hakka dialect group, according to the inscription on its cornerstone. In 1857, a guild called Li Yeung Tong was established by Cantonese actors and actresses.

According to a trusted informant many Chinese associations in fact evolved from temples and shrines, originally set up in reverence to

Above: The Tsao Clan Association's former premises in Lavender Street. It was founded by one T'sao Ah Chih, who was a member of Stamford Raffles' party to land in Singapore in 1819.

Left: The tablet of Tso Foo Sing, a key member of the Tsao Clan Association, reputed to be the oldest clan association in Singapore.

The Thian Hock Keng in Telok Ayer Street served for
a long time as the meeting place and temple of the
Singapore Hokkiens. It was completed in 1842.

some mythical protector gods and/or ancestors. Some associations also
evolved from coolie-keng (literally coolie quarters), cramped surroundings where destitute bachelor migrants spent their days. The Kiung
Chow Hwee Kuan in its early days provided both religious services as
well as accommodation for Hainanese migrants. The Po Chiak Keng
(Protect the South Temple) was at one time the assembly hall and
ancestral temple of the Tan clan in Singapore. The Thian Hock Keng
was the most important Hokkien temple and headquarters of the
Hokkien Association in the nineteenth century. The Ning Yeung Wui
Kun, by all accounts, continues to this day to be the meeting place
and ancestral temple of Cantonese immigrants from the Taishan district of Guangdong province.

Yet another organization is the well-known and feared secret
society, otherwise known in America as *tong* (hall). It is generally
believed that all such societies were offshoots of the parent society
called the Triad, also variously known as the 'Society of Heaven and

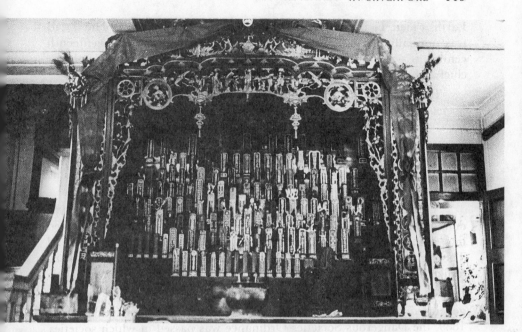

Above: The altar commemorating deceased ancestors of the Kong Chow Wui Kun. This *hui-kuan* organized immigrants from Xinhui district of Guangdong province.

Left: The old premises and temple of the Ning Yeung Wui Kun. One of Singapore's more prominent associations, it represents the interests of Cantonese immigrants from Taishan district in Guangdong province.

Earth' (Tien Ti Hui), and the Hung League (Hung Men). The Triad was orginally a quasi-religious sect but at the end of the seventeenth century it was transformed into a secret political organization with the chief aim of overthrowing the Qing dynasty.

Because of their revolutionary activities, elements of the Triad Society were forced to flee overseas. There, in an environment with a high concentration of lonely male immigrants, they soon involved themselves in protection and gambling rackets, brothels, opium dens and the control of the coolie or 'pigling trade'. They became nothing more than criminal societies, though all or nearly all employed some versions of the Triad rituals.

Throughout most of the nineteenth century, Singapore was dominated by secret societies. Hapless migrants were often coerced into joining, physical violence being a popular recruitment measure! The secret societies were therefore not strictly voluntary organizations, unlike the clans or *hui-kuans*.

The criminal activity of these secret societies and the unrest they generated finally led to an attempt to register and control them. In 1889, the Dangerous Societies Ordinance was passed in which societies classified as dangerous, including the Triad Societies, were required to register. Registration as a means of control, however, proved unsatisfactory. After an attempt was made on the life of the then Protector of Chinese, W. A. Pickering, the Secret Societies Ordinance was passed, which meant that institutionalized and legal power now existed to deal with these societies. They were banned and their members liable to arrest and persecution. For all effective purposes, the activities of the influential Triad societies in Singapore, with nearly a century's history, officially came to an end in 1890. This, however, did not by any means affect the total extinction of these societies. They continued to operate underground in a restricted way and do so even until the present day. They became secret societies in the actual sense of the word, indulging in petty crimes.

After the suppression of the secret societies in 1890, the clans, *hui-kuans* and dialect associations gradually became more prominent. From this date, these voluntary associations provided the major framework for mutual aid for the immigrants. The immigrants turned to the clans, and in their absence or weakness, to the *hui-kuans* and dialect associations for help and assistance.

The traditional associations held little political clout with the British administration. Being essentially welfare and community organizations, it was in these areas that they contributed most. In contrast, a Straits Chinese British Association was set up in August 1900 to foster the interests of the Straits-born Chinese, and loyalty to the British crown. Its founder members were Straits-born, English-educated Chinese leaders led by Tan Jiak Kim, Seah Liang Seah, Lim Boon Keng and Song Ong Siang. British policy consciously cultivated them in opposition to the immigrant Chinese by bestowing them titles, status and positions. Many served as unofficial members of the Straits Settlements Legislative Council, Municipal Commission, Chinese Advisory Board, and Governor's Straits Chinese Consultative Committee.

Being intimately attached to the authorities, these leaders tended to identify their interests with those of the British government. For example, in response to the Boxer Rebellion in 1900 some Straits Chinese agitated for the dispatching of a contingent of Straits-born Chinese volunteers to serve the British troops in fighting against the Boxers and the Manchus. They were deeply critical of the traditional leaders and the associations, accusing them of 'preferring inactivity to change and blind respect for authority to reasoning.' Of the clan associations an anonymous Straits Chinese wrote in 1899, 'their interferences in local quarrels and lawsuits and their organized intimidations and oppositions to government measures make them as obnoxious as the Triads . . . An *imperium in imperio* should never be tacitly tolerated.'

Second Phase, 1900–1949 : *Political Involvement*

While the traditional associations catered primarily to the socio-economic needs of the overseas Chinese in the nineteenth century, the next half century saw these associations at the forefront of political agitation for the motherland. The origins of political consciousness and nationalism among the overseas Chinese in Singapore and Malaya occurred during the period 1895–1911; between the Sino-Japanese War and the Chinese revolution.

The humiliating defeat by Japan stirred reformist and revolutionary fervour in China. Both shared the common aim of strengthening China and saving her from further depredations from the imperialist powers, though the reformists emphasized internal reforms and preserving the imperial monarchial system, while the revolutionaries were for radical change to a republican democratic system.

These political factions recognized early that the overseas Chinese presented a ready and fertile ground for the canvassing of funds and support for their activities. Within the Chinese community, the best way to mobilize the immigrant Chinese appeared to be through their traditional associations which were the mainstay of the Chinese community structure.

The Teochew Poit Ip Huay Kuan brings together Teochews
from the 8 districts of north-eastern Guangdong province.

The traditional associations play a pivotal role in Chinese community life. The first half of the nineteenth century saw not only a phenomenal growth in traditional Chinese associations in Singapore but more significantly the consolidation and amalgamation of existing associations into larger groupings. For example, in 1929, the Hokkiens established the Chang Chow General Association, catering to immigrants from the ten southern districts of Fujian province. In the same year, the Teochews started the Teochew Poit Ip Huay Kuan, bringing together members from eight districts of eastern Guangdong province. The Hakkas also had their Nanyang Khek Community Guild (the Hakka general association), founded in 1929 by eight earlier associations; the Yin Foh Fui Kun, the earliest Hakka association, being one of these. In 1938 the Singapore Kwangtung Wui Kun was founded to represent the interests of all immigrants or their descendants who came from the province of Guangdong.

Many small, localized clans also combined to form a general surname association. There are many examples of such amalgams, two of the larger ones being the Singapore Lee Clan General Association set up in 1907 and the Singapore Chong Clan General Association in 1938.

The development of larger groupings could be interpreted as a natural outcome of increased numbers of immigrants and the need to organize them in some larger umbrella organizations. Larger clans, *hui-kuans* and dialect associations meant greater resources and clout in meeting immigrants' needs and in dealing with external agencies, like other clans and dialect associations. In addition, scholars like Png interpreted this consolidation movement, especially during the period 1931 to 1940, as the response of the overseas Chinese to China's plight in the face of Japanese aggression. Uniting to form larger associations, the reasoning goes, enabled the Chinese to give their maximum support to their motherland.

On the basis of these developments, *bangs* or literally group or cluster of associations, emerged during this period. *Bangs* often have prefecture- or provincial-level associations at their centres, with other associations like the clan or surname associations, schools, hospitals, clubs, temples, cemeteries, pugilistic or recreational associations serving myriad purposes at the periphery. To give an idea of the size of a *bang*, the Teochew *bang* had the Teochew Poit Ip Huay Kuan as its headquarters, with one charitable association, six *hui-kuans*, one borough association, five village/town associations, twenty-three clan and surname associations, five guilds and eight cultural and recreational associations as affiliated associations in 1969. While the Teochew had fifty associations in its *bang*, the smaller Hakka *bang* had only thirty-eight.

The only superordinate association above these *bangs* is the Singapore Chinese Chamber of Commerce (SCCC), whose membership is restricted to Chinese firms, factories, professional companies and commercial associations that are registered with the Singapore government. After having been affiliated, member organizations may nominate a Chinese individual as their representative. There are no traditional clan, locality or dialect associations involved in the SCCC. However, since the towkays (bosses) of the commercial organizations are at the same time the leading officials of the traditional high-level voluntary associations, the SCCC actually has a controlling influence over the traditional clans, locality and dialect associations. The supremacy of the SCCC is based more on tradition than on legality due to a caveat in its written charter which gives it no power to dictate policy or issue orders to other associations.

新嘉坡中華商務總會

This photograph shows the 49 founding members of the Chinese Chamber
of Commerce, Singapore's premier Chinese association, in 1906.

What comes across is a loosely structured hierarchy of Chinese
associations, with the SCCC at its pinnacle because its management
committee comprises the most important leaders from the major dialect
groups. At the other end of the scale are the localized clans,
where membership is restricted to kinship and previous places of
origin.

The need to mobilize this loose federation of traditional associations became more urgent for the revolutionaries when the reform-
minded Emperor Guangxu died in 1908, and with him the entire
reformist movement led by Kang Youwei. Disillusionment with the
monarchial system under the reign of Empress Cixi drove many
patriotic Chinese into the revolutionary's camp. Under the dynamic
leadership of Sun Yat-sen, the revolutionary activities expanded and
spread overseas to the Chinese communities. Sun himself visited
Singapore eight times in the first decade of the twentieth century to raise
funds and support for the ongoing revolutionary activities in China.

In 1906, he set up the Singapore branch of the T'ung Meng-hui
(TMH), Sun's revolutionary party first formed in Tokyo in 1905.

Located in Wan Ching Yuan (a prominent private mansion off Bales-
tier Road), the Singapore TMH almost immediately became the headquarters of the Southeast Asian branches of the TMH. After setting up
TMH branches throughout Malaya, the revolutionary leaders accelerated their crusade to drum up nationalism among the overseas
Chinese against the Manchus. They attacked the Manchus through
the Chinese newspapers, through mass rallies, activist teachers in
Chinese schools and through different front associations, like the reading clubs.

One of the most effective media used by the TMH revolutionaries
to infiltrate the traditional associations was the setting up of the
so-called reading clubs. Between 1908 and 1911, more than fifty such
reading clubs were established throughout Singapore and Malaya.

In Singapore, the most famous of the reading clubs was the T'ung
Te Reading Club, otherwise called the United Chinese Library, which
was formed in 1911. Begun as a revolutionary propaganda organization, it served also as a cover for political activities for the Kuomintang (KMT), the successor to the TMH, until its proscription by the
British colonial government in 1949. It is still in existence in Armenian
Street though it is now an educational society.

Activities of the reading clubs were specifically aimed at leaders of
the *hui-kuans* and dialect associations, as these were the biggest and
most powerful social groups with which the greatest number of people
were associated. Through their propaganda efforts the revolutionaries
were successful in inviting individual representatives of the Cantonese,
Hokkien, Teochew, Hakka and Hainanese communities to give
speeches in support of the revolutionary cause. In this way large sums
of money were raised. After a few false starts, the revolutionaries won
in 1911.

The success of the revolution in China was greeted with much
rejoicing. Describing the scene in the streets of Singapore, Song Ong
Siang wrote:

> Red bunting and new blue and white revolutionary flags were displayed
> everywhere, and the ceremonious burning of the Imperial Dragon Flag
> took place in front of one of the leading Chinese banks in Kling Street.
> The debris of crackers lay ankle-deep in Market Street and covered the
> long line of North and South Bridge Roads like a carpet. Hundreds of
> Chinese residents lost no time in removing their queue without troubling
> about their hair in front of their heads. In some cases, enthusiasts went
> to the length of dragging passing Chinese, who wore *towchang* (or plaited
> hair), into neighbouring shops, where much against their will, amateur
> coiffeurs relieved them of their appendage.

China's troubles however were far from over. Yuan Shikai attempted to set himself up as Emperor. After his death, the whole country receded further into an era of warlordism, during which different factions struggled for control of China. After the KMT managed to unify China the Japanese invaded Manchuria and later China proper and the latent KMT-Communist conflict again erupted into open warfare.

With the Japanese invasion of China in 1937, Chinese nationalist activities reached their peak. In August a massive relief convention took place at the Singapore Chinese Chamber of Commerce (SCCC), attended by some 700 Chinese representatives from 118 participating bodies, consisting mainly of clans, *hui-kuans*, dialect associations and guilds, The Singapore Chinese China Relief General Association (SCCRGA) was formed, headed by Tan Kah Kee and headquartered at the Ee Hoe Hean Club. The 32-member committee was made up of representatives of various dialect groups in Singapore. This impressive line-up of dialect leaders underlines the fact that associations like the SCCC or the SCCRGA were influential only because the *hui-kuans* and associations had the allegiance of many Chinese.

Prominent Chinese leaders at the multi-dialects cooperative level invariably had the backing of their own associations. This was the case of Aw Boon Haw who was the President of the Nanyang Khek Community Guild, Tan Kah Kee, President of the Hokkien Huay Kuan, or Lum Mo Tin, the prime-mover of the Kwangtung Wui Kun and President of the Ning Yeung Wui Kun. The decision to fall back on the traditional association structure, in particular that of the *hui-kuans* and dialect associations, as bases of mobilization and operation could be regarded as a natural development for a society so tightly knit by dialect ties and in which wealth and status commanded great respect. The *hui-kuans* and dialect associations, being the centre of dialect groupings, had to assume the leading roles in the China-relief efforts. Any attempts to bypass them would have been ineffective.

However, by this time, leaders of the Chinese community realized the need for some form of co-ordination so as to increase the efficiency of fund-raising and other relief work. With the KMT's encouragement from China, overseas Chinese came together to form the Federation of China Relief Fund of the South Seas (FCRFSS). As one local newspaper aptly stated: 'The Conference marks a new era in the history of the overseas-Chinese National Salvation Movement, and is the culmination of overseas-Chinese unity.' The Federation was represented by various national salvation associations throughout the South Seas, and thus ranked above the SCCC which represented the interests of the Chinese dialect associations and business community. While the SCCC was the rallying point for Singapore overseas-Chinese nationalism, this role was replaced by the SCCRGA and the FCRFSS. There were, however, close ties between the SCCC, the SCCRGA and the Federation because many members of the executive committees of the SCCRGA and the Federation simultaneously held official positions in the SCCC. The headquarters of the FCRFSS was also at the Ee Hoe Hean Club.

The Federation functioned more as a general policy-making body and co-ordinator of patriotic activities of the Nanyang Chinese than a superior organization with absolute powers over its members' branches. However, as a result of better co-ordination and organization, relief efforts and patriotic activities like boycotts, fund-raising and labour walkouts were stepped up. In particular, the Chinese guilds and merchant houses provided the backbone to the more organized aspects of the anti-Japanese economic boycott. By the end of August some forty Chinese guilds and businesses had ceased dealing in Japanese goods. The FCRFSS, following an appeal from the government in China, even dispatched overseas drivers and mechanics for the transportation of crucial war supplies by road. It was reported that over 3,000 volunteers were sent to China in 1939.

While the KMT was at the forefront to mobilize overseas Chinese support for China, it was at the same time attempting to widen the KMT's political and ideological influence over the immigrant Chinese. This it did in various ways, one of which was the setting up of the San Min Chu I Youth Corps, the KMT's youth organization in 1940. Youths were recruited and given political and military training and encouraged to take part in anti-Japanese activities.

The KMT, however, scored its greatest success in infiltrating the traditional Chinese associations, instilling in its leaders and members love and concern for their motherland. The leaders were rewarded with Chinese honorary titles and some were elected as overseas Chinese representatives to the National Congress Conventions at Nanjing. These were tangible rewards given by the KMT government to the overseas Chinese leaders for their contributions to China's relief and for their allegiance to its government.

In contrast to the KMT, the Malayan Communist Party (MCP) made little headway with the traditional associations. Except for the guilds, which organized the generally poorly paid workers and craftsmen, the MCP met with little success. This was principally because the traditional associations were conservative welfare and social organizations concerned at this period of their history with the plight of their kinsmen back home in China. The KMT, as the sovereign government in China, was able to appeal to the overseas Chinese sentiments and patriotism. The communists, in contrast, had anti-British, pro-working class proclivities as compared to the traditional leaders who were mainly wealthy Chinese and pro-KMT people.

It was even more difficult for the MCP to penetrate the SCCC, because wealth and status, together with dialect group affiliations, were the key criteria for membership. The communist leaders, with their working class backgrounds, were in no position to qualify as leaders in the SCCC. In the end, the MCP had to rely on their own independently organized or infiltrated trade unions and Chinese school organizations to extend their influences in Singapore and Malaya.

When the Japanese captured Malaya and then Singapore in 1942, all anti-Japanese activities of the traditional associations came to a halt. As the vanguard of the National Salvation Movement, the leaders of the traditional associations came in for special treatment from the Kempeitai, the Japanese military police. Many had, like Tan Kah Kee, earlier fled or gone into hiding; however, a few were captured and killed, the most prominent of whom was Lim Bo Seng. To this day, a memorial stands in Lim's honour at Queen Elizabeth Walk, an esplanade opposite the City Hall in Singapore.

The post-war period from 1945 to 1949 saw a brief resurgence of political activities. The KMT in Malaya and Singapore and the MCP, which had helped the British in liberating the countries, were both reactivated. The Chinese community was seriously split at this time between pro-KMT and pro-communist factions. In 1949, the communists took the reins of power in China and this effectively led to the demise of the local KMT. Unlike the KMT, the MCP was not wholly oriented to China but was committed to wrestling political power from the British. The communists grew from strength to strength in the following decade and it took the British and the local governments 12 years of incessant struggle to suppress their activities. Finally in 1960, the 'emergency' was lifted and henceforth the communists were reduced to small, disorganized forces operating in the jungles of Central Malaya and the borders of Thailand.

Third Phase, 1949 to the Present : *Cultural Bridge*

During the decades after the war, the traditional Chinese leaders began to suffer a gradual decline in influence among the Singapore Chinese. Influence shifted to a younger generation of local-born Chinese whose interests were oriented towards Singapore as a homeland. Her independence and welfare became a matter of great importance to their own lives. A study by Yeo of the PAP leadership in Singapore from 1954 to 1955 revealed that sixteen of the seventeen leaders were either born in Singapore or Malaya. They were also better educated, about half possessing a university or college degree. Their bases of support came from the Chinese middle-schools and trade unions rather than from traditional Chinese voluntary associations.

As pointed out by Yeo, pre-war political activities in Singapore were largely an extension of politics in China, while post-war activities had acquired local roots. They were essentially issues relating to the preservation of the Chinese language and culture in an independent Singapore, immigration and citizenship rights for disfranchised China-born Chinese, and bread and butter issues among the poorly-paid manual and white-collar workers during the fifties and sixties.

This shift to indigenous concerns can be attributed to the British policy of preparing Singapore for self-government which compelled the younger generation to relate their political role to their future in that country. However, the main reason was that the Singapore Chinese had become a permanently-domiciled community. This phenomenon can undoubtedly be traced to the Immigration Restriction Ordinance of 1930 which limited the number of male immigrants who could land on Singapore annually. Its aims were to design migration policy to relate labour supply to demand, to achieve a better sex ratio, and to create a more stable population. Its effect was dramatic; within three years, the number of Chinese immigrants fell from 242,000 to 28,000 per year. Furthermore, by allowing women immigrants to continue to enter the island freely, the Ordinance enabled the sex ratio of the population to be corrected. From 1934 to 1938, when female immigration was relatively unrestricted, about 200,000 women emigrated to Malaya and Singapore. Their reasons for emigration varied from economic hardship, reunion with husbands or families, and escaping from ill-treatment at home.

At the beginning of the twentieth century, the ratio of male to female was about 3.9:1. This however fell to 1.1:1 by 1947. Two years later China closed her doors to immigration and repatriation. All forms of communication slowed to a trickle. Even family remittances from Singapore back to China suffered a drastic decline. In 1948, S$10,228,010 was repatriated back to relatives in China. In 1949, it dwindled to a mere S$2,596,683 as communication was disrupted by the communist takeover of the mainland. The net result of all these changes was that more and more Chinese immigrants were prepared to settle in Singapore and to raise their families here.

There was also a dramatic demographic change in the population. The 1957 census showed that Singapore's population had risen sharply from 938,144 in 1947 to 1,445,929. Of this, some 42 per cent of the population fell below age 14. Singapore in the 1950s was an island teeming with young people under the age of twenty-one. And it was this group of young people, many from Chinese middle-schools and the trade unions, who became the major force in Singapore politics in the fifties and sixties. Although basically Chinese in outlook and sentiment, they did not favour the nationalist China-oriented politics of the 1930s. They saw Singapore as their home since many of their families were permanently domiciled here, and many had been born as well as educated in Singapore.

The traditional Chinese leaders in the clans, *hui-kuans* and guilds and in the SCCC were looked upon differently by the new generation of young people. They saw them as appendages of old China, still oriented to the pre-war politics of the Kuomintang era. Many of the traditional leaders were indeed supporters of the KMT and as its political fortunes declined, they also suffered a corresponding lowering of status and reputation. It was from the younger and comparatively better educated Chinese leaders, like Lee Kuan Yew, Lim Chin Siong and Fong Swee Suan that the younger generation drew their inspiration. These leaders were characterized by their involvement in leftist politics and in their championing of the common workmen.

The roles of the traditional Chinese associations began to change. These associations were no longer the arbiters of political power, which had shifted to newly emergent trade unions and student organizations. New power bases had emerged and had to be reckoned with if any political party wished to capture power in Singapore. They either had to be co-opted or neutralized. They could not be ignored as could the traditional Chinese voluntary associations which had been sidelined by the more modern associations.

The traditional Chinese associations increasingly turned to cultural activities as a *raison d'être* for their existence. They provide a cultural bridge to Singapore Chinese, who politically may be Singapore citizens, yet were ethically and culturally Chinese in outlook and sentiment. The purposes and goals of joining the traditional associations, which had previously only been meaningful in relation to the immigrants' residence in China, were now given new meaning in a soon to be independent Singapore where they had taken up permanent residency and nationality. For example, second-generation immigrants were now faced with the problem of the death and burial of a parent in Singapore, and the subsequent difficulty of finding an appropriate place for the ancestral tablet.

As a result, one significant post-war development was the introduction – on a large scale – of mutual aid sections in traditional associations. The mutual aid sections organized planned insurance schemes for the specific purpose of providing funeral benefits. This enabled members to obtain a definite sum, plus their shares of dividends for the particular year or term when they died, provided they paid the specific amount of contributions. Some mutual aid schemes also allowed members to nominate one or two close relatives to participate in the scheme so that their funeral expenses would be paid when they passed away. Thus erstwhile sojourners who were now permanently domiciled in Singapore were assured of a decent burial. This was important because, according to the Chinese, without proper funeral arrangement and worship for the dead, the soul will be restless in the other world. For a small fee the wooden tablet cenotaphs of the deceased could be placed in the associations' shrines for worship in perpetuity.

More important, however, was the cultural link provided by the traditional Chinese associations. From the very beginning, immigrants from China regarded themselves as firmly Chinese and they had no real alternatives for other identities, save perhaps for the Baba Chinese who came to Singapore from Malaya where they had adopted certain Malay cultural traits. This was abetted by the PAP government's emphasis on a multi-racial society where each ethnic group was encouraged to maintain its native traditions and moral strength while promoting modernization and industrialization in the economic and technological spheres. The government's emphasis on bilingualism in the sixties – with one's 'mother tongue' as one and probably English as the other – also supported and encouraged the somewhat elusive search by the Chinese to-rediscover and preserve their cultural traditions.

Cultural and social activities like the Chinese art of self-defence, lion dances, dragon dances, Chinese opera and music, also gained popularity and many traditional associations began to organize such activities. The Kong Chow Wui Kun's lion dances and Cantonese opera troupe which has performed overseas are probably the most famous.

The mutual aid or 'burial' societies also flourished, and some Chinese derisively called them 'chap sie huay' (literally ten surnames societies), as they would take in any Chinese who could pay their dues without referring to kinship, places of origin or dialect ties. In fact, according to one study by Kwok, the main purpose of setting up the mutual aid sections in the traditional associations was to prevent their members from departing to join those mutual aid societies that were being set up like business ventures.

THE FUTURE

The erosion in our Chinese roots is reflected in the decline of the traditional Chinese associations in Singapore. The traditional Chinese associations embody certain key Confucian ideals, principally the notions of mutual help, collective responsibility, filial piety, reverence for ancestors, respect for authority and sacrifices for the common good.

Recruitment has become a problem. Many association leaders have voiced the difficulty of recruiting young members. One leader felt that those from the older generation were more prepared to offer their services for others' welfare. The younger generation, in contrast, are very conscious of personal benefit in joining any organization.

This opinion is shared by another association leader. He felt that individualism and materialism of our youths have overcome the older generation's spirit of communal sacrifice. As a result, 'the first thing the young look for when they join clan associations is what they can get from them, and not what they can give.'

The government shows considerable concern over the new spectres of fiercely competitive adults, pleasure-seeking and seemingly aimless youths and old parents being pushed into old age homes. It has therefore attempted to inculcate some good old-fashioned Confucian virtues into a somewhat renegade lot of Singaporeans.

Throughout this exercise of moral education, the traditional Chinese associations were singled out by the government, and constantly exhorted to be bastions of old-world Chinese virtues. They were called upon to promote a greater awareness of Asian values like filial piety, and to teach the young better human relations and work attitudes.

Ironically, while the associations are being called forth into battle against 'modern' values, their foundation is becoming increasingly shaky. The government keeps a tight control over the registration of societies and organizations in Singapore. It has the power to refuse applications for registrations and to deregister societies. From 1969 onwards, the government has forbidden the registration of new societies if they are formed on racial or dialect lines. The aim of the policy is to prevent the proliferation of associations catering to narrow sectional interests while encouraging the general public to join government-sponsored 'free-for-all organizations' like the Community Centres and the Residents' Committees. There is therefore a lack of free and spontaneously generated associations in Singapore, which in countries like the United States, form a necessary part of the democratic infrastructure.

The government's urban renewal programme also has had its

repercussions on the traditional associations. The compulsory acquisition of old pre-war houses, which housed many associations at below-market rate, render those affected associations 'homeless'. The clearance of areas of high Chinese concentration in Chinatown also cost the associations a large portion of their membership as the residents began relocating to far-flung HDB estates.

Another loss is the association graveyards to urban redevelopment. This loss has removed one key function of the associations, this being the administration of the graves and the carrying out of the biannual Spring and Autumn ancestral rites at the association cemeteries. Association leaders believe that potential members will not be attracted to join as they are now unable to be buried with their fellow clansmen in a common cemetery and be accorded the ritually important ancestral rites.

The third- and fourth-generation Chinese born after the war and mainly educated in English, do not have a close cultural affinity with these associations. They live in a rapidly modernizing society with no personal recollections or memories of China. Given the permanently domiciled population and an even sex ratio, most of the young Singaporeans were the offspring of intact family units and thus see no need to maintain their ties with clansmen and dialect group members. The social welfare role of the associations was increasingly being picked up by specialized government agencies as Singapore stepped up its pace of modernization. A genre of modern associations also appeared to take care of the needs of a younger, English-educated population of Singaporeans. These modern associations included trade unions, sports clubs, YMCAs, and the government-sponsored Community Centres and Residents' Committees.

Traditional associations, being organized on the basis of dialects, will find it progressively difficult to survive as Mandarin replaces dialects as the *lingua franca*. This means that the younger generation will end up using Mandarin, besides English, and see even less need to join the traditional associations.

In tandem with the Mandarin campaign is the campaign to use the Hanyu Pinyin system for the spelling of Chinese names. This means that a Chinese surname like 张 will be Zhang in Hanyu Pinyin instead of Chang, Teo or Cheong, et cetera, in the different dialects. Clan associations organized on the basis of dialect surnames will therefore slowly wither away as the present generation of children begins to adopt Hanyu Pinyin names.

In the light of these recent developments, the leaders of the traditional associations have been responding to the plight of their associations. A forum organized in December 1984 to explore ways to revitalize these associations led directly to the formation of the Singapore Federation of Chinese Clan Associations in January 1986. Its inauguration dinner was attended by more than 1,000 Chinese leaders from 127 traditional associations in a rare show of solidarity.

The Federation intends to preserve and disseminate Chinese culture and traditional values to a younger generation that was thought to be heavily dosed with western culture. It is noteworthy that the Federation Chinese language quarterly, which incidentally made its debut at the dinner, is called *Yuan* (source). Its programmes call for the organizing and support of cultural and art activities, performances, publications and forums. Ties would be forged with other traditional associations and grassroot organizations.

The success of the Federation's activities ultimately depends on their appeal to young Singaporeans. Perhaps this can only be achieved if the traditional associations cater to all Singaporeans, irrespective of race, dialect group, religion or sex – a point which the leaders of the Federation appear to recognize.

Even before the inauguration of the Federation, reforms had already begun in at least two Singapore associations. Kong Chow Wui Kun, a Cantonese *hui-kuan*, and Chin Kang Huay Kuan, a Hokkien *hui-kuan*, share the common characteristic of allowing all Singaporean citizens, irrespective of race or dialect, to join their recreational and cultural activities. In the case of the Kong Chow Wui Kun, however, people from other localities of origin in China are not allowed to vote or to stand for election. In 1983, when I visited the association, I even met a German associate member. He was then fully engrossed in painting the Kong Chow's *papier-mâché* dragon, which is reputed to be the longest in Singapore. He told me that he had been visiting Singapore regularly during his university vacations, each time performing odd-jobs for the association.

However, it should be pointed out that a change in the constitution of the traditional associations would in fact mean a change in their identity as they are traditionally based on kinship ties, place of origin or dialect group. Yet if the associations do not initiate reforms, they will probably fade away as the current members are old and ageing and the younger persons are unwilling to join. The traditional associations are therefore caught in an unenviable position. One road points to the preservation of their identity and may signify death. The other points to change, and possibly a new role in modern Singapore.

8
TRADITIONAL ASSOCIATIONS IN AMERICA

CHINATOWN, AMERICA

CHINATOWNS in America basically came into being through the process of self-insulation and segregation. The cultural tendencies of the Chinese to replicate their traditional structures have been commented upon. These traditional structures have a larger role than the immigrant aid societies formed by the Europeans in America. In the first place, the Chinese do not recreate their traditional associations anew, but model them upon those found in their homeland. In addition, their functions are diverse. Beyond the basic functions of fulfilling the material or social needs of the immigrants, these organizations reaffirm the basic Chinese beliefs about the world and inculcate values like the importance of kinship, filial piety and mutual responsibility.

Chinatowns also developed in America because of the impact of persecution wrought against the Chinese in the late nineteenth and early twentieth centuries. Forbidden to own land and shut out of trade after trade, the Chinese were gradually squeezed into a ghetto-like existence in some urban centres. Some of these Chinatowns are small – maybe only a street with a few shops, a restaurant or two and rooms for the clan or district association headquarters. Signs that a Chinatown exists are not apparent until one notices the Chinese characters on the signboard. As the Chinese moved away from the pioneering towns of the Wild West and into the big cities, such small Chinatowns disappear altogether. Examples of those are the Chinatowns of Butte, Montana, Boise, Idaho and Denver, Colorado, which no longer exist. In a survey of Chinese churches for the National Council of Churches in 1955, one author found 16 cities with Chinatowns compared to 28 cities in 1940.

The two most prominent Chinatowns today are in San Francisco and New York City. San Francisco Chinatown is the oldest and largest Chinese community in America. Established in the 1850s with an initial population of 700 Chinese, Chinatown grew rapidly until it was destroyed in the great earthquake of 1906 that took along most of San

Francisco as well. Rebuilt on the original site, San Francisco China-town has grown and expanded into a core area of 12 blocks bounded by Columbus Avenue, California Street, Powell Street and Broadway. Like New York Chinatown, it is located in the blighted, low-rent downtown area of the city, in a mixed residential and commercial zone area, near the central business and financial district. The city itself grew out of the flock of miners that descended upon California in the early nineteenth century and quickly became the labour and supply base to the goldfields.

As for New York's Chinatown, it was the result of the anti-Chinese violence during the 1870s and 1880s, when many flocked to New York from the West Coast. Located near the East River on downtown Manhattan, it is bounded by East Broadway and Canal Street. Within this small area is a thriving community. It abounds with garment workshops, restaurants, banks, retail stores and wholesale outlets. Due to the influx of new immigrants it is currently bursting at the seams and expanding outwards to encroach on the Italian and Jewish sectors. There is some urban renewal, like the Confucian Plaza, but due to its limited area, real estate has skyrock-eted. Many people are prepared to fork out US $5,000 in irretrievable 'key money' for the chance to buy old one-bedroom apartments. Com-mercial space goes for even higher – a well-located restaurant runs to US $300,000 to US $400,000 'key money'.

Both Chinatowns are major tourist attractions with millions of tourists coming through annually from sightseeing tour buses and the subways. They are places of quaint architecture, Chinese characters on vermilion red signboards, garish neonlights, and narrow, winding streets, some of which in New York's Chinatown are hardly more than cobblestone paths, barely wide enough for one car to squeeze through.

Chinatowns also have a fine reputation for their superb res-taurants, representative of each regional cuisine – from Cantonese to Szechuan, Shanghainese and Hunanese. Even curries and Hainanese chicken rice, Southeast Asian favourites, are available. If you would rather do your own cooking, there is a wide and bewildering array of fresh produce – fish, meat, poultry, vegetables, fruits and exotic whole Chinese herbs and delicacies like birds' nests, Chinese mushrooms and sharks' fins.

Within their small confines, many languages and dialects are spoken, a variety of newspapers and magazines are published locally or imported, and until recently San Francisco Chinatown even had its own telephone exchange manned by Chinese telepone operators, with the convenience of a completely hand-written Chinese directory.

Grant Avenue – in the heart of San Francisco Chinatown.

The buildings of Chinatown are actually old and decrepit, many of them more than a hundred years old. They are usually three to four storeys with dormered attics. The stairs one enters from the streets are black and warped, with uncarpeted, crooked, narrow treads. Most of the ground floors are occupied by shops, though there are also a great number of traditional associations and churches. An extra large and impressive building housed the consolidated Chinese Benevolent Association (in San Francisco it is called the Chinese Six Companies), which once aspired to speak for the Chinese community.

Due to the political situation in America, the Chinese in Chinatown have been left very much on their own. The Chinese community is isolated and self-sufficient and functions more like a separate immigrant settlement in an open society. Except during periods of anti-Chinese riots and campaigns, the Chinese carved out their own existence. Deprived for many years of the rights of naturalization and the franchise, they could not effectively voice their grievances to politicians, who generally ignored them. Unlike the other immigrants, like the Italians, the Chinese were not wooed or solicited by local politicians who were interested in winning elections, and therefore had to fall back on their own resources.

CHINESE TRADITIONAL ASSOCIATIONS

In structure and function, the traditional associations parallel closely those found in Singapore. There are the usual clans (sometimes called family associations in America), *hui-kuans* (referred to as district associations by some authors), guilds and dialect associations.

A large proportion of the immigrants were Cantonese from Guangdong province in China; specifically from the Sze Yup and Sam Yup districts. In America, therefore, Cantonese dialect-based associations predominate. In other words, the clans, *hui-kuans* and guilds usually comprise only Cantonese-speaking Chinese, unlike some associations in Singapore which are exclusively Hokkien, Teochew, Hakka, etc., or a composite of various dialect groups.

The Chinese group in America is therefore considerably more homogeneous in dialect and customs than that in Singapore. It was not until the first repeal period, after 1943, that a more varied group of Chinese arrived in America. The immediate years after 1943 were characterized by a great influx of women, wives and children with their consequent favourable implications for Chinese family life. Before the communist takeover of China in 1949, a large contingent of professionals, scholars and students arrived from all parts of China. Chinese students and intellectuals who had arrived before 1949 were now 'stranded' in America without an opportunity to return home. Their lot was a depressing one as almost overnight they not only lost their families but had to reorientate themselves politically, economically and socially to a life of permanent exile overseas.

Many of these students and intellectuals migrated from provinces and cities outside Guangdong province. Thus they did not speak Cantonese but rather the southern Fujian dialect and Mandarin. These minority groups generally stayed aloof from the lowly educated or illiterate coolies who arrived in the earlier waves of immigration. They formed their own social clubs but among the more conservative, a few clans and *hui-kuans* were set up.

Without a doubt, the Cantonese bloc is by far the most powerful among the dialect associations, politically and economically – despite there having been later waves of immigrants from other parts of

China. In the Singapore situation, the supremacy of the Hokkiens is not as absolute as they are challenged by the sizeable Teochew community. This is not to say that in American Chinatowns no conflicts occur over the struggle for economic or political power. In fact, the tongs were involved in many nefarious activities, sometimes involving the leaders of the traditional associations. There were also conflicts within the Cantonese bloc, especially between the Sze Yup and the Sam Yup factions. Generally speaking, however, whether in Singapore or America, when it came to confrontation with the external world, the Chinese were often able to unite themselves and present a united front.

A hierarchy of associations exists to organize and police the community. On the lowest level there is the *fong* (room) which is rapidly dying out as it exists to serve a few individuals coming from the same village who are invariably bonded by the closest kinship ties. Next come the clans, which numbered about 50 associations in San Francisco. The most prominent clans were those formed by the more common surnames such as the Lees, Wongs and Chins. The Lee clan claims a nationwide membership of 35,000 with the national headquarters located in San Francisco. The size of its membership is seen in the fact that at the time it was the only traditional association with a youth section. The Wong clan is also large and is distinguished by the fact that it was the only one with a women's section in the 1960s. (There are now probably more associations with youth or women chapters.)

Leadership is usually assumed by the wealthier merchants or businessmen. The smaller clans are located in the upper floors of shophouses. Associations with larger memberships could operate an association building in the heart of Chinatown. In these simple clan premises there would typically be mahjong tables, and some rough tables and chairs for reading and chit-chatting. The corner of the room is usually devoted to the ancestral tablets while the richer clans may devote a whole ornate room to ancestor worship. Space is generally not differentiated for use – part of the room may be used for storage and turned over at night to be used as a hostel.

Members would come together to sit and chat, hail the new arrivals, exchange news and gossip, read the papers or join in a game of mahjong, cards or *pai-gow*. These were places which members could go to if they needed a place to sleep or cook a simple meal. In the old days, if they had just arrived from China or were temporarily out of a job, the clan served as a haven until they had time to settle down and provide for themselves.

Chinese immigrant Huie Kin arrived in San Francisco in 1868. This was his experience:

> Somebody had brought to the pier large wagons for us. Out of the general babble, someone called out in our local dialect, and like sheep recognizing the voice only, we blindly followed, and soon were piling into one of the waiting wagons. Everything was so strange and so exciting that my memory of the landing is just a big blur. The wagon made its way heavily over the cobblestones, turned some corners, ascended a steep climb, and stopped at a kind of clubhouse, where we spent the night. Later, I learnt that people from the various districts had their own benevolent societies, with headquarters in San Francisco's Chinatown. As there were six of them, they were known as the 'Six Companies'. Newcomers were taken care of until relatives came to claim them and pay the bill. The next day our relatives from Oakland took us across the bay to the little Chinese settlement there, and kept us until we found work.
>
> In the sixties, San Francisco's Chinatown was made up of stores catering to the Chinese only. There was only one store, situated at the corner of Sacramento and Dupont streets, which kept Chinese and Japanese curios for the American trade. Our people were all in their native costume, with queues down their backs, and kept their stores just as they would do in China, with the entire street front open and groceries and vegetables overflowing on the sidewalks. Forty thousand Chinese were then resident in the bay regions, and so these stores did a flourishing business. The Oakland Chinatown was a smaller affair, more like a mining camp, with rough board houses on a vacant lot near Broadway and Sixteenth Street. Under the roof of the houses was a shelf built in the rear and reached by a ladder. Here we slept at night, rolled in our blankets much in the manner of Indians.

Further removed in the hierarchy of Chinatown organization are the *hui-kuans*. Like their Singapore counterpart, they accept for membership all those originating from the same district or county in China. Because they usually have a larger membership, they command greater respect among the Chinese. This is generally true of *hui-kuans* in other countries where the Chinese settled in sizeable numbers.

The *hui-kuans* cover the usual clans' functions of fellowship, a place to stay and ancestor worship, though the latter is generally not emphasized. One of the most important functions is the provision of capital for business ventures. The *hui* typically operates within the framework of the *hui-kuans* as memberships in these associations provide the approbation needed in the assessment of an individual's credit rating.

The *modus operandi* of a *hui* is as follows:

> A person in need of money works out an agreement with a number of
> friends or relatives whereby each pays a stipulated sum of money into a
> common pool. The organizer gets first use of the entire sum, and a
> month later the *hui* meets again and receives another sum through equal
> contributions and another member – chosen by bidding, election or lot –
> receives the whole sum. The meetings continue until each member has
> had full use of the total sum.

The widespread use of rotating credit among the Chinese in America
has been widely documented. It appears to provide one of the most
important savings and capital-raising institutions in Chinatown. For
older Chinese, it is probably the most important institution as they rarely
utilize the services of American banks.

The *hui* is by no means confined to *hui-kuans* but because they are
usually richer and have more members, they typically operate the *hui*.
The organizer of the *hui* is usually a widely respected and trusted
individual, because he is responsible for collecting subscriptions from
the members of the *hui*. (In Singapore, rampant cheating has led to
the banning of the *hui*. This fact plus the presence and use of banks
and pawnshops accounted for the lesser role of *hui* in capital formation
among the Chinese community in Singapore.)

One Chinese American writer, Betty Lee Sung, wrote about the
role of her father as the organizer of a *hui* for his village association.

> Because my father was widely respected and trusted, he ran the *hui* for
> many, many years. To the best of my knowledge, there was no formal
> organization or charter to this banking arrangement. Members who
> wanted to join merely signed up, and when enough members indicated
> an interest, the *hui* began. Bids were opened at 3 o'clock each Sunday
> and deposits made between 3 and 5. Members who could not make it
> down to Chinatown would call a relative at the *fong* or at a business
> nearby and arrange for the deposit to be made. Sometimes when a
> shareholder who had already received his pool defaulted in his pay-
> ments, his nearest relatives or his guarantors would put up the money
> and get after the delinquent shareholder to pay up. He usually did,
> because the other share-holders were his own village people, and he
> could not risk their ostracism.

Another organization more important than the *hui-kuans* in its range
of functions is the Chinese Benevolent Association (CBA), found in the
bigger Chinatowns like San Francisco, New York and Chicago. In San
Francisco, the Chinese Benevolent Association is known to the American

which amalgamated – the Ning Yung, Kong Chow, Young Wo, Shiu Hing, Hop Wo and Yan Wo. Of these, the biggest and most powerful is the Ning Yung, the association of people from Taishan, formed in 1853 as a breakaway from the Sze Yup Association. On a basis of one representative per 500 members, the Ning Yung has more representatives on the Board of Directors than any other *hui-kuan*.

The Six Companies is considered by the Chinese as the supreme organization over the local CBAs in large American cities where there are sizeable Chinese concentrations. The Six Companies was the first to be founded by the Chinese, though in recent years the New York and Chicago CBAs have risen in importance. The affiliation of the different CBAs was in part prompted by the passing of the Exclusion Act in 1882 when anti-Chinese agitation reached its height. There was then a greater need to co-ordinate the different CBAs to fight for Chinese rights in America.

The premises of the Kong Chow Wui Kun and temple located at the junction of Stockton Avenue and Clay Street in San Francisco.

Within the local CBA, many separate groups are represented – this could be most of the Chinatown organizations including the Chambers of Commerce, women's club, the traditional associations, the *tongs* and even the Chinese schools and newspapers.

The CBAs have many functions. At one time the Chinese Six Companies even assumed consular duties, before China had established formal representation in America. Until the formation of the Chinese Chamber of Commerce in 1910 the Six Companies, together with the guilds, also performed Chamber of Commerce functions, like the registration and regulation of businesses. A prior agreement with the shipping companies also ensured that all returning Chinese paid their debts in America before the requisite clearance from the Six Companies allowed them to buy a passage back. The Six Companies had on record arbitrated disputes among individuals and groups, arranged for burials of deceased immigrants, expedited the return of bones to native villages, run hospitals and schools, hired men to police Chinatown, undertaken to support the claims of alien Chinese for residence, initiated charity drives for China, celebrated China's Independence Day, organized reception of visiting dignitaries and the celebration of the Lunar New Year.

The leaders of the CBA are popular figures as they are the official spokesmen for the Chinese community. Their opinions and decisions carried great influence and power. Without a doubt their quasi-judicial role had helped in the resolutions of conflicts within Chinatown. There were also many instances in which the Six Companies and local Benevolent Associations had arbitrarily and covertly usurped community power to favour particular groups or individuals. Collectively the boards of control have suppressed the voices of Chinese who dared to protest against their pressures, threats or intimidations. The CBAs tend to represent partisan interests, particularly that of the Kuomintang and the local wealthy merchants and employers. As a result they spend too much effort forcing the Chinese regardless of political interest, to be pro-Kuomintang or to put the interests of the propertied class before their interests.

The *tongs* are not properly considered traditional associations. However any account of community life in American Chinatowns would not be complete without mentioning the *tongs*. *Tongs* (literally, halls), were transplanted from China as elements of the anti-Manchu organizations. In an immigrant society of a largely illiterate, male population, they soon capitalized on men's vices – in rackets involving prostitution, opium smoking and gambling. They also provided protection services for illegal activities – some of their clients were alleged to be important leaders of the Chinese community.

Tongs provided an alternative form of organization for the Chinese. Those who came from small or weak clans could join the *tongs* to represent their interests, as otherwise they might not find a voice in the community. Also attracted to join were those who had a score to settle with the established leaders, as well as the riff-raff and discontented elements of society who found the illegal activities an easy and lucrative business. The *tongs* generally enrolled members according to interest, rather than by kinship ties as was the case with traditional associations.

The *tongs* in America, the most prominent being the Chee Kung Tong, were also noted for their political activities outside of involvement in their own communities. At the end of the nineteenth century, their members were recruited by Sun Yat-sen's revolutionary movement in its fight to overthrow the Manchu dynasty. Their political involvement however soon declined after the successful revolution in 1911.

In the early days, the Six Companies and the CBAs were hard put to check the abuses of the *tongs*. *Tong* wars were epidemic and the community was terrorized to submission. The city officials were either indifferent to what happened within Chinatowns or else involved themselves in bribe-taking and payoffs. Fortunately the effect of exclusion on membership plus counter-efforts of the consular representatives of the Chinese Imperial government, local Chinese leaders, missionaries and police officials managed to curb their influences. There was however a resurgence of *tong* criminal activities in the 1960s and 1970s, concomitant with the rise in juvenile delinquency and youth groups in Chinatowns.

Nowadays the *tongs* do not even want to be called *tongs* with its connotations of their nefarious past. Some masquerade as merchant or mutual aid associations – for example, the On Leong Tong is now called the On Leong Merchants Association and the Chee Kung Tong, the Chinese Freemasons. All of these *tongs* in fact take care of the welfare of their members, though shady activities are presumably not a thing of the past.

EVOLUTION

The Chinese in America are a small minority in a predominantly White Anglo-Saxon-Protestant (WASP) society. The two most important concentrations of Chinese are in the Chinatowns of San Francisco and New York, each numbering about fifty to sixty thousand Chinese. Being a disfranchised minority for many years, the Chinese in America were unable to articulate and assert their rights and shape the destiny of the community as well as influence political events in China as much as the Chinese in Singapore with its Chinese majority were able to do.

From about the late nineteenth century, political events in China also caught up with the Chinese in America. Liang Qicao and Kang Youwei, the two most important reformers, took their causes to America to appeal for support among the *huaqiao* (overseas Chinese). Sun Yat-sen soon followed their example. In Hawaii, Sun equipped himself with Chee Kung Tong's credentials as the Triad there belonged to the same lodge as those in America. He was in fact conferred the important title of *hung-kun* (red staff) – in Triad parlance denoting a disciplinary officer of high military rank.

In 1895–96 and again in 1903–04, Sun travelled through the United States, lecturing and canvassing for support. During the latter trip, he was accompanied by an important leader of the Chee Kung Tong on their nationwide registration drive. Initially unsuccessful, Sun was later able to harness the anti-Manchu ideology of the Triads for his own use and turn it into a revolutionary movement. He drew many of his followers from the Triad members who came mainly from the labouring class. These people gave Sun his broadest support in the Chinatowns as opposed to the Six Companies in San Francisco or the Chinese Benevolent Associations elsewhere as they already had strong ties with the established government of China.

The lower-class Chinese had no stake in the Chinatown establishment, as leaders of the important traditional associations controlled all the lucrative businesses. They felt beaten and rejected by the White society around them, yet the Chinese establishment did not represent their interests; it was ineffectual in dealing with the Whites on issues like naturalization or the Exclusion Act. China was in a deplorable state, under a foreign dynasty, which gave them no rights, freedom or pride in being a Chinese. Thus in spite of the death penalty set by the Manchus for any member of the T'ung Meng-hui, or his relatives, the common labourers, together with Sun's Christian friends and supporters, raised funds, set up newspapers and even returned to Guangzhou during certain periods of the struggle to overthrow the Manchus.

After the victory of the revolution in 1911, political activities among the Chinese in America did not cease. As in the Chinese communities in the Nanyang and elsewhere, they were caught up in the turmoil following the revolution. The new Republic was unable to raise China's stature in the world of nations. Instead it degenerated into warlordism and imperialist predations; at the end of which China appeared more vulnerable to foreign aggression than she had been at the beginning.

In America, the Chinese watched developments in China anxiously as up until the Second World War, they were denied citizenship rights. Going back to China continued to be a viable option as long as they were not accepted by the White society. During the 1920s and 1930s, it seemed that every political party had opened a branch or set up their publications in one of the American Chinatowns to canvass support.

In 1927, in the wake of the Kuomintang-Communist split, the KMT which was the dominant party in Chinatowns, broke into the rightist, centralist and leftist factions, each of them setting up branches and newspapers in San Francisco, Chicago and New York.

Spearheading the leftist movement in Chinatown was the Chinese Workers' Mutual Aid Association (CWMAA) made up of the many Chinatown men who were employed by Alaskan salmon canneries during the winters but who tided themselves over during the off season on whatever work they could find in Chinatown. At its height the CWMAA held lectures on Marxism, the labour movement and other topics, convened weekly meetings to discuss problems of Chinese workers and operated a press which printed the first Chinese-language editions of essays by Mao Tse-tung ever published in America.

The Japanese invasion of China in 1937 led to widespread *huaqiao* activities. Some of these were not KMT-dominated but were in fact critical of Chiang Kai-shek and the KMT for their failure to negotiate a second united front with the communists. Some of the groups coalesced to form the Chinese Youth League (CYL) in 1942. Clearly not under the influence of the KMT, the group sponsored drama and choral performances to raise funds for the war effort, sent publications and letters to servicemen and maintained contacts with liberal and progressive groups outside of Chinatown. In its modified form after the war, the CYL is now called the Chinese American Democratic Youth League (Min Qing), and continues to be active in San Francisco. It is reported to have the largest Chinese-language library in America. Many of these more leftist associations were to fade away with the end of the war and the victory of the communists in 1949.

Ironically, the KMT in America rode an even higher crest after they were defeated and had taken over Taiwan. The mood in America after the loss of China was virulently anti-communist. Even before the loss of China, the KMT had pressed their advantage with the dominant merchant class through a combination of veiled threats and rewards. Titles, preferential tariffs and exclusive rights to import popular Chinese food and merchandise were given to co-operative Chinatown leaders. After a new KMT headquarters was established in January 1938, special commissioners were appointed by the Central Committee of the KMT in China. Those Chinese leaders appointed were considered by the local community as holding the highest influence and prestige. Such posts were therefore eagerly sought after.

For a time the KMT commission was headed by a local Chinese who was simultaneously the leader of the biggest clan, the Wong Family Association, the largest *hui-kuan* Ning Yung, and president of the most powerful secret society, the Bing Kung Tong, besides being on the Board of Directors of the Six Companies. This man, Wong Goon Dick, was directly responsible to the Central Executive Committee in China, and in the eyes of the community was virtually the most powerful man in Chinatown.

After his death, his successor who similarly held high positions in the Wong Family Association, the Ning Yung and Chinatown's underground, was given an even higher position. He became a member of the Chinese Nationalist government, with the title of National Policy Advisor to Chiang Kai-shek.

Leaders like him and others of his kind in the merchant community in Chinatown regularly organized fund-raisings, demonstrations of support for the Republic of China and elaborate welcomes for visiting Chinese officials. Chinese schools were established under their supervision with KMT support. After 1949, the surveillance of suspected Chinese radicals were added as one of their responsibilities.

The conservativeness of the KMT-dominated leaders led to the Chinese Six Companies' sponsorship of the Chinese Anti-Communist league in all American Chinatowns in the 1950s. The league carried out a systematic purge of Chinatown leftists and in collaboration with the FBI and the Immigration office, was responsible for the closing down of leftist groups and newspapers.

The CBAs also fought off union inroads among restaurant workers and garment workers. In the late 1960s, when the garment unions attempted to organize Chinese women garment workers in Chinatown, the Six Companies and the factory owners stepped in to thwart its attempts at unionization for better pay and working conditions. This was in spite of the fact that Chinese women garment workers were the lowest paid among all ethnic groups in the industry. Employers' falsification of workers' time cards to avoid prosecution for illegal working hours and wages beyond the minimum stipulated were common practices.

The merchant leaders were naturally suspicious of grassroot participation and populist movement which were inspired from the nationwide movements for minority rights spawned by the civil rights movements of the early sixties in America. This approach to community work is totally alien to the Chinese way of doing things. Social services were part of the traditional patronage system which see the leaders periodically handing out largesse and their constituents playing the role of grateful recipients. It is not surprising therefore that when the Economic Opportunity Council's anti-poverty programme took off in San Francisco Chinatown in the 1960s, the Six Companies attempted to co-opt their leaders or put in their own directors on the Council's Board.

In recent years, there have been some signs of change in the traditional leadership in Chinatowns. Younger, English-educated and American-born Chinese with more liberal views have moved in to positions of power within the traditional associations and the CBAs. Independent voluntary groups have made their appearance to challenge the dominance of the traditional leaders. As a result the traditional associations have loosened their grip on the Chinese community and are unable to speak with one voice for the Chinese people in America.

LOOKING FORWARD

Two important events were to change the power alignment in American Chinatowns. The first was in 1965 when President Lyndon Johnson abolished permanently all laws limiting immigration on the basis of race or nationality. The subsequent flood of Chinese immigrants helped to revitalize Chinatowns while at the same time disrupted the traditional relationship between their denizens. Another huge wave in the late 1970s had much the same effect, but this latest wave to hit America's shore had nothing to do with the easing of immigration regulations. The migrants were refugees from Vietnam, Laos and Kampuchea; the so-called 'boat people', and many were actually ethnic Chinese.

Certain features distinguished the post-1965 waves of immigrants and refugees. A large proportion of the new immigrants were from Hong Kong and Taiwan, who had fled from mainland China. The refugees from Vietnam, Laos and Kampuchea were an assortment of dialect groups – Cantonese, Teochew, Hokkien, etc. A few traditional associations were set up by the new immigrants and refugees, but they were small and weak in comparison to the established ones. Some were from the northern Chinese cities, mainly Shanghai. These spoke only the Shanghai dialect or *guo yu* which put them at odds with the intensely clannish Cantonese. Those from Hong Kong fared better as Cantonese was their *lingua franca* (albeit a different variety from the Taishan Cantonese spoken by the Chinese in America).

Another feature was the immigration of whole families, unlike the earlier immigration of single able-bodied men. The established traditional associations, which had been spawned by the bachelor society of the past, found themselves less relevant in meeting their needs. Further, many of these immigrants had lived in Hong Kong for years and were therefore familiar with the urban economy and setting. There was less need therefore to rely on the traditional associations for adjustment or adjudication of their problems.

Generally these immigrants held high expectations of life in America. Having to live in cramped housing with poor sanitation amidst the squalid surroundings of Chinatown soon dashed their hopes. They were invariably stuck at the lowest rank of society working at jobs in the garment factories and restaurants. Some did seek help from the traditional associations but met with disappointment. Instead they went away harbouring the impression that these associations were in the hands of wealthy individuals, more concerned with enhancing their own positions than with the plight of the needy. Association leaders, on the other hand, felt that these newcomers were too anxious to get ahead, to the extent of expecting and even demanding immediate assistance, something which they were not prepared to accede to.

There was much disenchantment with the Chinatown establishment, especially among the immigrant youths. Many had little education, were unable to speak English and had no saleable skills. Youth gangs flourished, juvenile delinquency shot up and New York and San Francisco Chinatowns experienced a wave of youth crimes and muggings in the 1970s.

The *tongs* soon got into the act, using the gangs as guards and enforcers of their gambling operations. 'Shake-downs' broke out which sometimes culminated in murderous shootings, the death toll often including innocent bystanders. One shoot-out in a San Francisco restaurant in the late 1970s involved many innocent diners. More recently, several Chinese men in a New York Chinatown's gambling den were shot and killed.

Generally anti-establishment, these youth gangs, like the Wah Ching (China's youth), the Black Eagles and the Flying Dragons feel alienated both from the American-born with their smooth manners, snazzy dressing and good education, and the traditional leaders who symbolized the wealth and power they were unable to attain for themselves. The Wah Ching had been known to hold the Six Companies to ransom and also to disrupt traditional Lunar New Year parades.

Part of the post-1965 wave was a group of highly qualified Chinese with professional or technical backgrounds. In 1970 for example, 3,715 Chinese professionals and technicians entered California as compared with 2,098 service workers. They were generally able to find suitable jobs outside of the traditional set-up in Chinatown. Chinatown became, then, a place which they may periodically visit with their families and friends for a meal or to buy provisions. For these people and the American-born Chinese, who are able to work and move freely in all areas of American society, Chinatown is slowly losing its significance as the centre of Chinese life.

The American-born Chinese, immigrant youths and middle-class Chinese, together form a bloc that cannot easily identify with the traditional associations and their merchant-businessmen leaders. They tend to see the associations as tradition-rooted and their leaders as a bunch of well-moneyed, conservative representatives of some conglomeration of Chinese family associations and groups.

Another wide-ranging event in the 1970s was to further erode the credibility of the Chinatown establishment. This was America's rapprochement with Communist China which resulted in the Shanghai Communique in 1977 and the normalization of relations by 1979. The KMT-backed Chinatown leaders staged nationwide campaigns to protest the admission of the People's Republic to the United Nations and the normalization of relations but to no avail. The younger, more leftist leaders of the Chinese community, on the other hand, appeared to favour normalization, even going to the extent of pressurizing the Ford and Carter administration for an early solution.

The traditional associations and their leaders were left on a limb. After almost eight decades of supporting the KMT they were suddenly left in midstream after the sudden and abrupt change in America's foreign policy.

The new younger leaders, not tainted by the KMT past, began to set up a whole host of organizations that bypassed the CBA, the *hui-kuans* and clans. Some of these groups included the Organizations of Overseas Chinese (OOC) with about 3,000 members and the National Association of Chinese Americans (NACA), which were spearheaded by intellectuals and business leaders residing outside Chinatowns. Other associations included the YMCA and YWCA, churches and religious groups, the Chinatown Planning Council, the Chinese for

Affirmative Action, the Asian-American Legal Defense and Education Fund.

They were concerned with a motley of issues ranging from low-cost housing, public health, non-discriminatory practices, crises of the garment industry, preservation and conservation, and bilingual education for Chinese American children. The radical left-wing group set their roots in the international workers movement against racism and economic exploitation symbolized by American imperialism, while the more conservative church-based groups were bent on spiritual salvation and saving souls. No project was considered too small. One group conserved San Francisco's famous International Hotel, which had for decades been providing housing for elderly residents in the community; it also subsequently set up a co-operative garment factory in its basement. Another prevented the removal of a Chinatown Playground. This group later amalgamated with others to form the Chinatown Neighbourhood Improvement Resource Counter which has lately been successful in their applications for federal, state and city funding for new bus lines, low-income housing and street improvement projects.

With increasing numbers and economic clout, the Chinese Americans began to involve themselves in political activities of their adopted country. In the past the immigrant Chinese had been inspired by the Chinese revolution and the KMT government. Their orientation was towards China and later the Republic in Taiwan. Now a new generation has begun to relinquish ties with their ancestral land and increasingly direct their energies towards maximum participation in American political life.

The earliest Chinese organization with political connections was the Chinese American Citizens Alliance (CACA) formed in 1915 from another group called the Native Sons of the Golden State. Its main aim was to promote assimilation of the Chinese into American life through its influential newspaper *The Chinese Times*, and through community work. The latter involved a broad range of projects – the Ping Yuen Housing Project, the creating of new job opportunities for Chinese, scholarship funds, voter registration and endorsing of election candidates.

As the CACA is seen as being Republican, Democratic clubs have been set up in all major Chinatowns. Addressing issues of minority rights, the Democrats emphasize what they see as the problem of Asian-Americans as a whole. These issues could be Japan-bashing that creates hostility against Japanese Americans, attacks on Vietnamese American fishermen, shortages of bilingual teachers, discriminatory college-admission policies and employers who hire but fail to promote

The earliest Chinese organization in America with political connections, the CACA is involved in a wide range of community projects.

Ping Yuen Housing Project – finding solutions to the
congestion in San Francisco Chinatown.

Asian-Americans. Differing in emphasis, the common platform of the
Republicans and Democrats appear to be to make racism politically
unpalatable and to get more Asian-Americans elected into political
office. Out of this political involvement has come such success stories
as March Fong Eu, presently Secretary of State of California and
Michael Woo, the first Asian-American to win a seat on the Los
Angeles City Council.

What we are seeing in American Chinatowns today is a new
generation that is more assertive and assimilated and willing to raise
its voice for greater recognition, just as other minority groups like the
Jews have received in the United States. As more and more Chinese
are able to move freely in American society, the Chinatown establishment as embodied in the traditional associations become less and less
relevant except for the trapped – the poor immigrants, the aged
bachelors of pre-exclusion days and those who continue to live there
by force of circumstance.

In the past the traditional association leaders adopted a strategy of withdrawal into the confines of Chinatowns where the Chinese live their own lives apart from the wider society. Politically apathetic, only a few thousand of Chinatown's residents voted regularly. Such a separation only served to accentuate the inscrutability and alien nature of the Chinese. Critics were quick to point to these unassimilable features and to demand the expulsion of the Chinese race.

Today this siege mentality of the Chinese American is over. The power of the traditional leaders and their associations is on the wane. The younger generation, at least, is more aware and is beginning to get involved politically in American society. As Betty Lee Sung has pointed out, the functions of these traditional associations today are not to provide shelter or give aid to their needy sons, nor to provide interpreting services or settle disputes, but merely to stand as a symbol of common origin.

9

TRADITIONAL ASSOCIATIONS IN AUSTRALIA, NEW ZEALAND AND BRITAIN

LIKE the Chinese pioneers in California, the early Chinese immigrants came to Australia and New Zealand as gold miners. Formed into distinct clans of working men hailing from the same area in China, the Chinese often worked away from the Whites in their own valleys. They built their own huts from castaway items such as crates, rice-sacks, and stones.

In their settlements, they organized their lives in accordance with the age-old principles of lineage and village ties. The clans set up their own temples, with the canonization of common real or mythical ancestors as the central focus of worship. Places of worship, called 'joss-houses' in Australia, were also set up everywhere for popular deities like Guan Gong, the God of War and Justice, and Guan Yin, the Goddess of Mercy. These temples served as a gathering and meeting place for all Chinese. Matters common to them were discussed under the auspices of clan elders or 'village' headmen. The occasional festival, like the Lunar New Year, was celebrated in the mining camps with a gathering of miners from the surrounding areas. A pig would be roasted, red papers with auspicious inscriptions pasted on the doors, crackers were lit, greetings exchanged, and for a moment the miners would forget that they were in a foreign land.

The early years saw a proliferation of traditional associations, mostly *hui-kuans* or district associations. Although most of these associations made their appearance in the mining communities, they soon became an important basis of organization in the cities. In Sydney alone, it was reported that there were 16 Chinese *hui-kuans* by 1891. One of the earliest *hui-kuans* to be formed is the Kong Chow Association founded by immigrants from the Xinhui district of the Guangzhou prefecture. The Sze Yup Association, probably the biggest and most powerful, was founded in 1854 by immigrants from the four counties south of Guangzhou.

In New Zealand, where there were fewer Chinese, only a handful of traditional associations existed. According to an authority on New Zealand Chinese there were only 4 *hui-kuans*, the most prominent being the Sze Yup Association in Wellington.

Apart from the usual social functions, the other activities of the associations were overtly political – raising funds for the reformist movement under Liang Qicao, and the later Republican cause. The bigger associations were also involved in economic activities, like being shareholders in the China-Australia Mail Steamship Line, set up after the war in 1921.

As was true for the overseas Chinese elsewhere in the world, the burial function of the associations was one of the most important for the Chinese in Australia and New Zealand. The old and the feeble were provided with funds to go home to die; or were ensured, upon their demise, that their remains would be despatched to their home villages. An accident in 1904 illustrated the importance of the shipment of bones to the Chinese. The steamship *Ventnor*, laden with the remains of over 400 Chinese, struck a rock off the New Zealand coast and sank without a trace. The Chinese in New Zealand and relatives in Guangdong province were devastated. Rewards were posted and efforts made to recover the mortal remains but to no avail.

For many years the traditional associations also organized the Ching Ming festivals during which members of the Chinese community would visit the graves of their deceased relatives. Visitors would burn offerings at the graveside, and eat the food brought for the worship. In both Australia and New Zealand, however, the graves of the Chinese are now in a state of neglect and the festival is slowly losing its significance.

Unlike the Chinese community organizations in America and Singapore, the associations in Australia and New Zealand were less well-developed in terms of hierarchy and specialized functions. In America, the Chinese associations were organized from the lowest level of *fong*, which was literally a room or headquarters for people from the same village who are usually bonded by closest kinship ties. Next on the hierarchy are the surname associations, called family associations in America and clans in Singapore. After this level comes the *hui-kuans* which generally assume wider functions as they are bigger and stronger. The apex of the Chinese organizational pyramid is the Six Companies in America and the Chinese Chamber of Commerce and Industry in Singapore.

In Australia and New Zealand, the smaller number of Chinese precluded the possibility of fine-tuning the Chinese community life at the lowest to the highest level. Clans, not to mention *fong*, are largely missing or unimportant as a basis of organization.

The highest level of organization in Australia appears to be the Masonic Society which had its beginnings in a secret society – the Yee Hing. It became the most powerful secret society after the dissolution of its rival, the Bo Leong, and was able to hold sway over the Chinese community. According to Chinese scholars, the violence and bloodshed often associated with the *tongs* in America and the secret societies before they were banned in Singapore and the Straits Settlements, was largely absent in Australia. This is due to the exclusive control enjoyed by the Yee Hing after 1912 and its able and popular leadership. In Australia and New Zealand, the *tongs* with their associated feuds and wars have never been active, as they were in America and the Nanyang.

Most of the functions of the Yee Hing were broadly the same as in the *hui-kuans* except that its concept of brotherhood was wider and encompassed Chinese from different parts of China. Like the American *tongs*, the Yee Hing was in the thick of the political fray during the turbulent years from 1900 to 1949. The leader of the Melbourne Yee Hing was instrumental in forming a united front with the Young China League against the Qing regime in China.

After the fall of the Qing regime, and the establishment of the Chinese Republic, the Yee Hing underwent a metamorphosis and reappeared as an overt political party. It was variously called the Chinese Masonic Society, the Chung Wah Ming Kuo Kung Hui, and the Chee Kung Tong. Its main aim was the support of Sun Yat-sen for the establishment of a true Republic of China. Some of its fund-raising activities included canvassing for the revolutionary armies in southern China and the launching of the northern expedition against the Chinese warlords. In order to ensure the success of the campaign, Sun Yat-sen in fact sent his personal representative to Australia in 1918 to raise funds.

Two papers published under the auspices of the Chinese Masonic Society were the *Chinese Republic News* and the *Chinese World News*. The emergence of the popular *Chinese World News* was especially significant because it represented the interests of a political force which could make its voice heard in the Australian Chinese community. Today, however, no Chinese papers are published in Australia or New Zealand.

The association in New Zealand most identified with the Kuomintang is the Chinese Association. It is a conservative association which strove to protect and improve the rights and privileges of the Chinese in New Zealand through petitions, and the cultivation of influential government MPs, ministers and clergymen. Its main orientation was however towards China, and for many years the association had a close relationship with the National Chinese Consulate in Wellington. On a non-political tone, the Association was responsible for organizing celebrations for the Lunar New Year, and the Double Tenth (founding of the Republic). It also welcomed visiting Nationalist Chinese delegations and visitors on behalf of the New Zealand Chinese.

Like their counterparts in America and the Nanyang, the Chinese Association, the Masonic Society and other traditional associations were active in raising funds and supporting China in the war with Japan from 1937. The end of the war saw the associations pitching for the Kuomintang in their struggle against the communists in China.

With the fall in China in 1949, a new political reality made itself felt. The prestige of the KMT plummeted and with it the political interests of the small overseas Chinese community in Australia and New Zealand. The traditional associations no longer have the large following they had when they were a centre of patriotic anti-Japanese organizations.

Several factors contributed to this. China appeared to be happy to let the overseas Chinese be on their own in reversal of the previous dynastic policy of considering them as ethnic Chinese and harnessing their support. In fact the Beijing government since the early 1960s has encouraged the assimilation of overseas Chinese to their own host societies.

The policy of the Beijing government has also alienated the overseas Chinese in other ways – for instance, in the large-scale land reform which saw the elimination of large land holdings, especially clan land and the weakening of the family lineages in southern China, which was the home of the immigrants. Many immigrants dared not return to their villages as they were afraid of being put on trial as landlords. Anyway, China's strict control over migration made returning home a remote possibility. Instead many immigrants attempted to save the day by settling permanently abroad and subsequently bringing their wives and children out of China.

Fortunately for the Chinese in Australia and New Zealand, the post-war period saw a liberalization of immigration laws. Doors were thrown open to different categories of people and the granting of naturalization rights greatly facilitated the transition to the founding of new homes away from their ancestral land.

In May 1986, while in Australia for the Commonwealth Study Conference, I had the chance to spend ten days in Sydney. Sydney is

A Chinese antique shop at the junction of Dixon Street
and Little Hay in Sydney Chinatown.

Australia's oldest city with a population of over 3 million people.
Sydney Chinatown itself is roughly bounded by Pitt, Goulburn, Hay
and Harbour Streets. Much of the happenings are centred in Dixon
Street, the main focal point. Dixon Street was recently beautified and
opened up for public use in 1980. The street is now tiled, flowering
plants adorn the sidewalks with intermittent ornately decorated telephone booths in between. High above, Chinese lanterns are hung,
crisscrossing the entire length of the street. The street itself is flanked
by two lovely arches. On both arches, there are inscriptions in English
and Chinese. One inscription spells the hope for better Australian and
Chinese friendship, another is inscribed with 'Understand virtue and
trust', no doubt a beckoning back to old Confucian ideals.

Chinatown is clearly a vibrant commercial centre. The restaurants, as is true everywhere else in Chinatowns all over the world,
make their presence felt with their Chinese roof, vermilion red lentil,

and their carved dragon, phoenix and cloud motifs. In Sydney China-town, there are also more modest joints with formica tables in a crowded seating area. Besides restaurants, many shops there cater to the more modern tastes of the younger generation – like photographic equipment, computer and video outfits.

I walked through the length and breadth of Chinatown and could only find one traditional association – the Chungshan association, tucked away in a large building at the quiet end of Dixon Street. While finding my way to the association, I stopped a young Chinese boy working in a garment shop. Directing me on my way, he had a last word of advice: 'Don't speak English to those old people there. They'll get very angry with you.' It is perhaps symbolic of the retreat of Chinese age-old culture and tradition that I found the association located in an inconspicuous basement far away from the main bustle of Chinatown.

The Chungshan Wui Kun located in a basement at the wrong end of Dixon Street. A sign of hard times?

Street scene on the main thoroughfare of Sydney Chinatown. The patch on the left is smoke from exploding firecrackers, set off to welcome the Lantern Festival.

Sydney Chinatown comes in a glittering, celluloid package. It leaves a plastic taste in one's mouth as much of it is facade and style. To be sure, the names of the restaurants, like Imperial Palace, May Sun, and Shanghai Village, as well as the red firecrackers I saw for sale for the coming Lantern Festival, conjure up images of old Cathay.

However, on closer observation, very few Chinese actually live in the area, which is given mostly to commercial uses. A contrast is clearly seen in Chinatowns like those in New York and San Francisco, where the places are teeming with Chinese living in tenements and shops. Traditional trades like making bean curd and salted eggs or vegetables are mixed with more modern shops, banks and factories. The streets are alive with hawkers and market gardeners. For all their grime and dirt, these Chinatowns have an authenticity that is largely missing in Sydney Chinatown.

A stirring Lion Dance performance in the streets of London Chinatown during the 1985 Lunar New Year celebration. Considered to be the most important annual celebration, the Lunar New Year brings colour and a festive air to Chinatowns all over the world.

It is not surprising then that there are no Chinatowns matching the scope and vitality found in America in these countries. New Zealand's Chinatowns are properly called streets while the bigger Chinatowns in Melbourne and Sydney are more ornamental graftings on essentially Occidental cities.

The main gathering point for the Chinese in Britain, is in the West End, London's entertainment and theatreland district. London China-town is a small boat-shaped area bounded by Shaftesbury Avenue, Charing Cross Road and Leicester Square. Gerrard Street, which is marked by two beautiful Chinese gateways, lies in the heart of Chinatown.

Called by the Chinese as Tong Yahn Gai (Chinese People's Street in Cantonese), it has an interesting history. First laid out in the late 1670s, the street boasts a number of seventeenth- and eighteenth-century houses, with an assortment of famous people, like John Dryden, living there through the ages.

This famous street now houses a number of prominent Chinese restaurants, like the New World Chinese Restaurant, and the Dumpling Inn, serving Cantonese and Peking cuisine respectively. Restaurants such as these also serve a vital social function. Chinese businessmen, proprietors of catering establishments and ordinary Chinese from as far as Europe, gather to exchange gossip, entertain or strike business deals.

Interspersed with the resturants are a variety of recreational or service facilities like gambling halls, cinemas, grocery stores, travel agencies usually with Chinese proprietors and office staff. The gamb-ling halls are a major attraction catering to the Chinese fondness for chance and risk-taking.

The overall impression is of an incipient Chinatown minus the excitement and dynamism of San Francisco or New York Chinatown. In these two Chinatowns, the Chinese immigrants could live fairly self-contained lives. All the major institutions of Chinese life are in-corporated – from the basic unit of the family to clans, *hui-kuans*, benevolent associations, Chinese factories, groceries, banks, newspapers and Chinese temples. London's Chinatown is quite different, as it is little more than a small ward (Tong Yahn Gai being only 2 blocks long interspersed with foreign shops and businesses). Rather than a residen-tial area, it serves more like a meeting place for the Chinese.

The community organization in Britain is even less developed compared to Australia and New Zealand. One of the more prominent clan associations is the Cheung Clan Association which brought together those with the surname Cheung. Its functions are limited to an annual dinner, welfare work and Chinese language classes for the

Chinese community in London. The Oi T'ung is the oldest Chinese association, founded in 1907, with the aims of organizing overseas Chinese in England for mutual benefit and welfare. Its constitution paid much attention to sickness and death benefits, ensuring its members a decent funeral. It still observes traditional Chinese festival days, like Ching Ming and Lunar New Year.

Some of the associations in Britain were embroiled in political activities in the past. The Chung Sam Workers' Club, which organized emigrants from San Tin in the New Territories was, in the early days, staunch supporters of the KMT and active in patriotic fund-raising efforts. After the communist victory, the KMT party and its branches in Britain were disbanded. In recent years, the reputation of the People's Republic has risen in the immigrants' eyes. Through its representative in Britain and the left-wing oriented Tai Ping Club, which are predominantly Hakka, they organized cultural activities, propagated the achievements of the People's Republic and its standing in international politics. The Club also has a library well-stocked with communist literature.

The associations and clubs that survive in Britain today are mainly recreational centres and/or gambling halls. The modern-day Chinese in Britain appear to be apolitical, mainly interested in business and financial matters. Places of recreation became needed outlets for letting off steam and for associating with fellow Chinese. Other notable associations in Britain are the trade organizations like the British Chamber of Chinese Traders or the Association of Chinese Restauranteurs.

According to Watson, the Chinese community in Britain is different from almost every other settlement of first-generation Chinese migrants in that it is not organized on the basis of traditional associations. The Mans, a lineage which he studied, for example, do not form organizations or formal activities overseas because the locus of their traditional loyalty and affiliation is in Hong Kong, where the ancestral temples are located. The incipient Chinese community in Britain is considered a backwater, not worth the expending of time and energy to replicate a lineage organization that is viable and accessible back home. Most came to Britain with good job prospects and accommodation and did not need the services of traditional associations.

In fact, Watson argued that the impact of emigration on the home villages of San Tin was the reinforcement of traditional patterns of social organization, many features of which were disappearing in other parts of rural Hong Kong. The early emigrants from China to places such as Singapore and America did not wish to stay permanently abroad. Unfortunately, their dreams and fond hopes to return home were not to be realized when the 1949 revolution closed the doors back to China. Emigrant Chinese in Britain in the 1960s however were a different breed. Many returned home on visits regularly due to the availability of cheap charter flights. They were thus able to exercise a direct and active influence on their village affairs in Hong Kong.

The emigrants' ties to their home villages were evidenced by their support of the construction and renovation of public projects such as temples, schools and ancestral halls. A conspicuous symbol of the emigrants' stake to the home community was the construction of 'sterling houses' named after the remittances from abroad that paid for their construction. These were modern spacious two-storey houses different from the traditional single-storey village houses. According to Watson, the orientation of the emigrants was to San Tin even though they lived and worked in Britain. San Tin, for example, was economically dependent on emigrant remittances. It would appear that working in an alien environment further reinforced traditional values and commitments to the home community.

However, the fateful year of 1997 is drawing near. If and when the People's Republic reclaims British Hong Kong, the Chinese in Britain and Europe will have to make some difficult decisions about their future. Those with families overseas would probably opt to stay on. Judging from the mini-panics in Hong Kong over the past few years, those emigrants without families overseas would try to get their families together and depart to safer havens.

THE FUTURE

In Australia, the last discriminatory rule against the Chinese was removed with the promulgation of the 5-year residency requirement for citizenship. In New Zealand the naturalization of the Chinese which was stopped in 1908, resumed again in 1952. In both countries, Chinese are no longer considered alien in status and are entitled to all the rights of citizenship.

Structurally the lack of sizeable Chinatowns in both countries have helped their assimilation. The Chinese are found in all parts of the two countries. In Australia, Melbourne and Sydney have areas that are distinctively Chinese, but these are small and sparsely populated. Most of the Chinese live in the suburbs of these cities even though there is still a concentration of Chinese businesses in other areas. In New Zealand, the Chinese are even more scattered. Auckland and Wellington have 'Chinese streets' but these consist only of a few Chinese shops and residences alongside other European business premises and residences. The Chinese shops typically cater to a mixed clientele and are indistinguishable from the other shops. Chinese schools have completely disappeared though *ad hoc* Chinese classes may be conducted in churches and association premises.

Chinese children and adolescents mix freely with Australian and New Zealand kids in integrated schools. These children of immigrants are hardworking and disciplined and pose no problems for teachers. They mix well and many form lasting friendships with members of other ethnic groups. Chinese professionals are found at all levels of Australian and New Zealand society and are well integrated. Quite often, too, the Australian and New Zealander would come into contact with the Chinese in restaurants and vegetable cum fruit stores owned by the Chinese. Intermarriage is on the increase in both Australia and New Zealand. A recent survey in Australia found that 36 per cent of the Chinese surveyed do not mind marrying Australians of a different racial origin or ethnic group.

A group of Australian kids in Sydney Chinatown. It is difficult to distinguish children of Chinese descent from other White Australian children.

The traditional associations appear to have the support of only a dwindling group of old immigrants. Associations like the Masonic Society or New Zealand Chinese Association are no longer widely supported by the Chinese; nor are they empowered to speak for all age groups. Popular during the time when the Chinese were discriminated against and in need of fellowship and mutual help in a strange land, the associations today have declined in importance. Many second- and third-generation Chinese cannot speak or understand Chinese. Though they may know their surnames, they would not know which clans or district-of-origin they belong to. As a result these associations are considered old-fashioned by the new generations. They would rather join professional associations, YMCA, churches and clubs.

With the passing of the old generation, the traditional associations will probably disappear unless they are reconstructed to suit modern conditions. The more successful associations attract the young with a host of activities like dances, balls, tennis and football games. They are slowly being transformed into ordinary social clubs though they purportedly cater to members who are Chinese or of part Chinese ancestry. A few Chinese association buildings like the Melbourne Sze Yup Association have been rebuilt or upgraded. A joss house has recently been restored in Brisbane. But these association premises and temples are little used and in time to come may become museum pieces.

Younger Chinese in Australia and New Zealand do not affiliate with the traditional associations. These associations, based on ethnic lines, tend to keep the Chinese apart from the rest of the population. Changing situations since the war, however, have helped in the assimilation of the Chinese in both countries. As integration proceeds apace, the Chinese are entering all walks of Australian and New Zealand life. As the memory of their ancestry faded, the past which is embodied in the old ethnic associations becomes irrelevant to their lives.

In Britain, the Chinese do not originally depend on the traditional associations as a form of social organization. The majority of the immigrants came to Britain much later than those in America or Australia. They came with good job prospects, joining kinsmen already well-entrenched in the catering business. Most of these immigrants look to Hong Kong society for the affirmation of their status – the traditional associations thus do not figure in their lives as viable or relevant organizations.

But there are already signs of change in the nature of Chinese emigration. As noted by Watson there was a marked rise in family emigration as the Hong Kong Chinese began to bring in their wives and dependents as helpers in their catering business. It also appeared that the Chinese were keeping their children abroad with them instead of having them educated in Hong Kong. These children, usually a small minority in the overall student population, were placed in English schools. As the mores and language of the dominant culture are gradually absorbed, it is unlikely that the relative imperviousness of the Chinese in Britain will last beyond the first generation. These children would not be likely to succeed their fathers in the catering trade, but would probably find a niche for themselves, preferably in the higher echelons of British society. The 1997 reversion of Hong Kong to mainland China's rule would further accelerate the assimilation of the Chinese in Britain by cutting off their ties with their home villages and by the possible stopping of all emigration of the Hong Kong Chinese to Britain or any other countries. The assimilation of the Chinese in Britain, however, will not spell the death of Chinatown because the ever-ready supply of tourist dollars and the Chinese fondness for good food and companionship will probably keep London Chinatown on an even keel.

Part IV
TRACING YOUR ORIGINS

The American movie *Roots* . . . motivated
myself and many others to visit China to find our
family roots. Many of us that had gone to China
in 1980 and the years thereafter, had been raised
in lands that were thousands of miles away.
Many of us being 2nd, 3rd or 4th generation
Chinese had assimilated quite comfortably into
American and Canadian lifestyles. We came to
China, because the Chinese nation, perhaps
more than any other nations, instills in her
people a sense of respect and pride towards her
history, culture and people.

Wayne Wong
California, U.S.A

10
YOUR ANCESTRAL HOMELAND

CHINA'S large land area is divided up into administrative provinces called *sheng*. The immigrant coastal provinces of Fujian and Guangdong are both considered *sheng* (省) and placed under the jurisdiction of an imperial appointee based in the capital cities.

Below the province in administrative size is the prefecture, *zhou* (州), followed by district or county, *xian* (县), borough, *qu* (区), and village, *xiang* (乡) or town, *chen* (城).

To give an example, Taishan (Toishan), the most prominent of all immigrant districts, was in fact one of the ninety-eight districts in Guangdong province. Within Taishan, as in all other districts, there were numerous boroughs (clusterings of villages) and individual villages or small towns.

Above the district in administrative size was the prefecture. Examples of prefectures in Guangdong province were the Guangzhou and Zhaoqing prefectures. Each prefecture could have a few to more than ten districts. In the case of the Guangzhou prefecture, there were fourteen districts including Taishan and Xinhui. Zhaoqing prefecture had sixteen districts, including Kaiping and Enping. Taishan, Xinhui, Kaiping and Enping, taken together as Sze Yup (Four Districts), was the source of the most immigrants to countries such as America, Australia and New Zealand.

Generally, the entire Chinese immigrant population throughout the Nanyang and other oversea communities came from South China, particularly the provinces of Guangdong and Fujian. There were a few immigrants from some of the other southern provinces – but these were rare exceptions. The great majority of the Chinese immigrants were from rural villages or small country towns of these two major provinces.

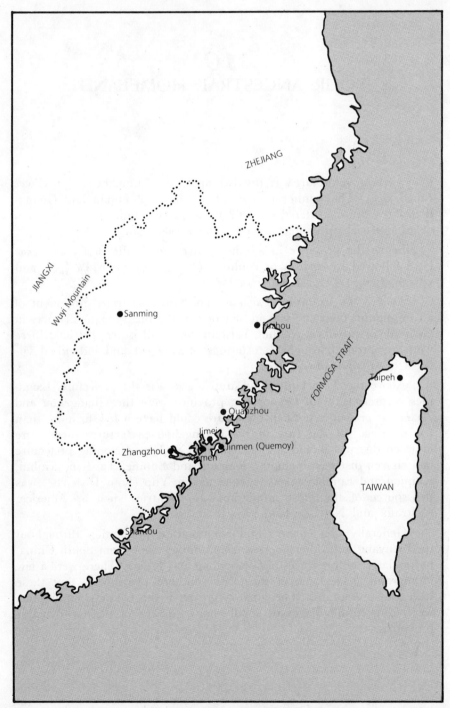

FUJIAN PROVINCE

FUJIAN

Fujian province is situated in the south-east corner of China, facing the islands of Jinmen and Taiwan. Historically, it was considered a backward province, far away from the more developed northern provinces with their great cities like Beijing and Shanghai.

The climate of Fujian is sub-tropical, which is hot and humid throughout the year, with plenty of rainfall. The soil is not too arable though in pockets in the south, where the land is flatter and more fertile, two or three crops a year is not uncommon. Crops grown are tobacco, tea and sugar, the last two being the province's main cash crops.

Due to its generally poor soil and hilly terrain, Fujian suffered from insufficient harvests. It was for centuries acutely short of rice, a staple crop in the south. Happily, the province is now self-sufficient, thanks to better grain stock, improvement in the method of farming and water conservancy projects.

The terrain of Fujian province is rocky and uneven, capped by crags and plateaus. Farming is difficult especially in the northern and western parts of the provinces, which is mainly given to the timber industry. The scenic Wuyi Mountain forms the boundary between the provinces of Jiangxi and Fujian. The mountain ranges a thousand miles with the main mountain tops rising thousand-odd metres above sea level, covering a land of seventy kilometres. Curiously-shaped mountain peaks amount to thirty-six in number, and strangely formed crags number ninety-five. Serene streams form nine zigzagging watercourses, with an abundance of luxuriant flowers blooming nearby. Wuyi Mountain is not just famous for its picturesque scenery but for its tea leaves, which are superb in quality due to the mountain's high latitude, spare air and misty weather.

Fujian is blessed with good natural harbours found in Fuzhou and Xiamen. Until recently these two cities had been major trading centres for centuries.

Fuzhou has the reputation of being a 'garden city'. The city is full of plants and flowers, which bloom the whole year round so that their fragrance permeates throughout this fair city. Formerly one could only go to Fuzhou by water transport; now, it is also accessible via trains and planes. Formerly an old city, Fuzhou is now full of modern buildings and factories. Just a few miles from the city proper is the Gushan area, which is a famous tourist spot. People come from near and far to this scenic area and to pray at the magnificent Yung Chuan Temple.

Xiamen is a beautiful island, covered with evergreen trees and shrubs. The harbour of Xiamen can accommodate big ocean liners, and serves the province and the surrounding area as a centre of import and export. Xiamen was in fact one of the five major ports opened up for trade with the foreigners under the terms of the 1842 treaty which ended the Opium War. The famous Amoy University, of some one hundred and thirty-three thousand square metres, is located just a few miles from the city. The island of Xiamen is surrounded by hundreds of small islands, providing ideal fishing spots for trawlers and boats.

In 1955, a bridge was completed linking Xiamen to the interior of Fujian. The bridge, built of more than seven hundred pieces of granite, runs a course of 2,212 metres and can accommodate pedestrians, railway trains and motor cars. On the mainland is Jimei village, the hometown of the famous overseas Chinese businessman and patriot, Tan Kah Kee. Today a memorial hall stands in his honour in Jimei, near the cluster of schools and colleges he founded.

Like many other cities in China, industrialization has changed Xiamen's face. In 1979, Xiamen was declared as one of the special economic zones open to foreign businesses. The city now has many modern buildings and factories, dealing in all kinds of production, one of the most prominent being the food packing and processing industry. Elsewhere in Fujian, industrialization has kept pace. For example, Sanming district, formerly a desolate area in West Fujian, is now a centre for heavy industry.

Further south in Fujian is Quanzhou, which is, incidentally, the former home of many Chinese now resident in the Philippines. A historic city, the Italian traveller Marco Polo first entered its waterway during the Yuan dynasty. Though its position as a foreign trading port is now lost, its historical beauty still exists. Among its ancient relics is the famous Kai Yuan Temple which contains many precious Buddhist ornaments and religious objects.

GUANGDONG

Guangdong province was more important than Fujian as a source of Chinese immigrants. It is isolated from central China by vast mountain ranges but the excellent and strategically located port of Hong Kong served as the springboard for the immigration of millions of Cantonese not only to the Nanyang but to countries further afield.

The climate of Guangdong is generally hot and humid with rainfall in the monsoon months. The cold spell comes in November and December. The Pearl River has three main tributaries – the Xijiang (West River), Beijiang (North River) and the Dongjiang (East River) – which flow into the inland districts. It is from the delta area, around the confluence of the three large rivers that most of the immigrants come. Surrounding the delta is the mountainous region; here, inaccessibility and poor communication generally precludes the immigration of the villagers. In the past, it took up to three days of trekking for the immigrants from the delta area to reach Guangzhou for the onward journey by junk to Hong Kong. From Hong Kong, the immigrants would then board their vessels for the Nanyang, America and other parts of the world.

The immigrant delta area which was approximately south of Guangzhou and west of Macao was divided into twelve main districts. The most important of these twelve was the Sam Yup (or Three Districts), which includes the provincial capital of Guangzhou. The people of the Sam Yup were considered by others as more urbane and educated and they tend to pride themselves on their polished manners and more sophisticated outlook. This was probably due to their being located near to Guangzhou, which was the capital and the cultural centre of Guangdong province. They regarded their southern neighbours, in particular the Sze Yup (Four Districts) people as loutish and uncultivated. Their variant of the Cantonese dialect appeared to the Sam Yup people as being more coarse and less refined and thus more difficult to understand.

The whole delta region is made up of small tributaries, creeks and foothills in which nestled hundreds of villages and towns, each with a population of 1,000 or more. In these hamlets, the hardworking peasants cultivated rice and grew mulberry bushes as silk is an important export commodity. Other staple crops include vegetables and sweet potatoes. There are also livestock like chickens, pigs, buffaloes and fish farms. Well-cultivated orchards also produced vast quantities of fruits.

The Pearl River delta is generally fertile land, producing two rice crops and one dry crop a year. However, in the nineteenth century severe

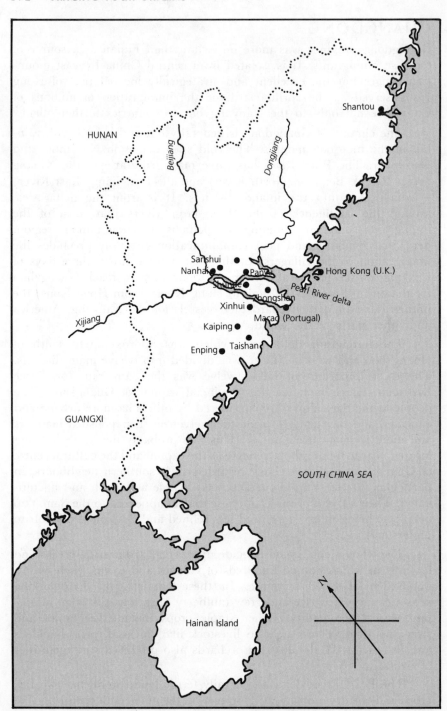

GUANGDONG PROVINCE

droughts and floods had occurred, leading to massive destruction of crops and livestock. In addition, the Taiping Rebellion took its toll of life and property while opium smoking sapped the productive energy of many people. To cap it all, overpopulation rapidly outstripped the ability of the land to feed the peasantry. Immigration then became the only viable alternative for many Cantonese.

Taishan

Generally, the whole 7,000 square miles of the Pearl River delta consist of fertile farmland. However, districts like Taishan, on the outskirts of the delta area, was not favoured by lowlying, cultivable land. Taishan, which was estimated to have some 60 per cent of all immigrants to America before 1914, is located in a hilly and rugged part of Guangdong province.

Taishan in fact means 'elevated mountain' – rising 800 to 1,000 feet above sea level. Its total area is about 3,000 square kilometres with an estimated population of 680,000 in 1853.

The peasants eke a difficult existence from farming the rocky mountainsides. The hills are terraced and planted with sweet potatoes, peanuts and vegetables. Where there is some level ground, rice would be planted. Each family, in addition, might grow some vegetables and keep a few chickens.

Taishan's agricultural output can only feed her population for four months per year – such was the plight of the villagers who stayed in Taishan. Her people were forced by circumstances to engage in other trades so as to earn a living. They acted as middlemen between buyers and sellers, and their jobs took them to big cities and coastal ports of China, principally Guangzhou and Hong Kong. There, as merchants and seamen, they came into contact with city folk and White men, and grew familiar with the art and technique of bartering, trade and financing.

Guangzhou (Canton)

Here and there in the delta region, can be found populous hamlets and townships. In these urban centres, merchants, shopkeepers, barbers, cobblers and many types of artisans can ply their trades and make a living off the concentration of the population. Itinerant workers and travellers make these locations their stops for selling or bartering of their wares or merely as a resting place on their way to the provincial capital at Guangzhou.

Guangzhou is historically China's official 'back door' serving as the main point of contact between China and the West. It was and still is today, China's most modern city. In ancient times it was a walled city of approximately six miles in circumference on the northern corner of the Pearl River delta. The poor lived in mud hovels while the rich could afford mansions with many rooms and quarters, orchards and gardens all fenced up and surrounded by walls. Narrow streets and canals crisscrossed this charming city with its tiled roofs and public squares.

Guangzhou has been largely rebuilt and is now a city of broad boulevards, lush gardens, rambling colonnades and pavilions. Its taxi fleet consists of modern Japanese cars. Modern hotels and office buildings have also made their appearance. As the gateway for foreigners for the last 150 years, Guangzhou maintains intricate financial and commercial ties with ritzy, glittering Pearl of the Orient, Hong Kong.

Hong Kong

Hong Kong itself was the gateway through which many immigrants left Guangdong province. It was a cosmopolitan city where people of many nationalities congregated. In the harbour, merchantmen and warships of many nations were anchored, together with many seagoing junks, flower boats, lorchas and sampans.

A mixture of rich and poor people, traditional and modern elements – the city was a microcosm of Imperial China buffeted by change and foreign influences. A hybrid of East and West, Hong Kong was like Shanghai, a facsimile of both European and Oriental cities. Today, of course, Hong Kong is a very urbanized and modern city of towering skyscrapers, five-star hotels, jam-packed crowds and a multi-billion tourist industry.

11
YOUR DIALECT GROUP

THE Chinese in the Southeast Asian countries do not form a homogeneous group. The most pronounced differences stem from their identification with various dialect groups. In contrast, the Chinese in North America, Canada, Australia and New Zealand are almost homogeneously of Cantonese descent. Collectively, the following are the major groups of Chinese that migrated to the Nanyang and countries further afield.

Hokkien (Fukinese)
From the vicinity of Xiamen, Fuzhou and Quanzhou in Fujian province, they are numerically dominant in Malaysia, Singapore, Java and the Philippines. Spoken Hokkien is quite similar to Teochew (Swatow) but it differs so greatly from the speech of other Chinese that it can be regarded as a distinct language. The term 'Hokkien' is the pronunciation in this dialect of the province of Fujian, though sometimes the term 'Chinchew' is also used. ('Chinchew' is the pronunciation, again in that dialect, of the prefecture of Zhangzhou.) They are probably the oldest settlers from China in Southeast Asia.

Teochew
The most numerous group in Thailand, Sumatra and Cambodia, the Teochews originated from the prefecture of Chaozhou, particularly from eight of the ten districts within it near the Fujian border. It is situated in eastern Guangdong province. In Southeast Asia, they are sometimes referred to as 'Swatow people'.

Cantonese
This dialect group comes from around the city of Guangzhou, particularly in South-west Guangdong in the Pearl River delta. It is the most

numerous group in South Vietnam, Hong Kong, North America, Canada, Australia and New Zealand, where Cantonese is the lingua franca among the Chinese. Sometimes they are referred to as Macaos, as a result of their embarking overseas from the port of Macao before the opening of Hong Kong in 1842.

Hakka

Unlike the other dialect groups, the Hakkas are not concentrated in any particular urban or rural centre. Their migration to Southeast Asia was a continuation of an earlier southward movement within China; hence the name Hakka (or Khek) which means 'guest'.

The hardy and adventurous Hakkas are known as the nomads of China. Strong concentrations can be found in the prefecture of Jiaying-zhou and the other two districts of Chaozhou prefecture, while smaller pockets are found in some of the other eight districts of Chaozhou and in parts of Fujian and Guangdong provinces.

There are six different types of Hakka – those from Taipu (太浦), Huizhou (惠州), Fengshun (丰顺), Meixian (梅县), Popo (婆婆) and Yongding (永定). Those from Yongding comprise the only group of Hokkien Hakkas.

Hainanese

They are emigrants from the island of Hainan in Guangdong province. Those in Singapore came mainly from 2 districts, Wenchang in the north-east and Qiongshan in the northern part of the island. As late participants in the coolie emigration, they were historically limited to more menial occupations in the Nanyang.

Miscellaneous Dialect Groups

Besides the five main dialect groups, there is also a miscellany of minor groups that migrated. These consist of the Foochows (or Hok-chews), Henghuas, Hokchias and the Waijiangren (i.e. people of the provinces in central China beyond Guangdong and Fujian).

The Foochows, Henghuas and Hokchias came from the northern reaches of Fujian province. All these groups migrated to the Nanyang in sizeable numbers only in the early twentieth century but even then they are numerically smaller than, say, the Hokkiens or Teochews. For example, the Henghuas numbered only 1,659, while the Hokchias had 3,845 members in Singapore in 1921.

The Foochows and the Hainanese are both noted for their concentration in the humble coffee-shop trade. The Henghuas and the Hokchias on the other hand made a strong showing in the road transport, bicycle and spare parts trade, not just in Singapore but in Malaysia and Indonesia as well. Before the introduction of the bicycle in Singapore at the beginning of the twentieth century, a lot of Henghuas and Hokchias were also engaged in the rickshaw trade, which was considered too demeaning to the other dialect groups.

Finally there are the Waijiangren who are involved in diverse occupations ranging from tailoring and leather goods to publications. The Shanghainese, for example, are best known for their craftsmanship in furniture making and furnishing. Generally these immigrants from the northern part of China come from the cities and speak a common language, Mandarin. Most came even later than the dialect groups mentioned so far – that is, before the communists took over power in China in 1949.

The following table gives the major sources of Chinese immigrants by the countries they migrated to.

Main Chinese Immigration Population by Originating Areas and Destination			
DESTINATION	ORIGINATING COUNTY/DISTRICT	PROVINCE	DIALECT GROUP
Singapore, Malaysia, Java, Philippines	Jinmen; vicinity of Xiamen, Fuzhou and Quanzhou	Fujian	Hokkien
Thailand, Sumatra, Kampuchea	Chaozhou Prefecture (especially 8 of its 10 districts)	Eastern Guangdong	Teochew
America & Canada	Sze Yup (4 Districts, especially Taishan)	Guangdong	Cantonese
	Zhongshan (especially in Hawaii)	Guangdong	Cantonese
	Sam Yup (3 Districts)		
Australia	Sze Yup (4 Districts)	Guangdong	Cantonese
	Sam Yup (3 Districts)		
New Zealand	Sze Yup Sam Yup (especially Panyu & Nanhai)	Guangdong	Cantonese

12
ABOUT SURNAMES AND THEIR ORIGINS

THE CHINESE SURNAME

THE surname is of the utmost importance to the Chinese in fixing one's identity in the constellation of so many different dialect groups. One of the first things for a Chinese to ask another, after the necessary formalities, is 'What is your surname?' (您贵姓?). After establishing your surname, he may be induced to throw up his hands, smile all over and exclaim, 'Ah, kinsman!' (阿! 亲人!). Hospitality and co-operation would not then be slow in coming. He would go out of his way to meet your every request; from buying you a meal to granting you business favours.

The bond of kinship ties is so strong that even today it is considered mildly incestuous for a couple sharing the same surname to marry. The same bond also means a mutual sharing of misfortune and honour. A virtuous widow or an eminent scholar share their merit and achievement with all their clansmen, just as shame and dishonour brought about by another clansman would cast its own baleful ripple.

A Chinese name is made up of a family name (or surname), which takes precedence and is thus written first, in the Chinese style, followed by the personal name. Family names are usually of one character each, though two-character family names like Ouyang (欧阳) and Situ (司徒) are quite common.

Nobody knows for sure how many Chinese family names there are. Over 6,000 surnames have been collected, but no doubt many have already become obsolete. Because of its heterogeneous population, Singapore has more Chinese surnames than overseas Chinese communities like America. A count from the Singapore Telephone Directory listed some 500 surnames. Among the more common ones are Tan (陈) and Lim (林). One of the rare surnames is Che (车), which literally means 'vehicle'. Legend has it that the surname was adopted when its ancestor was given the then unheard of privilege by the emperor to be driven to court in a carriage.

According to Chinese legends, Chinese surnames originated from the legendary Yellow Emperor, Huang Di, who had 25 sons. Feudal plots were given to 14 of his more capable sons, who took on new surnames after the geographical locations which they were given. This tradition persisted so that it is estimated that more than 60 per cent of the new surnames were named after some geographical locality or other.

Other common origins of surnames include following the designation of an official position or title, changes in order to avoid political persecution, and surnames bestowed by the emperor on loyal officials and generals. The feudal practice of that time also disallowed ordinary citizens of a state from having the same surname as the throne unless they were given special permission to do so. Hence the expedient switch of surname for many.

Traditionally, people with the same surname were forbidden to intermarry as they supposedly shared the same ancestor. In ancient China, this injunction was carried even further in that related surnames were regarded as belonging to one clan and thus considered as non-marriageable kinsmen or brothers. The Liu (刘), Guan (关), Zhang (张) and Zhao (赵) surnames is a case in point. Chinese history recounts a story about a Hebei native, Zhao Yun, who saved Liu Bei's wife and son during the Three Kingdoms period. When Liu conquered Yizhou he made Zhao general. Because Liu was the sworn brother of Guan Yi and Zhang Fei – the four surnames have since been closely identified and considered as one clan.

The Chinese surnames found in the Nanyang, America and other overseas Chinese communities were predominantly brought over from immigrants of the two southern provinces of Fujian and Guangdong. Some of the more frequently occurring surnames found in Singapore, America, Australia, New Zealand and Britain are the following: Chan (陈), Lin (林), Li (李), Wong (黃), Huang (黃), Mei (梅), Yang (杨), Chin (陈), and Fong (方).

In the following pages, the origins and illustrious ancestors of a sample of surnames – forty-seven to be exact·– will be discussed. The maps overleaf show in a summary fashion, the geographical origin of most of these forty-seven surnames, matching them with their provinces of origin.

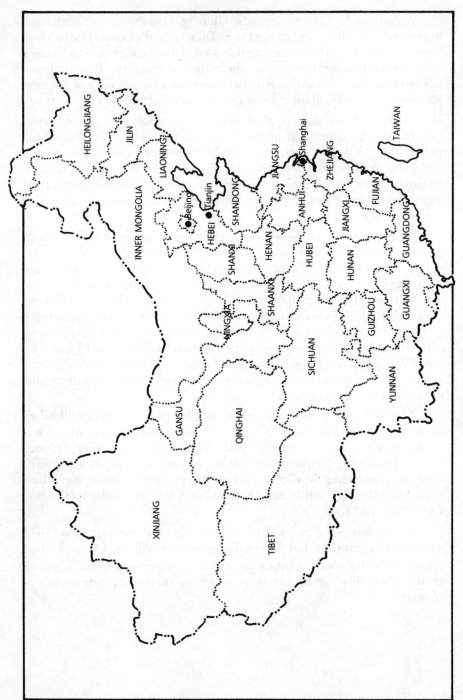

DIVISIONS WITHIN CHINA

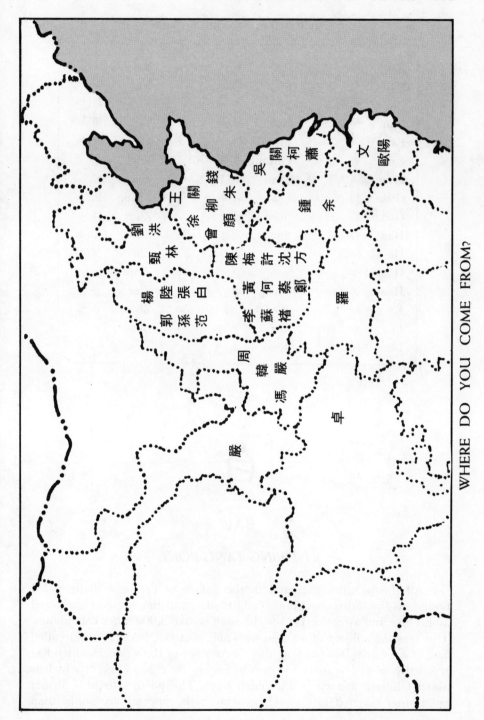

WHERE DO YOU COME FROM?

A Reference List of Surnames

Bai	白	Liu	柳	Xu	許(许)
Cai	蔡	Liu	劉(刘)	Xu	徐
Chen	陳(陈)	Lu	陸(陆)	Yan	嚴(严)
Chu	褚	Luo	羅(罗)	Yan	顏(颜)
Fan	范	Mei	梅	Yang	楊(杨)
Fang	方	Ouyang	歐陽(欧阳)	Yu	余
Feng	馮(冯)	Qian	錢(钱)	Zeng	曾
Guan	關(关)	Qiu	邱	Zhang	張(张)
Guo	郭	Shen	沈	Zhen	甄
Han	韓(韩)	Situ	司徒	Zheng	鄭(郑)
He	何	Su	蘇(苏)	Zhong	鍾(钟)
Hong	洪	Sun	孫(孙)	Zhou	周
Huang	黃	Wang	王	Zhu	朱
Ke	柯	Wen	文	Zhuang	莊(庄)
Li	李	Wu	吳(吴)	Zhuo	卓
Lin	林	Xiao	蕭(萧)		

BAI

INSPIRING TANG POET

All the beauties gathered in the palace of Emperor Tang paled beside his favourite concubine Yang Guifei, and the emperor showered all his love and attention on her although he had 3,000 other concubines. This was the subject of a poem by Tang poet Bai Juyi (白居易) called *Song of Everlasting Sorrows* (长恨歌). Another of Bai's poems which has reputedly moved readers to tears is *Song of the Pipa* (琵琶行) which is about Chinese women in the olden days. The poem tells of a former entertainer married to a merchant who 'cares more about money than parting with his wife'. Like Bai's other works, this poem became a source of colourful verses for present-day writers.

Bai, a native of Taiyuan district, Shanxi province, enjoyed mass appeal because of his simple yet touching language which struck a chord in everyone's hearts. It was said that he used to recite a few verses to illiterate old folk to make sure his poems could be understood by everyone. While serving in the imperial court, Bai became disillusioned with the lives led by the royal family and bureaucrats. He wrote revealing poems about their corruption and conspicuous consumption which contrasted with the people's misery, and political chaos. Some of these were *Heavy Taxes*, *The Wealthy* and *The Coalseller*.

Eventually, Bai was transferred from the central government to become an official in charge of arresting thieves in Jiangxi province. Compared to other poets of his time, he was far more fortunate.

But the first forefather of the Bai family, who lived more than 3,000 years ago, was no hero. This was Bai Gongsheng (白公胜), the notorious son of the crown prince of Chu state. Bai Gongsheng was executed after an aborted attempt to overthrow the king.

Presumably, the Bai family escaped from the state, thus spreading its family tree to Shanxi and Shaanxi provinces during the Warring States period.

Pak
Bak
Peh

CAI

THE PAPER-MAKERS

The Cai's have made a great contribution to mankind because one of them, Cai Luṇ (蔡伦), discovered the making of paper about 2,000 years ago, during the Later Han dynasty.

Paper was then made from floss silk; this technique, being expensive, could not produce a large enough quantity to meet the demands of society. So Cai Lun, a eunuch, decided to invent a method of producing cheaper paper. This he did by spreading the pounded pulp of materials like tree bark, rags and unwanted fishing nets onto small screens and draining off the water. The thin films of fibre left behind became paper when dried. This paper proved to be light, thin and long-lasting.

Cai Lun's method was adopted by the whole country. The eunuch was later promoted to a marquis and the people named the paper he invented Cai Hou Zhi (蔡侯纸) – literally, 'Marquis Cai's paper'.

But the ancestor of the Cai clan, Cai Shudu (蔡叔度) did not do as well. A brother of King Wu who founded the Zhou dynasty in 3100 B.C., Cai Shudu was given a piece of land in present-day Henan province and was conferred the title of Cai Shu. He became jealous of Zhou Gong (周公) who was asked to act as regent for the young successor after the old king died.

With another brother, Guan Shuxian (管叔鲜), he spread rumours that Zhou Gong was about to harm the young king. When this failed to get rid of Zhou Gong, they forced Wu Geng (武庚), the son of King Zhou, to join them in a revolt. The revolt was quickly suppressed. Wu Geng and Guan Shuxian were executed while Cai Shudu was sent away in exile until his death.

Cai Shudu's son, Hu, was given the place of Cai by Zhou Gong because of 'his good behaviour and virtues'. He was also named Cai Zhong (蔡仲) in order that the Cai surname may be perpetuated.

However, the Cai's soon had to move south to Anhui province to escape from the constant attacks of Chu state. Though the fiefdom of Cai was eventually destroyed by Chu, the Cai offspring continued to multiply and leave their mark in Chinese history.

There was Cai Yong (蔡邕), a great scholar and calligrapher of the Eastern Han dynasty who compiled an edited version of the six Confucian classics. Cai Yuanpei (蔡元培), 1868–1940, a renowned educationist, was the moving force behind China's educational reforms in the early twenties. As the chancellor of Beijing University, he played a great role in substituting the Chinese classical language – *wen yan* (文言) – with the vernacular form – *bai hua* (白话).

Chua (Hokkien)
Chai
Chye
Choy (Cantonese)

CHEN

THE REBELLIOUS CLANSMEN

There is a Chinese saying that the Chen's and Lin's share half the world. This is not so much of an exaggeration if one cares to enumerate how many Chens there are in Singapore alone. Its origins can be traced to King Wu of Zhou who conferred a city, Chen, to his son-in-law, Wei Man (妫满). But the people in Chen city did not adopt Chen as their surname. Ten generations later, Wei Man's descendant, Wei Wan (妫完), was forced by internal trouble to take refuge in Qi and changed his surname to Chen to avoid suspicion. Chen Wan was then given a piece of land at Tian city and he changed his surname to Tian (田). Thus the Tian and Chen clans actually share a common ancestor, and can be considered as one family 3,000 years ago.

The first Chen to make a name is history was Chen Sheng, a poor farmer who led an uprising against the Qin dynasty. Though he failed in his attempt, he paved the way for the setting up of the Han dynasty. Another famous Chen, Chen Kai led the Heaven and Earth Society to fight the Manchus at the end of the Qing dynasty.

This rebellious tradition was carried into the twentieth century by Chen Yingshi (陈英士) and Chen Tianhua (陈天华) who worked under Dr Sun Yat-sen, father of the Chinese Republic. Chen Yingshi was murdered by warlord Yuan Shikai in Shanghai while Chen Tianhua wrote several influential anti-Manchu books which were widely read.

In popularity, none beats Chen Yuanyuan, a famous songstress of the late Ming dynasty. She was at the centre of a tussle of love between Wu Sangui, a general, and Li Zicheng, a rebel leader. Desperate for this beautiful lady, Wu resorted to enlisting help from the Manchus which gave the latter a chance to invade China.

In Singapore, the best known Chens are of course Tan Kah Kee (Chen Jiageng) and Tan Lark Sye (Chen Liushi), famous millionaire and philanthropist who contributed greatly to its economy and education system.

Tan (Hokkien)   **Ting** (Hokchew)
Chan (Cantonese)   **Chin**

CHU

CLAN ORIGINATES FROM HENAN

The Chu clan got its surname when its ancestor was appointed to an official post called the *chu shi* (褚师) more than 3,000 years ago. *Chu shi* was a post equivalent to that of a mayor. The duke of Song appointed his son, You, as a *chu shi* and You's descendants later adopted Chu as their surname.

Chu was also believed to be a place south of Luoyang county, as was recorded in *Zuo Zhuan*. Chu's of either origin can however trace their ancestral home to Henan in the Spring and Autumn period.

During the Tang dynasty, the Chu produced a famous hero by the name of Chu Suiliang (褚遂良). Chu Suiliang was a palace official whose job was to act as an ombudsman and advised the emperor on national policies. He was noted for his fearless criticisms. Luckily for him, the emperor, Tang Taizong, was very receptive to his advice. Before Taizong passed away, he even trusted Suiliang with the responsibility of looking after the young emperor, Tang Gaozong (唐高宗).

A well-known case was when Gaozong wanted to make the ambitious Wu Zetian his empress. Suiliang thought it unwise and objected to the idea vehemently. Though the stubborn Gaozong refused to accept his advice, the people were impressed by Suiliang's courage and loyalty.

Chu Suiliang was also a gifted calligrapher. His writing style is still imitated by many calligraphy students. Besides Suiliang, the Chu clan also had Chu Da (褚大) and Chu Shaosun (褚少孙), who were outstanding Confucian scholars in the Han dynasty.

Chu Yin was the 'King of Chess' in the Five Dynasties period. Chu Hua (褚华) made his mark in Chinese history when he fought against the invading border tribes during the Song dynasty.

Choo (Cantonese)

FAN

CLEAR ORIGINS

For certain surnames, there is more controversy over their origins. Not for the Fan surname, though, which can be traced right back to Emperor Yao 4,000 years ago.

His descendants were first named Tang Du (唐杜), then renamed Du (杜) in the Zhou dynasty. Shortly after being vanquished by Emperor Zhou Xuan, Du Bo's son sought refuge in Jin state and became a tutor there. His surname was changed to Shi (士), based on his position, and thus it remained until his great-grandchild Shi Hui (士会) was given the Fan territory, which was later used by his descendants as the given surname. So it was that 2,000 years ago, the Fan surname originated in Jin state, which was situated in Gaoping county, Shanxi province.

Personalities belonging to the Fan clan include Fan Li (范蠡), Fan Qiao (范睢) and Fan Zeng (范增).

Fan Li was indispensable to King Gou Jian in defeating the king of Wu. By leading the army against Qi and Jin, he enabled Gou Jian to re-establish his Yue kingdom at the end of the Spring and Autumn period. To honour his achievements, he was offered the position of general. He was however shrewd enough to realize that Gou Jian was not a person to be trusted and that he was only relied upon in a tumultuous period. So he took the drastic step of relinquishing his post, and sailed away, never again returning to Yue state.

Warring States period's Fan Qiao was another important historical figure. King Qin Zhao made use of his abilities to strengthen the foundation of the state of Qin. This state was to annex the six states of Han, Wei, Chu, Zhao, Yan and Qi only 20 years after.

As for Fan Zeng, many people are no doubt familiar with his fate. Towards the end of the Qin dynasty, warring broke out between Chu and Han states. Fan Zeng was instrumental in helping Xiang Yu, king of Chu, at this time. In his fervour, he urged the king to eradicate Liu Bang, the king of Han, but Xiang Yu fell into Liu Bang's trap of setting one person against the other. He began to distrust Fan Zeng and stripped him of his powers. In a fit of rage and anguish, Fan Zeng took his own life. If Xiang Yu had only listened to Fan Zeng, he would not have played right into the hands of the consummate strategist Liu Bang.

In the Eastern Han dynasty, there came people like Fan Dan (范丹), Fan Shi (范式), and Fan Pang (范滂). Fan Shi and Zhang Shao (张邵) were bosom friends, and they are known to posterity as exemplifying the deepest bonds of friendship between two people.

Then in the Song dynasty, the Fan surname rose to fame with individuals like Fan Zhongyan (范仲淹) from Jiangsu province, governor of Herao prefecture, who was sent to watch over the border tribes of Xia and Jiang. He was an imposing figure and was regarded with much awe.

Fan Zhongyan suffered an unhappy childhood. His father passed away when he was only three, and his mother remarried. It is to his credit that he remained humble even after he had established a marvellous reputation for himself. All of his four sons, Chun You (纯祐), Chun Jiang (纯江), Chun Li (纯礼) and Chun Cui (纯粹) were court officials.

A contemporary of Lu You (陆游), Fan Chengda (范成大) from the Southern Song dynasty, was especially well-known for his idyllic picture of rural life given in a sequence of poems called 'The Farmer's Year'.

Fam

FANG

MANY MYTHICAL ANCESTORS

The Fang surname can be traced back to the legendary Shen Nong, who had the head of an ox and ruled by the element of Fire. As for the original ancestor Fang Lei (方雷), there appears to be differing historical evidence. Some sources say that Fang Lei was a man, and others declare that it was a woman. It has not been established if Fang Lei was in fact Xuan Yan's Empress, or Yu Wang's son.

It is however clear that one of the first ancestors came from the Western Zhou dynasty. Fang Shu (方叔), who was a minister serving under Emperor Zhou Xuan, helped to bolster the weakening throne. As his descendants were mostly to be found in the locality of Henan province, this can be considered the originating homeland. Seven hundred years ago, the Fang's had already moved to Fujian territories of Zhangzhou and Quanzhou.

Although the Fang surname developed long ago, its clan members did not feature prominently in China's early history – apart from Fang Shu. Besides, those who were mentioned were mythical figures like Fang Hui (方回), Fang Xiang (方相) and Fang Bi (方弼).

The Ming dynasty saw the appearance of many important Fang's in the fields of art and academia, like the loyal Fang Xiaoru (方孝儒), advisor to Emperor Minghui. He was consulted on all important state affairs.

One of Ming dynasty's four princes was Tong City's Fang Yizhi (方以智). After the Qing army had overrun the country, he left to become a monk.

Even more important personalities appeared during the Qing dynasty. There was Fang Bao (方苞) who made important contributions in Confucianist tradition, Fang Shin (方薰) an eminent painter who also wrote very good poetry, Fang Chenguan (方承观), a high official during Qianlong's reign who paid particular attention to irrigation. He was one scholar who, being highly practical, always applied whatever he had learnt.

Fong (Cantonese)

FENG

SEA GOD IS MYTHICAL ANCESTOR

King Neptune rules over the Seven Seas in Greek mythology. His Chinese counterpart is a god by the name of Feng Yi (冯夷). Legend has it that the goddess Nu Wo (女娲) sang while Feng Yi accompanied her on the drums. Such is the beautiful myth surrounding the legendary ancestor of the Feng clan.

The Feng clan is more fortunate than most because its origins are clearly outlined. It could be traced to Prince Bi Gonggao (毕公高), 15th son of King Wen of the Zhou dynasty. Bi's descendant, Bi Wan (毕万), was the marquis of Wei. His son later became the overlord of a city called Feng. Since then, his descendants adopted the city's name as their surname.

During that period, the Feng clan produced a famous figure in Feng Jianzi (冯简子) who was consulted by the king of Zheng state on all important matters. By the Han and Tang dynasties, the Feng clan had spread from Shaanxi, its place of origin, to Henan, Hebei, Shanxi and Fujian.

The *Xing Shi Kao Lue* (姓氏考略) said the Henan branch was descended from Feng Yi (冯异), an Eastern Han general who fought against the border minorities. Descendants of another Han general, Feng Fengshi (冯奉世), set up their homes in Shanxi province. The general was known for his military prowess and diplomacy. The ancestor of Fujian's Feng clan was Feng Can (冯参), marquis of Yidu, while Feng Shigu (冯师古), imperial inspector of the Tang dynasty, founded the Hebei branch.

Other famous figures of the Feng clan include Qing general Feng Zicai (冯子材) who led his troops to victory against the French in 1885 in Zhennan Pass (later renamed Friendship Pass), near Lang Song.

Feng Yunshan (冯云山) was one of the founders of the Taiping Heavenly Kingdom. He led about 2,000 peasants and coal-miners to join the uprising organized by Hong Xiuquan.

Feng Menglong (冯梦龙), A.D. 1574–1646, was a magistrate before he turned to writing novels, operas and prose about the common people's life. His works are still widely read even today.

Fung (Cantonese, Hakka)
Foong (Cantonese, Hakka)
Pang (Hokkien)

GUAN

SYMBOL OF PATRIOTISM

There has been no blue blood in the Guan clan. But patriotism is a marked feature of the clan. There is a saying which goes like this: 'In Shandong there was Kong Fuzi (Confucius) and in Shanxi, Guan Fuzi.'

Guan Fuzi, better known as Guan Gong or Guan Di, was the hero whose patriotism and righteousness had been idolized in the classic, *Romance of the Three Kingdoms*. The Song and Ming emperors also helped to reinforce this popular image.

Temples for the worship of Guan Fuzi can be found all over China, Malaysia and Singapore. Among the many worshippers are the secret society members who see him as a symbol of personal loyalty, a treasured asset to those who are always on the run from the law. But members of the Guan clan may take consolation in the fact that the police in Hong Kong also worshipped Guan Gong as their deity.

Another great patriot in the clan was Guan Longfeng, a loyal minister of the Xia dynasty who tried to bring the king's attention to the chaotic state of affairs. But the ungrateful ruler executed him instead. The event occurred in 1770 B.C. in Anyi, a capital city in the region north of today's Shanxi province.

A source said the surname Guan derived from an official title, *guan yin*. In the olden days, a *guan yin* referred to the official who guards the pass on the state border. If this is true, then this lineage dates back to about 2,400 years ago in the boundary area between Shandong and Jiangsu province.

A number of Chinese historical figures from the Guan clan were noted for their sense of justice and patriotism. A recent example was

Guan Tian Pei, a commander of the Qing navy who died while defending a fort against the British some time after the Opium War.

Among the literati, Guan Hanqing of the Yuan dynasty was a leading figure noted for his dramas. Even today, his works such as *Snow in Midsummer* are favourites with Chinese opera enthusiasts. Then there was Guan Tong who surpassed his teacher, Qing Hao, in the art of Chinese painting.

Kwan (Cantonese)
Kuan

GUO

TWO ORIGINS TO THIS CLAN

The Guo clan is more than 3,000 years old and an offshoot of the Ji royal family which ruled the Zhou dynasty, according to the Book of Surnames, *Xing Zuan*.

When the third brother of King Wen of Zhou state was conferred the land of Guo (虢), he adopted it as his surname. But as Guo sounded similar to Guo (郭), the latter was soon substituted for the former. Other historical records, however, showed that many small states during the early Zhou dynasty were also named Guo.

Nobody could tell the exact location of the Guo clan but it was very active around Shanxi, Henan and Shaanxi provinces.

Another account of the clan's origin came from the book, *Xing Shi Kao Lue*, which recorded that during the Xia dynasty some 4,000 years ago, there was already a group of people with the surname Guo. These early clansmen derived their surname from their place of abode because *guo* means the area outside the city wall. And as most of them lived outside the city wall, they took Guo for their surname.

Scholars have now accepted that there were probably two sources to the Guo clan's origin and that they developed independently of each other.

Like the other clans, the Guo migrated southwards from Shanxi province. By the Eastern Han period, the clan was to be found in Shandong and Anhui. By the end of the Jin dynasty, the clan had extended into Fujian province.

Among the famous personalities in the Guo clan was Guo Wei (郭隗) who helped to strengthen the state of Yan during the Warring States period. Guo Wei counselled the King of Yan to treat his officials well so as to attract more talented men to serve under him. This policy worked so well that Yan state became powerful enough to rival Qi state, the dominating power during the period.

Another well-known figure was Guo Ziyi (郭子仪) of the Tang dynasty. He defeated the rebel An Lushan and restored order to the crumbling Tang dynasty almost singlehandedly. He remained loyal to the Tang emperor all his life although the entire army was under his control. In fact, although Guo Ziyi was a reputedly wealthy man, nobody grudged him his wealth, considering this his just desert.

The Guo clan has also produced some distinguished and outstanding artists like Guo Xi (郭熙), a landscape painter of the Northern Song dynasty who was famous for his wall murals. Then there was the contemporary artist, Guo Moruo (郭沫若), who was also a writer, poet, historian and playwright. He passed away in 1978.

Kuok
Kwok (Cantonese, Hakka)
Kuo
Quek (Hokkien)

HAN

LOVE LASTS FOREVER

Like many other clans, the Han's originated from King Zhou Wen. Wu Zi (武子), one of his descendants, was the first man to change his surname from Ji (姬) to Han (韩), when he was offered the city of Han Yuan (韩原) in the Spring and Autumn period. Han Yuan city was located in present-day Shaanxi province. Later, Wu Zi's descendants set up the Han state and became very powerful. The Han's spread from Shaanxi to Shanxi and Henan, and later to the rest of the country.

When the surname Han is mentioned, many would think of Han Fei Zi (韩非子), a representative figure of the Legalist school of thought in ancient China. Although he was a reticent person by nature, he was a most prolific writer. Han Fei Zi was a prince of Han in the Warring States period. His writings attracted the notice of the king of Qin, who sent armies to attack Han state so that he could get to see him. When King Han realized this, he decided to send Han Fei Zi to Qin state. Unfortunately, King Qin's prime minister Lisi killed him out of jealousy.

Han Peng (韩朋) was an official who served under King Kang during the Zhou dynasty. When the king found out that Han Peng had a beautiful wife at home, he abducted Han Peng's wife and threw the husband into jail.

Han could not take the insult and committed suicide in prison. His wife, upon hearing this news, killed herself in the palace. The king was furious over this drastic turn of events, and even refused to let the dead couple share a common grave.

Though buried in different graves next to each other, the love between Han Peng and his wife did not cease. On the second day, trees sprung up on each grave and their roots and branches were tangled together. And above the trees were two mandarin ducks crying plaintively. It was said that the mandarin ducks were the souls of the couple. Nowadays mandarin ducks are symbolic of a pair of lovers.

Other personalities in the clan include the famous general Han Xin (韩信) who helped Liu Bang (刘邦) to set up the Han dynasty. Then there was Han Yu (韩愈), brilliant essayist from the Tang dynasty who was said to have driven away the crocodiles from Chaozhou prefecture in

Guangdong to Southeast Asia. He did this by writing an open letter to the species!

Han Yu's name is always linked with that of Han Xiangzi (韩湘子), his nephew, who is worshipped as one of the Eight Immortals. Be it myth or fact, Han Xiangzi was also said to have protected Han Yu on his journey to Chaozhou and helped to eradicate the crocodiles.

Hon (Cantonese, Hakka)

HE

WHO IS MY ANCESTOR?

The surname, He, came about quite by chance. It was an offshoot of the Han clan whose history could be traced to 3,000 years ago. The Hans were the descendants of the legendary emperor Huang Di.

According to the *Book of Surnames*, *Xing Zuan*, the He clan descended from Tang Shuyu (唐叔虞), who was appointed duke of Han Guo (韩国) by King Cheng of Zhou dynasty. When the lineage came to Han An, the clan was persecuted by the state of Qin and fled their homeland in Henan to settle elsewhere.

For those who settled around the rivers of Huai He and Chang Jiang, they adopted the name of He, for at that time, Han (韩) sounded similar to He (何).

The He's became a prominent family around Donghai in Jiangsu province and Lujiang and Hefei in Anhui province. But it would be a great task to trace their family roots. This was because the He's were originally Han's, who are of the Han nationality. But some Han people had intermarried other ethnic groups, making it difficult to ascertain their original ancestors.

To add to the confusion, the surname was adopted by Zhu (朱) and Suo (锁) families during Han and Ming dynasties respectively. A result of this is that the He clan became one of the more well-known clans in China.

Although it is not an established historical fact, the first recorded southbound migration was about 1,700 years ago, during the early Eastern Jin dynasty. There were two groups: one to Fujian province and the other to Guangdong province. He became a common surname in these two provinces.

Famous historical figures of the He clan include He Xiu (何休), A.D. 129–182 of Eastern Han dynasty. He was a great scholar and an avid researcher of most of the Chinese classics.

During the period of the Three Kingdoms, there was He Yan (何晏) who was fostered by Cao Cao and known for his talents and beauty. Another was seal-carver He Zhen (何震) who enjoyed a high social status during the Ming dynasty.

For the more contemporary figures, there was He Xiangning (1878–1979). She was a politician as well as an artist whose forte was landscape and flower paintings. There was also He Qifang (1892–1977) whose poems are still being studied in local schools.

Ho (Cantonese)

HONG

A FLOOD OF FURY

The surname Hong means 'flood' or 'vast', and this was unleashed in the nineteenth century when a young man from this clan stirred torrents of events which almost drowned the Qing dynasty. This was during the Taiping Rebellion, the only rebellion in Chinese history that used a western religion as an ideological weapon. And in that mass movement started by Hong Xiuquan (洪秀全) could be seen once again the strength and weaknesses of an intellectual-led rebellion.

A dropout from the mandarin examination, a disgruntled Hong turned to revolution. He borrowed the ideas of equality from Christianity and started preaching for the overthrow of Qing's rule. He could have succeeded were it not for the internal dissensions and factional in-fighting which plagued the Taiping Kingdom he established.

The movement was enough to make Hong a frightening word among the panicky Qing officials. Earlier, another anti-Qing movement led by Hong Menhui (洪门会), an underground organization, had given the surname enough publicity. Members of this organization all adopted Hong as their secret surname for identification among themselves.

Although this surname shot to fame only during the last dynasty in Chinese history, its origin went right back to the early part of Chinese civilization, long before the first dynasty – Xia – was established.

Ironically, the ancestor of this clan was Gong Gong (共工), a man who was supposed to have contained the perennial flooding of the Yellow River. As this was an important achievement in the agricultural society, the Hong clan had always enjoyed a prestigious status in the country.

During the period of Emperor Shun (about 4000 B.C.), Gong's ancestor made a serious mistake and the whole clan was exiled to part of present-day Hebei province and Liaoning province. Not long after, there was another dramatic turn in the development of the clan's history. To avoid their enemies, the clan added 3 drops of water and changed their surname from Gong to Hong.

In the Tang dynasty, two other surnames, 弘 from Jiangsu and 宏 (also pronounced Hong) from Jiangxi were incorporated into the family. Today, Hong is a major surname among the southern Chinese, especially the Hokkiens.

Besides Hong Xiuquan (洪秀全), the Hong clan is also known for producing loyal diplomats. Hong Hao (洪皓) in Song dynasty was an ambassador who was detained in Jin state because he had refused to surrender to its government. Hong Jun (洪钧) in Qing dynasty was also a famous diplomat. He represented China in several countries like Russia, Germany and Holland.

Ang (Hokkien)

HUANG

RISING TO PROMINENCE

Huang is an important surname in South China as there are many people in this clan. The Huang clan ranks fourth among the five main Chinese clans, the others being Chen, Li, Zhang and He.

But this must be a rather recent development because in the Song dynasty book, *The 100 Surnames*, Huang occupies the 96th position among over 400 listed surnames. This is far behind many surnames which are considered obscure among Chinese communities throughout the world. This suggests that the Huang clan was probably not a very important one in the twelfth to thirteenth centuries.

The origin of the Huang clan could be traced to the founding of the Zhou dynasty in 1122 B.C. when the royal families and their descendants were each given a small kingdom to rule.

One of them was given the state called Huang in Henan province. The people of Huang then adopted the state's name as their surname. Huang state was later annexed by the rapacious state of Chu in south China during the Warring States period.

The Huang people probably migrated from north China and gathered around Jiangxia in Jiangxi province around the time of the Han dynasty. Huang Xiang (黃香), a noted filial son in Chinese history, was made a prime minister during this period. Even today, to differentiate Huang and Wang in Cantonese, it is usual to refer to the former as Huang from Jiangxia. The Huang clan moved further downwards to Fujian and Guangdong provinces from the time of the Tang dynasty as recorded in a book on the Huang genealogy.

Many eminent people came from the Huang clan, like scholar- poet Huang Tingjian (黃庭坚) of the Song dynasty, whose works are widely read and acclaimed. He is often mentioned in the same breath as Su Dongpo.

In Southeast Asia, particular mention should be made of Huang Nai Shang (Wong Nai Siong). Having leased a piece of land from Raja Brooke of Sarawak, Huang gathered his fellow Fuzhou people to build a pioneer colony in Sarawak. This colony is today's Sibu, known also as New Fuzhou to many Chinese.

Wong (Cantonese)
Hwang
Ng (Hokkien, Teochew)
Wee (Hokkien)
Oei
Ooi (Hokkien)

KE

DESCENDANTS OF TAI BO

The family of Ke had their roots in southern China. They came from the state of Wu, which was a large territory roughly south of the Yangzi Jiang, in present-day Wuxi county, Jiangsu province.

History records that Wu state was passed down by Tai Bo (泰伯), uncle of King Wen, during the Zhou dynasty 3,000 years ago. Although the place did not attract much attention initially, generations of hard work in the country by Tai Bo's descendants paid rich dividends and developed it into a large piece of fertile land around the Zhejiang area. They later migrated southwards and became a prominent clan in southern China, especially in Fujian province.

Besides the people from the state of Wu, other groups like the descendants of Jiang Taigong (姜太公), a well-known statesman in the Zhou dynasty and some minority ethnic groups also adopted Ke as their surname.

As in other clans, the Ke's had their share of brilliant people. One of them was Ke Su (柯述), an official under Emperor Song Shenzong (1067–1085) of the Song dynasty. It was said that when he was an official, he often helped to raise funds for the poor. In a popular legend, two magpies built their nests on the beams of his house. Later, when his official term was up and he moved away from Huaizhou to another place, the birds also followed him.

In the Ming dynasty, there was a scholar of noble character named

Ke Qian (柯潜). His aloofness and casual attitude towards life, though quite uncommon in those days, was respected by many people. Another scholar who deserves mention was Ke Qian's great grandson, Ke Weiqi (柯维骐), who rejected an officer's post so as to concentrate on his historical research. He was so meticulous and serious in his work that it took him nearly 20 years to compile the histories of three dynasties – Song (960–1279), Liao (916–1125) and Jin (1115–1234) – into one book. The book, called *A New History of Song Dynasty* (宋史新编), was highly acclaimed in the academic world.

There was also Ke Tie, a patriot who came from Taiwan during the late Qing dynasty. When the Japanese put pressure on the Qing government to give up Taiwan to them in 1895, Ke Tie and a few others led an armed resistance against the Japanese.

Although Ke originated in the south, some Northerners also bear the surname. One of these was Ke Shaomin (柯劭忞), a contemporary historian from Shandong province in northern China. He was well-read and had a deep knowledge of history. In 1914, the Republican government appointed him head of a committee to compile the history of the Qing dynasty.

Ke Shaomin (柯劭忞) was also the author of several books. One of them was *Xin Yuan Shi* (新元史), a book on the history of the Yuan dynasty and the Mongolians, which was made the official history by the government.

Kua
Quahe

LI

TRACING ROOTS TO PLUM TREE

The surname Li owes its origin to the plum fruit. The first person to adopt this surname was a direct descendant of Zhuanxu (颛顼), an emperor who lived more than 4,000 years ago.

According to *Xing Zuan*, the dictionary of surnames, Emperor Zhuanxu had a great-grandchild whose son held a post similar to that of a judge. The man adopted his official title, Li (理), for his surname, as was the fashion then.

The lineage continued to prosper until the Yin dynasty. Li Zhi (理徵), then head of the family, offended the tyrant king and the family was persecuted. One of Li's sons, Li Zhen (利贞), managed to escape. While Li Zhen was hiding in some ruins he ate some fruits from a tree nearby to assuage his hunger.

Later, to avoid arousing the king's suspicion, Li Zhen changed his surname to Li (李), a combination of the two characters 木 and 子, as 木子 is the name of the fruit which saved him from starvation. Some people believed that the fruit that Li Zhen ate was in fact a plum (李).

The earliest emergence of the surname was in Henan province. Later on the Li clan developed into 2 distinct branches in Gansu province and Hebei province.

According to an ancient source, during the Tang dynasty the Li surname was bestowed on people with these surnames: Xu (徐), Shao (邵), An (安), Hu (胡), Hong (弘), Guo (郭), Ma (麻), Xian Yu (鲜于), Zhang (张), Ah Bu (阿布), Ah Die (阿跌), She Li (舍利), Zhu Xie (朱邪), Dong (董) and Luo (罗).

The most well-known of the Li's in Chinese history was Li Yuan (李渊), founder of the Tang dynasty and his son, Li Shimin, or Tang Taizong.

There were several well-known poets by that surname. The outstanding Tang poet Li Bai (李白) – probably better known as Li Po – was such a popular figure during his time that the Tang emperor did not dare to take any action against him though he had humiliated the imperial concubine.

Li Yu, the poet king, and Li Shangyin also left behind many great works. One of the earliest Chinese writers to speak up for the rights of women was the Qing writer Li Nuzhen. Li Zhen was a Tang painter noted for his portrayal of Buddhist themes.

There were also military personalities like Han general Li Guang (李广), an excellent archer, Li Xiucheng of the Taiping Rebellion and Li Zicheng, leader of a peasant's uprising against the Ming throne. In the field of medicine, Li Shizhen, pioneer of Chinese herbal medicine compiled a glossary of Chinese herbal medicine.

There were Li women of both brains and beauty. Among them were Song dynasty poetess Li Qingzhao (李清照) and the beautiful courtesan Li Shishi. From the Han dynasty there was the songstress Li Xiangjun who defied all pressure from a corrupted official to marry her.

Lee (Hokkien, Teochew)

LIN

IN THE SHADE OF TWO TREES

The surname Lim or Lin is a combination of two identical characters meaning 'wood' or 'tree'. The two trees planted side by side denote a forest (林).

As for the origin of this well-established surname, a popular story is often told. It was harvest time and all the people in the village were out in the fields gathering the ripe grain. One of the women was in an advanced stage of pregnancy. As she worked alongside the others, the labour pains started to come at rapid intervals.

There wasn't enough time for her to return to her village. So she was helped to the edge of the woods and there, in the shade of two trees standing side by side, a baby boy was born.

When the time came to name the baby, what could be more appropriate than 'Lin', a reference to the two trees which sheltered him and his mother when they most needed it. The baby grew up and succeeded in life. So great was his fame that his children and their children after them adopted his given name as their surname in order to perpetuate his memory.

Ancient records however maintain that the ancestor of the Lin clan was the loyal minister Bi Gan (比干), who was cruelly murdered by the tyrannical King Zhou. His son fled to the forests, and later on King Wu of Zhou gave him the Lin surname, and provided him with a place in present-day Hebei province. Thereafter, during the Spring and Autumn period, his descendants wandered to the northern parts of the country, to the provinces of Shandong and Henan, settling finally in Jinan district of Shandong province.

Of the famous Lins in history, eight or nine out of ten are Hokkiens. In fact, many of the prominent figures from the Lin clan came from Fujian province. Lin Chunpu (林春溥) was a great Qing dynasty scholar who wrote the famous *Gu Shi Ji Nian* (古史记年).

Lin Xu (林旭), a high-ranking Qing official, advocated constitutional reforms and modernization during the reign of Emperor Guangxu. He was killed when the conservatives regrouped under the Empress Dowager and reduced the emperor to a mere figurehead.

There was also the famous Lin Zhexu (林则徐) who, with the help of Lin Changyi (林昌彝), waged a bitter war against the British during the first Opium War. The renowned translator, Lin Shu (林纾), made a name for himself with his translation of many foreign literary works like *Camille* into Chinese, based entirely on oral narratives.

Lum (Cantonese)
Lam (Cantonese)
Lim (Hokkien)
Ling (Hokchew)

LIU

A SAINTLY ANCESTOR

Liu Yong (柳永) was the most well-known romantic poet in the Song dynasty. Typical of many poets, he did not fare well in his civil service career. But what he could not attain in his career, he made up by his poetry writing. His sentimental poems were the favourite of many young Han Chinese. Musicians looked for him to write lyrics for popular songs.

Liu Yong became so dejected after failing the national civil service entrance examination that he wrote a poem alluding that the emperor was foolish to have left out a brilliant man like him.

The emperor, on reading this, was very angry. When Liu's application for a government post came to him, the emperor laughed and said, 'Why should he apply to work for the government? Let him write poetry.'

But Liu immediately took this up and changed his name to 'Royal-commissioned poet Liu'. The emperor was stunned by his action but could not do anything.

The romantic but poor poet was much adored by the women in the 'green towers', a brothel cum nightclub in the Song dynasty. Even the responsibility for his funeral arrangements was shouldered by them. They collected money to put the handsome poet to eternal rest, in style.

It is thus difficult to link Liu Yong with Liu Xiahui, the common ancestor of the Liu clan and a most honourable gentleman in Chinese history. Apparently Liu Xiahui (柳下惠) was so well-behaved that he did not move a muscle when a beautiful girl sat on his lap. His behaviour naturally drew applause from the Confucian scholars. Confucius and Meng Zi praised him as being a saint and model worthy of emulation.

Liu Xiahui's original surname was Zhan (展) but as he was working in a city named Liu Xia (柳下), he then changed his surname. Liu Xia was in Lu state in the Spring and Autumn period. When Lu state was conquered by Qin, the descendants of Liu Xiahui moved to Chu state. But it was not long before Chu was also overrun by Qin. The Liu clan then had to move further to a large piece of land east of Yellow River, in present Shanxi province.

Most of the famous personalities in this clan had achievements in art and literature. There were Liu Zongyuan (柳宗元), a famous prose writer often associated with Han Yu, and Liu Gongquan (柳公权), a renowned calligrapher in the Tang dynasty.

Prose writer Liu Kai, story-teller Liu Jingting (柳敬亭) and artist Liu Yu (柳遇) contributed a great deal to the cultural development of China.

Leow
Liu (Hokchia, Foochow)

LIU

BLUE BLOOD IN THE VEINS

There is enough royal blood in the veins of the Liu clan to make it one of the most glorious in Chinese history. All in all, members of the Liu clan set up four dynasties and held the reins of power for about 500 years between the Warring States period to the end of Qing dynasty. But it was a long and winding road before Liu was established as a surname.

Historical sources say that the Liu surname has five different branches – descendants of King Yao, descendants of King Zhou Wen's father Wangji, the Lou surname which was changed to Liu, the Ding surname which was also changed to Liu, and Xiongnu's surname which was also changed.

Legends have it that 3,850 years ago, a cute baby boy was born with two words Liu Lei (刘累) written into his palm. His parents immediately used these as his name. This was the first time Liu was used as a surname in Chinese history. Unfortunately, it was relatively short-lived. Liu Lei's descendants, instead of continuing the surname, adopted others like Du (杜) and Shi (士).

Five hundred years later, a group of Shi clansmen moved over to Qin state. And to distinguish themselves from the rest of the Shi's in the other states, they checked their family records and decided to revive the surname Liu.

This time, the Liu surname had a more lasting and enviable life. It was quick to establish itself; only two centuries later, one of its clansmen became the emperor of China. Liu Bang (刘邦) led an uprising to overthrow the Qin dynasty and set up his Han dynasty. This is still the proudest moment of the Liu clan as China's power reached its height during the Han dynasty.

After the Han dynasty, the Liu's still maintained a strong interest in palace life. In the North-South dynasty period, Liu Yu (刘裕) founded the Liu Song dynasty. And in the Five Dynasties period, the Liu clan went one step further to set up three dynasties: Liu Zhi Yuan's (刘知远) Later Han, Liu Chong's (刘崇) Northern Han, and Liu Yin's (刘隐) Southern Han. The Later Han dynasty has no less than 24 Liu emperors.

But the Liu clan's achievements also extended to art and literature. Liu Ling (刘伶) was a famous poet in the Jin dynasty, while Liu Xie (刘勰) was widely respected as an authority in literary criticism in the North-South dynasty.

Lau (Hokkien, Teochew)
Liew
Lew
Low (Teochew)

LU

A PATRIOTIC PAST

The origin of the Lu surname is rather complex. The earliest source lies in Yongji county in present-day Shanxi province, northern China. There, a descendant of the royal Wei family was given a piece of land called Lu near a tributary of the Huang He (Yellow River). His family adopted Lu as their surname. This branch was related in blood to those Chen (陈) and Tian (田) branches whose progenitors shared the same father, Yu Shun.

Another Lu branch appeared some time during the Spring and Autumn period. A minority group living in the state of Lu Hun (陆浑) called themselves after their state when the Jin state annexed their land.

In the North-South dynasty period, a new branch emerged when a minority people simplified their surname from Bu Lu Gu (步陆孤) to Lu.

The early Lu clans were concentrated in Shandong, north-eastern China and in Henan province, central China. They later thrived in the provinces of Jiangsu and Zhejiang, hometowns of Lu Jiuling (陆九龄), Lu Jiuyan (陆九渊) and Lu You (陆游).

Lu You (1125-1210) was a poet distinguished by his poems of both patriotism and tragic love. He lived towards the end of the Northern Song period when the hostile Jin people attacked the Song empire.

The political situation worried Lu You, who was brought up in a family of patriots. Later, as an official in the imperial court, he strongly advocated military reinforcement for national defence. But he was opposed by those who suggested a compromise with the invaders.

Frustrated with the chaos and corruption of the government, the ignorance and incompetence of people in power and also his own helplessness, Lu You voiced his strong sentiments in poems. Of his 9,000-odd poems that still exist today, many told of the people's sufferings and destruction of war. He also hit out at those people in favour of a compromise with the enemy.

Lu You's marriage, unfortunately, was also a failure. He loved a talented cousin whom his mother disapproved of, and the couple eventually separated. The lovelorn Lu expressed his sorrow in several poems, the best known of which he wrote after he met his former wife by chance in a garden.

When Lu You was 81, the new Song emperor realized the influence of his ideas and appointed him to an important official post once again.

Twenty years after Lu You's time, there was another heroic Lu patriot, Lu Xiufu (1236–1278). Lu Xiufu (陆秀夫), a minister, died when the Mongolian invaders cornered him at Yashan. He ordered his wife to jump into the sea while he did the same, carrying a prince with him.

In academics, two Lu brothers, Lu Jiuyan and Lu Jiuling, came out with their own ideas on the study of *li* (basic laws of nature). These two 12th-century neo-Confucianist philosophers argued that the mind can understand these laws by mere meditation. They also contributed to the study of *yin-yang* (opposing forces in nature) and the five elements said to compose the physical universe.

Another interesting character in the Lu clan was Lu Yu (陆羽), venerated by generations after him as the 'Tea God'. Lu Yu was the person who elevated tea drinking into an art, and in his writings, wrote about the proper way to pour tea, the type of teapots and teacups to be used.

Loke (Cantonese)

LUO

DESCENDANTS OF THE FIRE GOD

The *Romance of the Three Kingdoms* (三国演义) is probably a familiar classic to many readers. Its popularity has gone beyond the printed medium – numerous films based on the intriguing plots from the book have been made. The man behind this great classic is Luo Guanzhong (罗贯中), a Yuan writer from Hangzhou, who lived from 1330 to 1400.

Luo had also written other books like *Sui Tang Zhi Zhuan* (随唐志传)

and *Fen Zhuang Lou* (粉妆楼), but they did not prove as popular as the *Romance of the Three Kingdoms* classic.

Luo Guanzhong's family history dated as far back as 2,000 years ago. The forefather was Zhu Rong (祝融), who was said to be a god of fire. During the Zhou dynasty, Zhu was given the city of Yi (in present-day Hubei province, Xiangyang district). This was renamed the state of Luo.

During the Han dynasty, however, the state of Luo was turned into a prefecture which became part of the property of the Chu state. When it was later replaced by another state, the progeny of Zhu Rongshi started to drift southwards and became a prominent clan around the region of Changsha and Nanchang.

Sui and Tang dynasties were important for the Luo clan, as this was the time they moved to the rest of China from Lianghu and Yuzhang.

For the Luo clan's share of respectable historical personalities, there were the three Tang scholars known as the Three Luos (三罗): Luo Yin (罗隐), Luo Ye (罗邺), and Luo Chou (罗虬).

Both Luo Ye and Luo Chou were poets in their own right. But the most well-known of the three was Luo Yin. Luo Yin (833–909) was a writer whose language was simple and colloquial and whose poetry was mainly satirical compositions about society.

Then there was Luo Longji (罗隆基), a contemporary figure. An American university graduate, he was the former lecturer of several universities in China as well as the chief editor of several Chinese national papers and magazines.

Law
Loh (Cantonese)

MEI

OF OPERATIC FAME

Chinese opera fans will surely have heard of Mei Lan Fang, who died about 20 years ago. His portrayal of ancient ladies on stage was so exquisite that his style has become a school.

The first ancestor of the Mei clan was enshrouded in legends. He was Mei Bo (梅伯), mentioned in the Chinese mythology *Feng Sheng Bang* as a marquis, who lived more than 3,000 years ago. Mei Bo served loyally under the tyrant king Zhou, only to be rewarded by the tyrant's order that he be hacked to death.

The earliest Mei clan lived in the region of present-day Runan county, Henan province, in central China. By the fourth and fifth century A.D., new branches joined the clan as some minority ethnic groups to the north and south of China proper adopted Mei for their Chinese surnames. By the end of Western Han, it had already spread from Henan to Jinjiang district in present-day Jiangxi province.

The Mei clan has its share of brilliant scholars. One of the more colourful characters was Mei Xun (梅询) from the city of Anhuixuan. It was said that Mei Xun used to light two urnfuls of joss-sticks every morning. He would let the fumes of the joss-sticks penetrate through his long sleeves. When he finally entered his study and flung his sleeves, the incense captured in his sleeves would perfume the whole room.

In the field of science, three Mei brothers made important contributions. Their discoveries, particularly in astronomy and almanacs, brought new knowledge to traditional Chinese society of the early Qing dynasty in the seventeenth century. All three, Mei Wending (梅文鼎), Mei Wennai (梅文鼐), and Mei Wenmi (梅文鼏), were learned men well-versed in the almanacs and the use of the lunar calendar. Wending, the eldest brother, wrote some 80 books on the different types of almanacs. To commend their contribution, the Qing emperor Kangxi presented Wending with a plaque.

Mui (Cantonese)
Moey (Cantonese)

OUYANG

EIGHT GENERATIONS OF SCHOLARS

People having the surname Ouyang are, like those with the Ou surname (欧), actually descendants of Gou Jian, the king of Yue, during the Spring and Autumn period. Seven generations after Gou Jian, one of his descendants Wujiang made his second son marquis of Ouyang pavilion on Ouyu Mountain. (Ouyu Mountain was located in present-day Zhejiang province, east of Wuxing county.) Not long after, King Wujiang suffered a crushing defeat under the mighty army of Chu, and thereafter his grandchildren adopted Ouyang as their surname.

Going even further back, the original ancestor of the Ou and Ouyang clans is the legendary tamer of floods Xia Yu, more than 4,000 years ago. However, the recorded history of the surname Ouyang dates back approximately 2,300 years.

Ouyang is a most illustrious surname, and from the Han dynasty onwards, was already acclaimed as the Eight Generations of Scholars – referring to the outstanding character Ouyang Sheng (欧阳生), and after him, Ouyang Gao (欧阳高), Ouyang Diyu (欧阳地馀), Ouyang Xi (欧阳歙), etc.

Ouyang Sheng's descendant Ouyang Xi was an especially well-respected individual. During the reign of Emperor Guang Wudi in Eastern Han dynasty, he was the official in charge of Runan. He taught 100 people over a period of 9 years, and as his reputation continued to grow, he was promoted to the rank of *da situ*. In that capacity, he was said to have despatched 1,000 people to prison.

Jin Wen Shang Shu (今文尚书) is part of the rich Chinese cultural tradition, and the fact that the Ouyang surname has been featured so prominently in it emphasizes the respect it has accrued over the ages.

Since the Ouyang clan was from the region of Gaoyuan in Shandong province, its members were called people of Bohai, which is the sea between Shandong and Liaodong.

Their migration took place this way – from Zhejiang to Jiangsu and then to Shandong, then southwards to many parts of Jiangnan. By the Tang dynasty, they had already moved south of Changjiang, even as far south as Jinjiang area of Fujian province.

Ouyang Shun (欧阳询) was from Linxiang in Hunan province, during the Tang dynasty. He excelled in history and literature. In fact, his literary merits spread so far and wide that even the Gaoli state sent envoys to ask for his help! Ouyang Zhan (欧阳詹) was a native of Jinjiang in Fujian province, and with others like Ruo Guan (弱冠) and Han Yu (韩愈), were praised as being exemplars in the literary tradition.

However, one of the most outstanding and distinguished figures to ever emerge from the Ouyang clan must be Ouyang Xiu (欧阳修), a native of Luling. He has been legendarily attributed with one thousand poems, ten thousand books, one zither, one game of Chinese chess, one bottle of wine, and one crane. Till this day, he is accorded the deepest respect of many Chinese individuals.

Ouyang Xiu ranks with eminent personalities like Han Yu, Li Bai (李白) and Du Fu (杜甫), and regarded as one of the eight great literary names of the Tang and Song dynasties. *The History of the Five Dynasties* and *The History of the Tang Dynasty* were his works of great renown. His other essays have gained widespread recognition as well. This distinguished statesman, philosopher and poet is almost as well-known for his delightfully written essays as for his lyric verse.

Apart from Ouyang Xiu, there was his father Ouyang Guan (欧阳观), uncle, son, and many other members of the family tree, all of whom were people of great repute.

All along, the Ouyang clan has produced fine men of letters and talent, like Ouyang Xian (欧阳玄) of the Yuan dynasty, the great poet Ouyang Lu (欧阳辂) from the Qing dynasty, just to mention a few.

Auyong
Owyang

QIAN

MANY LITERATI IN THE CLAN

The origin of the surname Qian, meaning 'money', is indeed closely related to money. According to historical writings, the ancestor of Qian was Fu (孚), descendant of an ancient emperor. He was a minister in charge of the treasury in the Zhou dynasty. Fu later adopted his title as his surname.

The early Qians were mostly residing at Xuzhou, Jiangsu province. Later, they moved to southern China, though there are still a number of Qians in some parts of Jiangnan province, especially in Wuxing and Wujin.

Strangely, the descendants of Fu were not outstanding in economics. Instead, they became more prominent in the literary circle.

About 1,000 years ago, during the Five Dynasties period, Qian Miao (钱镠) set up his own kingdom of Wu Yue (吴越) and added royal colour to the clan. In the Tang dynasty, poet Qian Qi (钱起) was one of the ten top gifted writers of histories.

The Qians have more outstanding personalities in the Qing dynasty – like famous painter Qian Tu and seal engraver Qian Song. Qian Dating (钱大昕) was a renowned historian.

The May 4th Movement saw the rise of Qian Xuangtong, who was the first to propose romanization of Chinese characters. He was a stalwart of China's New Cultural Movement. In recent years, Qian Xueshen and Qian Sanqiang are the two scientists responsible for the development of nuclear science in China.

History books recorded that people having the surnames Qian and Peng (彭) have the same ancestor. In the old days, intermarriage between the two surnames was prohibited. But this belief has dwindled with the passing years.

QIU

FOR THE SAKE OF CONFUCIUS

Until Emperor Yongzheng ruled China from A.D. 1723 to A.D. 1736, the Qiu (邱) family was known as Qiu (丘). Because Qiu happened to be the name of the sage, Confucius (孔丘), the emperor ordered that all those bearing this surname were to add the radical 阝 to the word as a form of respect for the great teacher. Thus, the surname Qiu (邱) actually came from 丘, both of which are pronounced in the same way.

To trace the origin of the Qiu clan, we have naturally to trace the root of Qiu (丘). History books recorded two origins. One came from the descendants of Qi Taigong (姜太公). Qi Taigong was conferred a place, Qiu, in present-day Shandong province, Changle county. So his offspring adopted the name of the place as their surname.

The second origin came from members of a foreign tribe. They changed their name from Qiudun (丘敦) to Qiu during the period of the North-South dynasties (581–420 B.C.).

Both groups changed their names to Qiu at the beginning of the Qing dynasty. From Shandong province, their family roots extended to Shanxi province and became a prominent clan there. It also stretched as far south as Fujian and Guangdong provinces.

The clan contributed much to Chinese history. When China came under the rule of Genghis Khan, many intellectuals refused to have anything to do with the tyrant. But a Taoist priest, Qiu Chuji (邱处机), volunteered his service and patiently taught him the substance of his faith.

Genghis Khan was deeply touched by Qiu's teachings and slowly began to show some respect for traditional Chinese morals and values. He even regarded Qiu Chuji as a sage.

Some people may be familiar with the name of Qiu Fengjia (邱逢甲), A.D. 1864–1912, a patriotic poet who led a resistance army against the Japanese invaders towards the end of the Qing dynasty. He left behind several poems expressing his love for his country.

Hew (Hakka)   **Yeow** (Cantonese)
Khoo (Cantonese, Hakka)   **Yow** (Cantonese)

SHEN

A SURNAME WITH TWO PRONUNCIATIONS

Although the more common pronunciation of this surname is Shen, it can also be pronounced Zhen.

The surname has two main sources. The Shen clan came from the descendants of the legendary emperor Huang Di, while the Zhen family came from the descendants of Emperor Zhuanxu.

Through the years, the groups that descended from Huang Di dominated the scene. Their origin was in the Runan county of Henan province. The Shen surname was actually taken from the name of King Wen's son of the Zhou dynasty.

Around the tenth century, the clan branched off into another family, the You (尤) clan. The reason behind this was that at that time, there was a ruler in Fujian province whose name was Shen (审). Though they had different characters, they sounded the same, and the Shen clan therefore removed the water radical (氵) from their surname. This also explains how the surname You (尤) was evolved. People with surnames of You and Shen could not marry.

A familiar figure in the Shen clan is Shen Congwen (沈从文), one of China's most well-known writers and the author of *Ancient Chinese Costumes*. Born in 1903 to a Miao minority group in Hunan province in southern China, Mr Shen started writing stories as early as the 1920s. Besides being an established writer, he is also a historian and researcher in his own right, having worked over 30 years as a researcher in China's Museum of Chinese History.

Besides Shen Congwen, there was Shen Kuo (沈括) of the Song dynasty, 1031-1095. A politician as well as a scientist, he was well-versed in literature, astrology, music and medicine.

In the contemporary field of entertainment, there was Shen Xiling (沈西苓), 1904–1940, a film director who gave us well-known movies like *Crossroads* and *Shanghai 24 hours*. Most of his films depicted life of the thirties and had anti-feudalism themes.

Another figure was Shen Xingong (沈心工), 1869–1947, a music

teacher who had been involved in the compilation and publishing of songs since 1904 and who wrote lyrics to foreign music for use in schools.

Sim (Hokkien)
Sum (Cantonese)

SITU

HOLDING ONTO THE TITLE

The chapter on kings and emperors in *Historical Records* put the legendary Chinese emperor Shun as the first ancestor of the Situ clan. But the term Situ comes from an official rank which existed in China during the Western Zhou dynasty, some 4,000 years ago.

The Situ clansmen were in fact descendants of the officials who held this senior post. By the Zhou dynasty, it was listed as one of the six most senior positions in the Chinese court.

A *situ* was responsible for farmlands and drafting serf labour for state projects. During the Western Han dynasty, the prime minister's post was replaced by the *da situ*.

Prominent figures of the Situ clan included Situ Ying (司徒映), a senior official in the court of Tang Emperor Wenzhong, who was renowned for his scholarship. Despite his rapid rise to the top of the power pyramid, he resigned at the peak of his officialdom to engage in literary work. Tang dynasty scholars respected Situ Ying's work highly.

Situ Xu (司徒诩) was a great official during the Five Dynasties period and was appointed head of the civil service. During the Ming dynasty, Situ Hua Bang (司徒化邦) was made senior prime minister and commander of the Liaoyang army. He was reputed for his filial piety and loyalty to friends.

Situ Ying came from Jezhou (in present-day Shanxi), Situ Xu hailed from Hebei and Situ Hua Bang was a native of Jiangsu province. Therefore, over a period of 4,000 years, the Situ clan has spread far and wide over China.

Szeto (Cantonese)
Seeto

SU

FAMOUS FOR HIS 'DRINKING POEMS'

Like the Tang dynasty, the Song dynasty saw the rise of many literary figures. Among them was a great scholar, Su Dongpo (苏东坡), a familiar figure with Chinese literature students.

Su was capable of expressing himself freely in prose and poetry. And as he loved wine, it was said that most of his inspiration came from drinking. Indeed he was particularly famous for his 'drinking poems'.

The successful scholar was less successful as a senior court official. In his drunkenness – though some said Su pretended he was drunk – he criticized the government's policies and was arrested and put in jail. He was demoted to a minor official and banished from the imperial court for 25 years.

Su Dongpo's father, Su Xun (苏询), was also an outspoken writer who dared criticize the government's rules. Su Xun and his two sons, Su Dongpo and Su Shi (苏辙), were known as the Three Su's (三苏). The Su family was also listed as one of the great eight scholar families of the Tang and Song dynasties.

The first person to adopt Su as his surname was Kun Wu (昆吾), an offspring of Emperor Zhuanxu who lived in the present-day Henan province, Linzhang county. Later, the Su clansmen moved to the region around Gansu province. After establishing a name for themselves in these northern provinces, the Su quickly headed south, and it is now the surname of many southern Chinese.

Even as far back as 3,000 years ago, during the Spring and Autumn period, the Su clan had enjoyed a high reputation. At that time, a Su clansmen and senior court official, Su Cong (苏从), helped the Chu state become strong and powerful by advising the emperor to pull himself together instead of neglecting state affairs.

During the Warring States period, there was Su Qin (苏秦), a political strategist who advocated that all small states combine forces to defeat the state of Qin. Later, he was appointed prime minister of six states – and the incident has been retold ever since through a popular Cantonese opera (六国封相).

Another historical figure was Su Wu (苏武) of the Han dynasty. He was captured by the Xiong Nu (匈奴) minority tribe which was then at war with the Han regime and was banished to the cold north (Beihai), where he tended sheep for 19 years. Still he refused to yield to the enemy. Finally, he was released and returned to his country.

Soh (Cantonese)

SUN

TRACING THE ROOTS TO A KING

The Sun clan has a history dated back some 3,000 years, and many of its ancestors were great politicians and were skilled in the art of war.

According to the *Dictionary of Surnames*, King Wen of the Zhou dynasty was the first ancestor of the Sun clan. The Zhou dynasty was a feudal society and King Wen's eighth son, Kang Shu, was conferred the dukedom of Wei, which is in present Taiyuan district, Shanxi province.

When the title was passed on to Duke Wu, his son Hui Sun (惠孙) became a senior official. Henceforth, Hui Sun's descendants adopted Sun as their surname.

Tang and Han dynasties' records disputed this version and claimed that the Suns were descended from the Bi clan. With so much controversy surrounding the ancestors of the Sun clan, it is indeed a trying task for the Suns to trace their roots.

One fact is certain though: due to the conferring of titles by the royalty and the practice of not allowing commoners to have the same surname as the emperor's, many people gave up their original surname to adopt the Sun surname.

Some of the Sun clan members could also be traced to the Chen (陈), Xun (荀), Xia (夏) and Hou (侯) clans.

Among the many renowned figures of the Sun clan was Sun Wu

(孙武), author of China's earliest military writings. Sun Wu, who lived during the Spring and Autumn period, used his clever strategy to lead the Wu army to victory over Chi state.

Sun Quan (孙权), founder of the Wu state during the period of the Three Kingdoms, was also another famous character. But his heavy taxation and frequent resort to severe punishment caused many people to rise against him.

Sun Wei (A.D. 1183-1240) was an expert in the making of armour. He had such a fine reputation that the Mongol ruler, Genghis Khan, once tried to pierce his armour with special arrows but to no avail. Sun Wei was then given charge of the armoury.

The founding father of the Chinese republic, Sun Zhongshan (Dr Sun Yat-sen, 1866–1925), came from Cuiheng village, Zhongshan county in Guangdong province. He added another glorious page to the Sun clan history. Dr Sun, who overthrew Manchu rule on October 10, 1911, was made the first provisional president of the Republic of China.

Soon

WANG

ROOTS HERE, THERE AND EVERYWHERE

Wang is one of the commonest surnames among the Chinese, and has a more varied origin than most. One group started more than 2,000 years ago with the 15th son of King Zhou Wen, the ancestor of the Zhou clan who changed his surname from Ji to Wang. The prince and his family lived in Hebei province.

Another source of the surname was in Beihai, Guangxi province. There the descendants of Shun, a tribal chief who lived more than 4,000 years ago, set up their own Wang community. Later, some ethnic minorities such as Gaoli (高丽) and Qian Er (钳耳) also adopted the surname when they settled in China.

In time, many Chinese were endowed with the surname by the emperor as a reward for loyalty and distinguished service.

With the many sources of Wang lines throughout China, a large number of personalities by that name are known in China. The teacher of the ancient military strategists Su Qin (苏秦) and Zhang Yi (张仪) was Wang Xu (王诩). In history, influential political figures included two Wangs, Wang Mang and Wang Anshi. Wang Mang seized the Han throne and set up an oppressive and ineffective government that finally caused his own downfall. Wang Anshi was noted for his land reforms to help the common peasants.

Among the literati, there were Wang Chong, a Han philosopher whose concepts on materialism were well ahead of his time; and Wang Fuzhi, an eighteenth-century Chinese thinker well-versed in literature, astronomy and mathematics.

In Chinese calligraphy, Wang Xizhi (王羲之) was one of the two top Chinese calligraphers. He made a breakthrough of the conventional style and established his own style of writing. Wang Mian was a painter cum poet of the Mongol empire who was distinguished in his ink paintings of plum blossoms. Last but not least was Wang Wei (王维), A.D. 701–761, a poet and writer whose painting had been described as being so vivid that it affects the senses like poetry.

According to *Guang Yun* (广韻), prominent Wang clan members came from 21 places in China: Taiyuan (Shanxi province), Liangya (Shandong province), Beihai (Shandong province), Chenlin (Henan province), Donghai (Shandong province), Gaoping, Jingzhao, Tianshui (Gansu province), Dongping (Shandong province), Xincai (Henan province), Xinye (Henan province), Shanyang (Shandong province), Zhongshan (Hebei province), Zhangwu (Hebei province), Donglai (Shandong province), Hedong (Shanxi province), Jincheng (Jiangsu province), Haihan, Changsha (Hunan province), Tangyi (Jiangsu province), and other places in Henan province.

Wong (Cantonese)
Heng (Teochew)
Ong (Hokkien)

WEN

A FAMILY OF PATRIOTS

The surname Wen originated from the region of present-day Shaoxing county of Zhejiang province in eastern China. The first Wen ancestor was a prince of direct descent from Huang Di.

The Wen clan was also said to have come from the Jing (敬) family, whose surname was banned because some emperors also had the same surname. One example was Wen Yanbo (文彦博), A.D. 1006–1097, who was originally Jing by surname. He was known for his outstanding official career, having served as an important minister in the imperial court for 50 years under four different rulers.

In Chinese, wen also means language and literature. There happened to be an early Wen ancestor who was a pioneer of education. Wen Weng (文翁), a learned official serving under the Han emperor in about 120 B.C., advocated the importance of education and set up schools in his prefectures. The popular education in Wen Weng's prefectures impressed the emperor so much that the imperial court ordered schools to be set up throughout the country.

The well-known eulogy on righteousness, *Zhengqi Ge*, was written by Wen Tianxiang (文天祥) when he was in prison. Wen was a patriot and prime minister to the last emperor of Song dynasty. Though he tried hard to resist the invading Mongols, his efforts failed and he was captured by the enemy.

Wen's captors tried to win over his loyalty through threats and temptations, to which he refused to give in. Although Wen Tianxiang was executed after three years of imprisonment, his spirits remained high.

In the fifth century B.C., there was a loyal minister who ended up sacrificing his own life. The minister, Wen Zhong (文种), was an important aide to the king of Yue, Gou Jian. When Gou Jian was held hostage by the enemy, he worked very hard to secure the king's release. It was also Wen Zhong who was chiefly responsible for the success of Gou Jian's military campaign when the king was later freed.

Gou Jian, however, was an ingrate who was only prepared to rely on friends in times of trouble. One of his right-hand men, realizing this, gave some excuse and resigned. Only Wen Zhong did not heed any advice. Finally, Gou Jian accused him of attempting to revolt and forced him to take his own life.

In the arts, the Wen clan had Ming painter Wen Zhengming (文徵明), A.D. 1470–1559, who was also good in poetry. In his younger days, he painted mostly scenery. When he was an old man, his best works were of plum blossoms, bamboo and man. His style evolved into a school of painting and attracted a large following.

Boon (Hokkien)
Mun (Cantonese)

WU

WHEN NOTHING IS GOOD ENOUGH

To coin an appropriate name is an agonizing experience for the Wu's, because Wu sounds like the character *wu* (无) – which means 'without' or 'nothing'!

Despite the frustrations caused by its Mandarin pronunciation, the Wu clan, like most Chinese, is quite proud of its surname because it goes back to a royal ancestor.

According to *The Record of Surnames*, Emperor Zhou conferred upon Prince Tai Bo a territory at Wu and his descendants adopted the territory's name as their surname. As the prince was the elder brother of the Zhou emperor, the Wu and Zhou clans are actually two of the branches on the same family tree.

Apart from carrying some blue blood, the Wu's are also proud of their renowned clansmen in history. The *Chinese Encyclopaedia Dictionary* has nearly 200 entries on the Wu's.

One of the earliest revolutionary leaders in Chinese history was Wu Guang (吴广) who led a peasant uprising against the tyrant Qin king in 209 B.C. During the Warring States period, Wu Qi (吴起) was a great military strategist.

In the field of fine arts and literature, Wu Daozi (吴道子) of the Tang dynasty was known as 'The Greatest Artist of All Time'. Wu Changshuo (吴昌硕) of the Qing dynasty was one of the most versatile artists China has ever produced. Wu Dacheng (吴大徵) was a great Qing dynasty scholar held in high esteem even by present-day scholars.

An infamous Wu was a uniformed man by the name of Wu Sangui (吴三桂). He started out as a general loyal to the Ming throne. A garrison commander at the north-east border facing the menacing Manchurians, he was widely acclaimed for his bravery.

But when he heard that his favourite concubine, Chen Yuanyuan, was seized by the revolutionary forces who aimed to overthrow the toppling Ming dynasty, he opened the country's door to the very invaders whom he was supposed to defeat, to give vent to his personal spite. This outburst of anger over a beauty helped to precipitate Manchu rule in Han China.

Goh (Hokkien, Teochew)
Woo (Cantonese)
Ng (Hokkien, Teochew)

XIAO

PRINCE CHARMING

The Xiao clan originated some 3,700 years ago. There was a Xiao state in the present Jiangsu province, Xiao county, and its residents were said to be from the Xiao clan.

After the downfall of the Qin dynasty, Xiao He (萧何) was the think-tank whose strategic planning proved an invaluable aid to Liu Bang in establishing the Han dynasty. Of the five dynasties in the period called the North-South dynasties, the Xiao's set up two dynasties, Liang (梁) and Qi (齐).

Prince Xiao Tong (萧统), or better known as Prince Zhao Ming (昭明), was born during the North-South dynasties (A.D. 420–581). His father Xiao Yan (萧衍) was the founder emperor of Liang dynasty.

He was said to have been a child prodigy. At the age of five, he had completed the Confucian classics that others took 20 years to do. His father once tested his capability to rule the country. Thousands of law suits or complex legal cases submitted by officers from all over the country were put before him. Most people would have collapsed under such pressure but Xiao Tong solved all the cases quickly and decisively. His liberal attitude in granting the guilty a second chance was also welcomed by his people.

In winter, he would provide the homeless with shelter. And proper funerals were arranged for unclaimed dead bodies found by the roadside. In his free hours, he took time to compile and edit classical writings and published them under his name. His collection of writings is still read by students of Chinese literature today.

He died at the young age of 31 and the whole country mourned for the loss of this charming and caring prince. Many believed that if he hadn't died so early, the Liang dynasty would have lasted beyond its 50-odd years.

Other personalities from the Xiao clan also came mainly from the North-South dynasties period. Two members of a royal family made their names in the academic world as well. Xiao Ziyun (萧子云) and Xiao Zixian (萧子显), both sons of emperor Xiao Daocheng (萧道成), were established historians. Ziyun wrote a book on the history of Jin dynasty while Zixian wrote on Later Han and Qi dynasties.

After Tang dynasty, the Xiao's started to move to southern China. In Song dynasty, the clan also incorporated some members of the Liao (辽) and Jin (金) tribes which had brought trouble to the northern part of China.

Siew (Teochew)
Siu
Seow (Hokkien)
Hsiao

XU

SELF-SACRIFICING SPIRIT OF ANCESTOR

The course of Chinese history would be very much different if not for Shen Nong (神农), the ancestor of Xu clan. Shen Nong is a legendary figure in the early Chinese civilization. He is said to be an emperor who governed the southern part of the world from the heavens. But his most important contribution was the invention of the plough that helped agricultural development in China.

Shen Nong is also widely respected by Chinese physicians. There are many folk tales of how he personally took different kinds of herbs, some poisonous, to find out more about their characteristics and functions.

Because of his important position in Chinese history, there were many descriptions of what he looked like. In some books, he was even described as a 'man with the head of a bull'.

Ironically, the long history of Xu clan helped to cause confusion over its origin. One account attributed the ancestor of this clan to Xu You (许由) of ancient China.

Ancient China was then ruled by the populist King Yao. He was so democratic that he wanted to pass on his throne to Xu You whom the people thought could rule better. But Xu You, for reasons known only to himself, declined the offer. He ran away and hid in Ji Mountain, refusing to emerge. He was eventually buried there, and in remembrance the mountain was renamed Xu You Mountain, which is in present-day Henan province, Dengfeng county.

Though some historians believed that Xu You was the Xu clan's ancestor, historical records later showed that he was not. So Shen Nong finally won in the tussle of ancestorship.

The descendants of Shen Nong only changed their surname to Xu during the Zhou dynasty. One of them, Sun Wenshu, was given the city of Xu by King Zhou Wu. Sun later set up Xu state in this city, located in present-day Henan province, Xuchang county.

Xu was such a small state that it was constantly invaded by the neighbouring states. By the early Warring States period, it was conquered by Chu state. The people of Xu state had to live in exile. And to make sure that they would not forget their country, they took Xu as their surname. The Xu clan is prominent in Hebei and Henan provinces.

In the Five Dynasties period, the Xu's first lived in Zhaoan in Zhanzhou, then Quanzhou, and later moved to Guangdong. The Xu's in Fujian and Guangdong can therefore be regarded as one family.

Famous personalities in this clan include Xu Shao (许劭), a famous political commentator in the Three Kingdoms period. His judgment of Cao Cao as the 'hero of the turbulent era' has been accepted by historians as the most adequate description.

Xu Heng (许衡) was a famous teacher in Yuan dynasty who attracted scores of students from all over China. Xu Jingdeng (许景澄) was a pioneer diplomat in the Qing dynasty.

Hui (Cantonese)
Koh (Hokkien)
Hsu

XU

MODEST CLAN ANCESTOR

Had the ancestor of the Xu clan been a little more ambitious, the surname might not have existed at all. He was Bo Yi (伯益), who was offered the crown for having helped Emperor Xia Yu to contain floods caused by the overflow of the Yellow River about 4,000 years ago. He not only declined the offer but retreated to the mountains.

Emperor Xia had no choice but to appoint his own son as the successor, thereby starting the tradition of dynasty rule. To express deep gratitude for Bo's achievements. Xia gave a county, Xu, to Bo's son. This was in present-day Anhui province. The county lasted more than 1,000 years before it was conquered by the Chu dynasty. Just like the fate of other small states in the Spring and Autumn period, after having been vanquished by a more powerful state, its people began to use the state's name as their own surname.

Its last ruler, Xu Yenwang (徐偃王), made history by surrendering himself to the enemy because he did not wish to sacrifice his people's lives. Since then, the residents of Xu county started to use Xu as their surname. Most of them settled down in the present Shandong province.

They came into the limelight again during Qin Shi Huang's reign. Emperor Qin, eager to rule China forever, craved for immortality. The man entrusted with the task of finding the medicine with such immortal properties was Xu Fu (徐福), a famous magician at that time.

It was said that there was an island east of China which produced the medicine Qin wanted. So with 3,000 young boys and girls, Xu Fu sailed east. They never returned. People believed that Xu, afraid of being punished for failing the mission, decided to remain on that island, which many still believe to be part of contemporary Japan.

By the Tang dynasty, Xu clansmen were found all over China and excelled themselves in many fields. Xu Yougong (徐有功) was a brave general who helped to found the Ming dynasty. Xu Gan (徐干) made his literary reputation in the Three Kingdoms period and was one of the 'Seven Prominent Scholars' then.

But it was Xu Guangqi (徐光启) in the Ming dynasty who had the biggest impact on the course of Chinese history. He was the first Chinese to acknowledge the importance of Western technology. Through his translations of Western works, China was able to have her first intellectual contact with the West.

Seah (Hokkien, Teochew)
Shu
Tsui (Cantonese)

YAN

DIGNIFIED AND FILIAL

The expression *zhuangyan* (庄严) means 'dignity' in the Chinese vocabulary. While *zhuang* (庄) and *yan* (严) make good sense when put together, as surnames, these two characters are also related to each other.

Although both surnames evolved quite independently, they both originated from the emperor of the Chu state during the Spring and Autumn period (771–476 B.C.). The surname, Yan, was said to be first used by the grandsons of Emperor Zhuang of the state of Chu, as a mark of respect to remember his death. Thus, the suggestion that both surnames shared the same roots. The ancestral home of the Yan's is in Tianshui district, Gansu province, and Shaanxi province.

That was perhaps the reason why the great scholars, Zhuang Guang (庄光) and Zhuang Ji (庄忌), chose Yan when they had to change their surname as the Eastern Han emperor then was Liu Zhuang (刘庄). (There was a rule at that time that no one was to use a name containing even one Chinese character which the emperor had in his name.) So the two scholars became known as Yan Guang (严光) and Yan Ji (严忌). Because of their popularity, many people from the Zhuang clan during that period took Yan as their surname, too.

Filial piety was almost synonymous with the Yan clan after the famous Yan Ximeng (严希孟) of the Song dynasty. One of the most filial sons known in Chinese history, Yan Ximeng was said to have cut flesh from his bottom to cook medicine for his mother when all forms of medical treatment failed. His act, it was believed, so moved the gods in heaven that his mother was cured. Much later, when his mother died, he mourned her so deeply that not a smile ever crossed his face again.

Other well-known names of the Yan clan included poets Yan Yu (严羽) and Yan Shengsun (严绳孙) of the Song and Qing dynasties respectively. A more recent example is one of China's most prominent translators – Yan Fu (严复), who during the last days of the Qing dynasty, held the post of president of the Beijing University.

Yim

YAN

UPHOLDING CONFUCIUS' TEACHINGS

This glorious surname actually has more than one origin. One was from the legendary fire god, Zhu Rong (祝融). It was said that one of the descendants of Jo had the character Yan in his name, so his descendants decided to use it as a surname.

Another branch of Yan's came from Bo Qin (伯禽), the son of Zhou Gong in the Zhou dynasty. As one of Bo Qin's descendants was conferred a piece of land at Yan city, he started this branch of the Yan clan.

Fortunately, as both these branches originated in Shandong province, the present Yan clan can safely trace their roots there.

The Yan clan has done much to uphold the teachings of Confucius. Starting with Confucius' favourite student, Yan Hui (颜回), the clan has produced many personalities who have made much effort in putting his preachings into practice.

Yan Hui was of course the person whom all staunch Confucianists worshipped throughout Chinese history. Confucius himself declared that Yan Hui was the model student among his 70-odd disciples. Yan Hui was also a person who was contented with what he had and was never lured by the temptations of money and status.

He was praised as a person who seldom got angry and never repeated the same mistake. One of his famous sayings was: 'Living in the slump, I am quite happy with a bowl of rice and a scoop of water. There are people who find this kind of life unbearable but my pleasure in living will never change.'

In the Tang dynasty, Yan Gaoqing (颜杲卿) rose to oppose the rebellion led by An Lushan (安禄山) although An was his superior and had just promoted him before the rebellion. When he was captured by An, Yan refused to be bought over. He said: 'My loyalty lies with the country and I would fight anyone who revolts against the emperor.' An killed him on the spot.

In the North-South dynasty, Yan Mao (颜髦) and his brother did what Confucianists praised as a perfect example of filial piety. It was said that while the two were at the funeral site of their dead father, a fire broke out and everyone started to run for their lives. Only the two brothers, hugging the coffin and crying, refused to budge. By a sudden stroke of providence, a heavy downpour put the fire out immediately. Confucianists claimed that the brothers' filial behaviour had moved the gods to stop the fire.

Another filial son was Yan Zhitui (颜之推) who wrote a book, *The Family Teaching of Yan Clan*, in which he outlined all the important points in Confucius' teachings and instructed his descendants to adhere strictly to the Confucian way.

Then there was Yan Yuan (颜元) in Qing dynasty who revived the orthodox Confucian thought from what he called the 'misdirection led by scholars in the Ming dynasty'. He started a school on his own and advised his students to read the original texts and not the 'misinterpretations' of the Ming scholars. Yan Yuan urged the students to adopt a more flexible attitude in their work. He said that reading without thinking as practised by Ming scholars only made people more confused and more incapable of understanding the real issues.

Chinese calligraphy enthusiasts will surely know of Yan Zhenqing (颜真卿) from the Tang dynasty, while other notables in the same dynasty included Yan Shigu (颜师古) who was known for his research in classical studies; Yan Yanzhi was a well-known Song poet.

YANG

THE PATRIOTIC CLANSMEN

There are many different versions of the origin of the Yang surname. Some said it came from an official position while others thought it was named after a place. But most believed that the Yang clan was an offspring of the Ji (姬) family which was said to have descended from the legendary emperor Huang Di. It was said that King Wu's grandson, Bo Qiao (伯侨) of the Zhou dynasty, was made marquis of the Yang county. He later adopted the county's name as his surname.

The Yang clan was very prominent in Shanxi, which was its homeland. Towards the late Tang dynasty, many people were forced to migrate to the south because of war. The Yang clansmen followed suit and settled in Zhangzhou, Fujian province. By the Song dynasty, Fujian virtually became the heart of the Yang's.

Yang Ye (杨业), a renowned general of the Northern Song dynasty, was captured by the invading Liao army during a battle. He was then 60 years old, but rather than submit to the invaders, he went on a hunger strike till his death. Several of his sons also died while defending their country's northern border. Yang Ye's northern exploits were widely proclaimed and he became a legend. His wife and daughters-in-law were also famed for their military prowess.

Besides Yang Ye, there were other famous figures produced by the clan. Among them were Yang Zhu (杨朱), a philosopher who lived during the Warring States period. Yang Zhu was against the concept of equal love for all as advocated by Mo Zi. He was also against Confucius' teachings. He advocated that one should value one's own life. One should resist those who do us harm but not to do harm to the innocent.

Another Yang, Yang Wanli (A.D. 1122–1206) was an outstanding poet during the Southern Song period. Concerned with the welfare of his country and people, he often spoke out against social ills. His poems are characterized by simplicity in style and by his closeness to the people's life.

Young
Yeo (Hokkien)

YU

A SIGNIFICANT CONNECTION

The Chinese surnames 余 and 佘 vary by a fraction, and it is difficult to tell them apart at a glance. Both however are pronounced very differently. Whilst one is pronounced yu (余), the other is pronounced *she* (佘). Delving into the background of these two surnames, one will discover that besides the superficial similarity, there is a surprising relationship between the two.

The character 佘 is in fact derived from the character *she* (舍), and that should have been its correct pronunciation, instead of *yu*. The other surname (which incidentally arose from a mistake in writing 余!) bears the *she* pronunciation. It has been substantiated that Yu and She surnames come from the same source.

The clustering of the Yu clan was mainly in Anhui province. Its ancestor was one You Yu (由余), who fled to Qin state from the Jin state 3,000 years ago. He rendered invaluable help in reinforcing the Qin state.

In north and south China, the descendants of the Yu clan continued to multiply, and the change of Yu (余) to She (佘) took place in Jiangnan. In the very beginning, there were no She's in the north, but they gradually migrated there from Jiangnan.

Although the origin of this surname dates back to about 3,000 years ago, the Yu's really only made a name for themselves after the Tang dynasty. During the Song dynasty, the Yu clan established itself in many ways. Yu Qing (余靖) was one of the Four Court Advisors held in high regard, the others being Ouyang Xiu (欧阳修), Wang Su (王素) and Cai Xiang (蔡襄). Yu Qing is also one of the eight sages venerated in The Hall of Eight Sages in Guangzhou.

Another famous Yu was the scholar Yu Qianyi (余谦一) from Putian in Fujian province, who contributed much to the development of education and culture in the south during the Song dynasty. He was later put in charge of the treasury.

Yew
You
Yee
Eu (Cantonese)

ZENG

PEDIGREES ALL THE WAY

Zeng Zi (曾子), a student of Confucius, was also said to be the author of the classic, *Great Learning* (大学). He was renowned for his filial piety and believed that one should seek self-criticism every day. Zeng Zi was a well-respected figure in his time. So was his surname, Zeng.

According to history, the Zeng clan from Shandong was filled with blue blood. The Zeng family history could be traced as far back as 4,180 years ago, during the reign of Emperor Shao Kang of the Xia dynasty.

When Shao Kang was in power, he conferred on his youngest son, Qu Lie (曲烈), a state called Zeng (鄫). His direct descendants lived in this state for nearly 2,000 years until it was destroyed by another state during the Spring and Autumn period.

The ruler of the state of Zeng was then King Wu (巫). He fled to the neighbouring state of Lu (鲁), in present-day Shandong province, and became an official there. He decided to adopt the name of his former state as his surname, but without the radical 阝. Since then, Zeng became the surname of his descendants.

As the state of Zeng was also in Shandong, it naturally became the homeland of all the Zeng clansmen. From Shandong, the descendants migrated to Fujian and Guangdong in the south.

Besides having a glorious past, the Zeng's, unlike other clans, had no records of other ethnic groups or clans adopting their surname. In other words, they are the pure descendants of King Wu.

Besides Zeng Zi, another well-known figure was Zeng Guofan (曾国藩), 1811-1872, a Qing general who organized armies to fight the Taiping Rebellion. Besides being involved in military work, he was also a scholar. He wrote good essays, mostly on moral values. Guofan's works were very well-received by the people of that time.

Cheng (Hokkien)
Chng (Cantonese, Hakka)

ZHANG

MARTIAL BLOOD IN THE VEINS

The Chinese character for the surname Zhang is made up of two parts. On the left is *gong*, which means a bow; on the right is *chang*, meaning long. This is truly significant because the clan's ancestor, Ji Hui (姬挥), was the inventor of the bow and arrow in Chinese history. People with this surname often introduce themselves as *gongchang* Zhang (弓长张) – to distinguish themselves from other Zhang's like 章.

Ji Hui was said to be the fifth son of Huang Di, the legendary ancestor of all Chinese. Ji Hui made his invention after studying astronomy. Apparently Huang Di was very pleased with his invention, and made him the duke of Zhang city which was in Taiyuan district, present-day Shanxi province. Ji Hui henceforth adopted Zhang as his surname. This is considered the mainstream of the Zhang clan. Some of Ji Hui's descendants also took Gong (弓) as their surname, whilst the rest stuck to Zhang (张).

About 3,000 years ago, two other branches of Huang Di's descendants also changed their surname from Ji to Zhang. They spread to Xiangyang and Luoyang counties, adding strength to this surname which already had a strong following.

During the Han dynasty, it was said that many people were so impressed by the clan's prestige that they took Zhang for their surname. For instance, Zhang Liao (张辽), the famous general who assisted Cao Cao, was Nie Liao (聂辽) until he changed his surname. And until the Ming dynasty, the Zhang clan was very powerful and well-respected in many cities.

The first prominent figure of the Zhang clan in Chinese history was Zhang Yi (张仪), a famous strategist during the Warring States period. He offered his service to the duke of Qin and helped him rule the country. Zhang Liang (张良) was an outstanding political adviser to the first Han emperor, Liu Bang. It was also during the Han dynasty that China's first goodwill ambassador, Zhang Qian (张骞), travelled outside the country's border to as far as Iran.

Zhang Zhi (张芝) was a master in Chinese calligraphy and Zhang Heng (张衡) made his name in astronomy.

The clan also produced many brave generals. Zhang Fei (张飞), the whiskered general in the Three Kingdoms period, is still a household name among the Chinese. During the Tang dynasty, general Zhang Xun (张巡) defended Suiyang city against the rebels. After being surrounded for a few months, the city ran out of food but Zhang Xun refused to surrender. He killed his pretty concubine to feed his soldiers and then committed suicide before the rebels caught hold of him.

Zhang Zidong (张之洞) of the Qing dynasty stirred up a row in the debate on China's modernization programme. He proposed retaining traditional Chinese culture and values while learning western science and technology.

In later years, Zhang Xueliang altered the course of Chinese history in the anti-Japanese war when he kidnapped Chiang Kai-shek (Jiang Jieshi) and forced him to co-operate with the communists.

Chong (Hakka)
Chang (Hokkien, Teochew)
Chiang
Cheung (Cantonese)
Cheong (Cantonese)
Teo (Teochew)

ZHEN

GODDESS OF THE RIVER

During the Three Kingdoms period, General Cao Cao of the Wei state had a talented son named Cao Zhi (曹植). Cao Zhi wrote many beautiful poems. The one which remains even today is a eulogy of immortal love: Goddess of the River – Luo Shen. It reveals Cao Zhi's love and admiration for Queen Zhen (甄宓).

Queen Zhen, or Zhen Mi, was the wife of a general's son in Hebei.

When the Wei army conquered that place, Cao Zhi saw and fell for the beauty. So did his father, Cao Cao, and his elder brother, Cao Bi.

Cao Cao gave Zhen Mi to Cao Bi. And when Cao Bi succeeded the throne, he sent the broken-hearted Cao Zhi on exile. Meanwhile, Zhen Mi gave birth to a baby boy and died soon after.

When Cao Zhi learned of her death two years later, he was grieved, and went to the banks of River Luo to mourn for her. It was said that in his sorrow, he saw Zhen Mi rise from the waters. With mixed feelings, he penned the tragic romance of *The Goddess of River Luo Shen*.

Zhen Mi was a native of present-day Hebei province. The Zhen clan was also said to have originated from there about 4,000 years ago, from the time of the Han dynasty.

The clan's earliest ancestors were craftsmen (*zhen* means potter) who made pottery for King Yu Shun. Another branch of the Zhen clan was said to be founded by a minister's son serving under the same king.

In *Ji Le Pian* (鸡肋篇), written in the Song dynasty, it was recorded that during the Three Kingdoms period, the character was read as *jian*. But as the emperor's name was Sun Jian, many intellectuals with the *jian* surname tried to avoid clashing with the king's name. Thus the pronunciation of the character was changed and became *zhen* thereafter.

In the early Tang dynasty, two Zhen brothers brought glory to their ancestry. They were Zhen Quan (甄权) and Zhen Liyan (甄立言) who contributed to traditional Chinese medicine with their findings on acupuncture and herbal medicine.

Most of the well-known Zhen clansmen in Chinese history were men of letters. Zhen Chen (甄琛), for example, was an upright and efficient official who was highly respected by three successive kings (孝文, 宣武, 孝明) towards the end of the Wei dynasty.

ZHENG

ADMIRAL BRINGS FAME TO CLAN

Around 830 B.C., the tyrant king of Zhou died and his youngest son ascended the throne. The new king then gave the dukedom of Zheng to his brother.

Zheng state lay to the south of Yellow River in Henan province, the Zheng clan's original home. The duke adopted Zheng as the surname of his family line. Later, one of the duke's sons moved to Luoyang and sowed the seed of the Zheng clan there.

Historically, two Zhengs were well-known scholars of the classics. They were Zheng Xua (郑玄) and Zheng Zhong (郑众) of the first century A.D. Zheng Zhong was noted especially for his annotation of many classics, including *The Analects* and *Yi Shou*.

In the Ming dynasty, Zheng Chenggong (郑成功), a patriotic general with troops based in Taiwan, fought against the Manchus who had invaded China.

Qing writer and painter, Zheng Xie, was an upright scholar who ranked among the 'Eight Prodigies' of Yangzhou, Jiangsu province.

Most Malaysians and Singaporeans will be familiar with Admiral Cheng Ho (Zheng He in Hanyu Pinyin). Legends of the Sam Po Cave in Ipoh and Sam Po Well in Malacca owed their origins to this Ming official who sailed south in the early fifteenth century. Zheng was a surname given to the admiral by the Ming emperor, Yongle.

The Zheng's in Taiwan are from Fujian province, who were originally from Henan province.

Cheng
Chng (Cantonese, Hakka)
Tay (Hokkien)

ZHONG

FAMOUS ZHONGS

In the Han dynasty, Zhong Limei (钟离昧) was a general working under Han Xin, the field marshal of Emperor Liu Bang. But Han was not really liked by the emperor. The arrogant general was always a thorn in the emperor's eyes.

Before Liu came into power, he could not do anything to Han, as Han was still needed in his military set-up. But when Liu had finished with his rivals, he decided that it was time to act against Han Xin.

The emperor then summoned Han to see him in the palace. Han was quite reluctant as there were rumours that he was staging a coup. Realising that Zhong was the right-hand man in Han's camp, Liu then spread rumours that Han would be spared if he killed Zhong and presented his head to the emperor.

In a moment of panic, Han decided to do just that. Zhong now realised how stupid was the man he wholeheartedly served. He told Han, 'Dear Sir, you are not a clever person. The emperor dares not touch you because he knows that I am by your side. If you kill me then you will soon suffer the same fate.'

But the simple-minded yet stubborn Han refused to listen. After presenting Zhong's head to the emperor, he was detained, and eventually killed.

Although Han and Zhong had a similar ending of their colourful lives, Zhong was praised for his farsightedness (though not far enough), and Han was denounced as a selfish and naive person.

After general Zhong's death, his second son then moved to the present Henan province, and from there, the Zhongs soon developed to a big clan. Before the resettlement, the clan members were mostly staying in Anhui province, a place where the surname originated in the Spring and Autumn period.

Like many other surnames, Zhong was used as a surname after its ancestor was conferred a land named Zhong Li (锺离). Initially, it was a double surname Zhong Li, but later, some descendants preferred a shorter surname, hence the birth of the surname Zhong.

The first famous personality in this clan was musician Zhong Ziqi

(钟子期) in the Spring and Autumn period. He was said to be very good in *gu qin* (a kind of ancient string instrument), and became a good friend of a fellow musician, Bai Ya (伯牙). They understood each other so well that when Zhong died, Bai Ya simply burned his *gu qin* as 'there is no one left in this world to understand and appreciate my music.'

Zhong Yan was a famous calligrapher in Han dynasty and Zhong Rong (钟嵘) in the North-South dynasties period was an authority in poetry criticism. In folk belief, Zhong Xi (钟馗) is a ghost catcher, who is supposed to keep the ghosts from disturbing the human world.

Chung (Cantonese, Hakka)

ZHOU

MODEL FOR CHINESE KINGS

All Zhou's should be justly proud of King Wen, the ancestor of Zhou clan. King Wen's original surname was Ji. He changed his surname to Zhou only after he was conferred the dukedom at Zhou city in the present Shaanxi province. He made Zhou the strongest among all dukedoms during the Shang dynasty.

King Wen's way of ruling his dukedom also made him the model emperor throughout Chinese history. His benevolent policy was constantly referred to in Confucian teaching as the best form of government. King Wen's rule was the ideal government that all emperors after him tried to attain. The Zhou surname became so well-known that even some barbaric tribes chose Zhou as their surname during the Five Dynasties period.

Besides King Wen, the Zhou clan also produced a good number of personalities who shaped Chinese history. King Wen's son, Zhou Gong (周公), was the founder of the Chinese bureaucratic system. He was the first to fix the different titles of mandarins and standardize the bureaucratic procedures.

Zhou Yu (周瑜) in the Three Kingdoms period was a famous general of Wu kingdom. He defeated Cao Cao in The Battle of Red Cliffs. Poet Zhou Bangyan (周邦彦) and philosopher Zhou Dunyi (周敦颐) from the Song dynasty, were figures to note in China's cultural history. In recent years, perhaps the best-known figure of the Zhou clan was the late Chinese premier Chou En-lai (周恩来).

Chew (Hokkien)
Chiu (Hokkien)
Chou
Chow (Cantonese)

ZHU

RAGS-TO-RICHES STORY

The surname Zhu came from the legendary Emperor Zhuanxu. The surname started 3,000 years ago when Cao Xie (曹挟), a descendant of Emperor Zhuanxu, was conferred the territory called Zhu (邾) during the Zhou dynasty. The place roughly corresponds to present-day Shandong province.

Later, Zhu (邾) state was destroyed by another state; its residents discarded the radical 阝 and adopted Zhu (朱) as the clan's surname. In Chinese, the radical 阝 usually represents a place. So, the removal of it is symbolic of the Zhu's having lost their land.

Although the name originated from Shandong province in the north, it was also a prosperous and big clan in the south, especially in Fujian province. This was because of the fame of Zhu Maicheng (朱买臣) of the Han dynasty. His victory over rebel troops enhanced the Han's image and its reputation spread far and wide, even into far-flung provinces like Fujian province where it became a prominent clan.

The Ming dynasty was established by Zhu Yuanzhang (朱元璋). Zhu came from a humble background and became an emperor. His success story is exemplary. He not only overthrew the unpopular Mongolian rulers, but improved the drainage and irrigation systems as well. He also brought about a more fair system of taxation and conscription, and improved the welfare of his people.

Zhu abolished the post of premier and gave more power to the throne. He also gave land as rewards to outstanding generals and officials. All these won him the confidence of the people and his surname became very popular. For the next 300 years, Zhu became a national surname.

Zhu Xi (朱熹) of the Song dynasty was a well-known name in classical literature and philosophy. He spent his life doing research on classics, history, literature and the natural sciences. He was well-read and had a sophisticated, analytical mind, which later had a great influence on scholars.

From this clan there was also Zhu Zhixin (朱执信), a contemporary revolutionist. He took part in the famous uprising against the Manchurians' rule at Huanghua Gang (Yellow Flower Mountain). He also played an important part in Dr Sun Yat-sen's revolution against the Manchus.

Contemporary writer and poet Zhu Ziqing (朱自清) was also a worthy figure of the Zhu clan. He started writing poetry when he was a student. His works were a reflection of the seamy side of life during his time and his desire for a better future. He died of illness in Beijing in 1948.

Chu
Choo

ZHUANG

BAFFLING CHARMER

Of all the ancient Chinese philosophers, Zhuang Zi (365–290 B.C.) was indisputably the most charming. His preaching of merging oneself with Nature and searching for individual freedom certainly raised the eyebrows of the Confucians.

Once Zhuang Zi said he had a dream about butterflies. But when he woke up, he was not sure whether he was still Zhuang Zi or if he had already become a butterfly! And this sometimes eccentric philosopher left behind scores of legends about his unconventional behaviour.

It was said that when he was criticized for not mourning his wife's death, he wrote a song in reply:

'Now I bury my beloved wife after her death but please think of what would happen if I were to die before her. I am sure she would remarry instead. / My property would go to another man, my horse would be ridden by him and my wife become his. Isn't it a big joke? / So, while you people may think that I am a heartless person, I think you are wasting your tears.'

Zhuang Zi was one of the forefathers of the clan. He was the descendant of Zhuang Qiao (庄蹻), the common ancestor of the Zhuang clan. Zhuang Qiao was the offspring of Chu Zhuang (楚庄), a king of Chu county in the Spring and Autumn period.

Unfortunately the use of the surname Zhuang was banned during the Han dynasty because one Han dynasty emperor, Hui Zhuang (讳庄) happened to have the word Zhuang in his name. The Zhuang's had to change their surname to Yan (严). Perhaps that was why they seemed to have kept a low profile for a number of years in Chinese history. The Zhuang and Yan clans are therefore actually related.

After the Tang dynasty, they resurfaced especially around the south of Changjing and once again became very active in various fields. Names like Zhuang Chunyu (庄存与) and Zhuang Yanlong (庄廷钺) were widely recognized as brilliant scholars in the Qing dynasty. Most Zhuang's are found in the locale of Zhangnan.

Chuang

ZHUO

PRAISED DESPITE HER ELOPEMENT

In the fifth century A.D., the Zhuo clan spread themselves to all parts of southern China. By the next century, Fujian province had the largest concentration. A number of Zhuo families in the neighbouring province of Guangdong were believed to have come from Fujian. The Zhuo clan is still a large one among southern Chinese.

It was iron which brought great wealth to the first ancestor of Zhuo. This wealthy ancestor passed his time hunting in the countryside and had thousands of child slaves to serve him.

The Zhuo forefather lived in Ling Qiong (临邛) in present-day Sichuan province, central China. Ling Qiong was also where the romance of Zhuo Wenjun (卓文君) and Sima Xiangru (司马相如), took place more than 2,000 years ago.

Zhuo Wenjun was probably the only woman the ancient Chinese glorified for her virtues despite her elopement. She was the talented daughter of a wealthy man. Her husband died when she was very young.

Zhuo lived with her father. One day, her father gave a dinner for a Chengdu scholar, Sima Xiangru, who had always wanted to meet her. During the dinner he played so beautifully on the zither that he stirred Zhuo's feelings. Zhuo understood his message, and, as she felt the same for the equally talented suitor, they eloped to Chengdu that very night.

Sima, however, was a poor man. Soon the couple had to return to Ling Qiong where Zhuo managed a small inn, cooking and serving, while her husband concentrated on his scholastic career.

Though Zhuo Wenjun's father was furious with their elopement, he could not bear to see his daughter suffer. He helped the couple by giving them a large sum of money. Living comfortably, Sima quickly worked his way up in the imperial court. Soon, however, he was tempted to take a concubine.

His grief-stricken wife wrote the poem, *Bai Tou Yin* (白头吟). The emotions in the poem about true love between husband and wife moved Sima Xiangru so much that he desisted. Zhuo Wenjun's romance is still a favourite topic for Chinese opera.

About 200 years after Zhuo Wenjun, there was another well-known figure from the same clan. Zhuo Mao (卓茂) was a Han scholar noted for his noble character and accurate calculation of the calendar. He was appointed to a very senior post in the government.

Zhuo Mao's two sons were also among the 28 generals decorated for having helped restore the throne to the Han emperor from the usurper Wang Mang.

TO CONCLUDE

THE decline of the traditional associations does not spell the death of Chinatowns. The major Chinatowns of San Francisco and New York will probably always remain with their famous restaurants, curio shops, picturesque houses and their little alleyways. Even though the inhabitants of Chinatown may move out, the millions of tourists who come in every year with their tourist dollars will ensure their survival.

Signs of revitalization in the American Chinatowns can be seen everywhere – in the expanding population and teeming crowds, the lively bartering and trading, the new buildings and developments and yes, even in the *tongs*, that continue to make good money out of their gambling rackets. Perhaps nothing symbolizes this vitality better than the Chinese Culture Center in Chinatown, San Francisco which is on the third floor of a 27-storey skyscraper linked directly to Chinatown's Portsmouth Square by a bridge, juxtaposing the supermodern Trans-American pyramid. Here a vigorous cultural life pulsates, with its world class exhibitions, presentation of Chinese arts and dances and lectures by eminent scholars. In San Francisco Chinatown itself, celebration of major festivals like the Chinese New Year is a total community affair. The community has excellent lion and dragon dance troupes, choruses and musical groups, a clutch of outstanding artists, painting in the traditional as well as the modern abstract styles and a first-rate children's Chinese orchestra.

Chinatowns embody the memory of a race, that crosses the wide ocean to cleave and hew a foreign soil, lay the tracks across the face of the earth, wait at tables, serve food and wash dirty clothes for a living. Through untold hardship and persecution, they persevere and prosper to implant their seeds and raise a new generation – black-haired, black-eyed children of Han, not completely Chinese and not quite American.

The ambiguity of their ethnic status has led to an intense exploration of what it means to be a Chinese American. This attempt by individuals and groups to grapple with the question of ethnicity and identity has been spurred by decades of discrimination and the awakening of black consciousness in the United States. Unashamed to be yellow, the Asian-Americans, like the blacks, seek to affirm their ancestry, and demand a recognition of their ethnic heritage and their cultural contribution.

The expression this newfound ethnic consciousness takes, comes in different forms. There was the much-heralded trip of a group of youths of Chinese descent from America and Canada, who visited their ancestral Xinhui and Enping counties in 1982. More often than not the Chinese American voice comes through in literary contributions, novels, dramas and poems. In a poem like 'Saying Yes', Diana Chang best expresses for post-war generations of Chinese Americans, the precise language and rhythm of their ethnic duality.

'Are you Chinese?'
'Yes.'
'American?'
'Yes.'
'Really Chinese?'
'No . . . not quite.'
'Really American?'
'Well, actually, you see . . .'

But I would rather say
Yes.

Not neither-nor
not maybe,
but both, and not only

The homes I've had,
the ways I am

I'd rather say it
twice,
Yes.

In Singapore, the Chinese have a greater control of their lives to determine their own destiny because they form the majority. Nowhere else besides Hong Kong is, in this tiny city-state, the ingenuity and entrepreneurial spirit so keenly manifest. A combination of affluence, English education and the purveyance of western lifestyles and values through the mass media, have eroded traditional Chinese values to shape a more individualistic lifestyle for the young. However, the teaching of Chinese language and Confucianism in schools, and the government's ever-vigilant attitude towards western fads, will slow if not stop the process of total westernization. In the end the young will have to make their own choice on the kind of life they want. In recent years, there is some evidence of a resurgence of interest in things Chinese, from resurrecting Chinatown and Asian values to visiting China, not only among the older generation but also young Singaporeans.

Even in the small half-assimilated Chinese communities of Australia, New Zealand and Britain the ancestral culture appears to linger on in the children. Invariably industrious, withdrawn and quiet in class and circumspect in public, their strength is anchored upon a culture that emphasizes strong families, self-help and devotion to education. As a result, in such countries and in America, they have on average outperformed all other ethnic groups in high school graduation rates, percentage of college graduates and in median family income.

The Chinese hold the economic clout in many countries they have settled in. Their businesses dictate or influence the pace of economic growth. In the fields of science, technology and the arts, they have made valuable contributions to their host societies. In countries where there are vast resources and an emphasis on private enterprise and individual initiative, the opportunities accorded the Chinese individual for growth and upward mobility are unparalleled.

CHINESE DYNASTIC CYCLE

LEGENDARY PERIOD

XIA	c.21st century–16th century B.C.
SHANG	c.16th century–11th century B.C.
WESTERN ZHOU	1027–771 B.C.
EASTERN ZHOU	771–256 B.C.
(SPRING AND AUTUMN PERIOD)	771–476 B.C.
WARRING STATES	475–221 B.C.
QIN	221–206 B.C.
Shi Huang Di	221–210 B.C.
FORMER HAN	206 B.C.–A.D. 9
Gaozu (Liu Bang)	206–195 B.C.
Wendi	180–157 B.C.
Wudi	141–87 B.C.
Xuandi	74–49 B.C.
Chendi	33 B.C.–A.D. 7
XIN	A.D. 9–23
Wang Mang	A.D. 9–23
LATER HAN	A.D. 25–220
Guang Wu Di	A.D. 25–57
Ming Di	A.D. 57–75
Huan Di	A.D. 146–167
Xian Di	A.D. 189–220
THREE KINGDOMS	A.D. 220–280
(Wu, Shu and Wei)	
WESTERN JIN	A.D. 265–316
EASTERN JIN	A.D. 317–420
LIU SONG	A.D. 420–479
SOUTHERN QI	A.D. 479–502 } South China
LIANG	A.D. 502–557
CHEN	A.D. 557–589
SIXTEEN KINGDOMS	A.D. 304–439
NORTHERN WEI	A.D. 386–535
WESTERN WEI	A.D. 535–557
EASTERN WEI	A.D. 534–550 } North China
NORTHERN QI	A.D. 550–577
NORTHERN ZHOU	A.D. 557–581

SUI	A.D. 581–618		
TANG	A.D. 618–907		
Taizong	A.D. 618–626		
Gaozong	A.D. 649–683		
Empress Wu	A.D. 683–705		
Xuanzong	A.D. 712–756		
TEN KINGDOMS	A.D. 907–960	–	South China
FIVE DYNASTIES	A.D. 907–960	–	North China
SONG	A.D. 960–1126		
Taizu	A.D. 960–976		
Taizong	A.D. 976–997		
Renzong	A.D. 1022–1064		
Shenzong	A.D. 1067–1085		
Huizong	A.D. 1100–1125		
SOUTHERN SONG	A.D. 1127–1279	–	South China
JIN (Tartar)	A.D. 1126–1234		North China
MONGOLS	A.D. 1234–1271		
YUAN	A.D. 1279–1368		
MING	A.D. 1368–1644		
Hongwu	A.D. 1368–1398		
Yongle	A.D. 1403–1424		
Chenghua	A.D. 1465–1487		
Jiaqing	A.D. 1522–1566		
Wanli	A.D. 1573–1620		
QING	A.D. 1644–1911		
Kangxi	A.D. 1661–1722		
Yongzheng	A.D. 1723–1736		
Qianlong	A.D. 1736–1795		
Jiaqing	A.D. 1796–1820		
Daoguang	A.D. 1821–1850		
Guangxu	A.D. 1875–1908		
REPUBLIC			
Kuomintang	1911–1949		
Chinese Communist Party	1949 onwards		

Footnote: The epoch following the fall of the Later Han dynasty is called the Six Dynasties period (Liu Chao) after the six successive dynasties that had their capitals at Nanjing between A.D. 222 and A.D. 589. Only the more prominent emperors are listed.

TRANSLITERATION CHART

PINYIN	OLDER ROMANIZATIONS	
Places		
Anhui	Anhwei	安徽
Fujian	Fukien	福建
Gansu	Kansu	甘肃
Guangdong	Kwangtung	广东
Guangxi	Kwangsi	广西
Guizhou	Kweichow	贵州
Hebei	Hopei	河北
Heilongjiang	Heilungkiang	黑龙江
Henan	Honan	河南
Hubei	Hupei	湖北
Hunan	Hunan	湖南
Jiangsu	Kiangsu	江苏
Jiangxi	Kiangsi	江西
Jilin	Kirin	吉林
Liaoning	Liaoning	辽宁
Ningxia	Ningsia	宁夏
Qinghai	Tsinghai	青海
Shaanxi	Shensi	陕西
Shandong	Shantung	山东
Shanxi	Shansi	山西
Sichuan	Szechwan	四川
Xinjiang	Sinkiang	新疆
Yunnan	Yunnan	云南
Zhejiang	Chekiang	浙江
Beijing	Peking	北京
Guangzhou	Canton	广州
Fuzhou	Foochow	福州
Shantou	Swatow	山头

PINYIN	OLDER ROMANIZATIONS	
Xiamen	Amoy	厦门
Nanjing	Nanking	南京
Taishan	Toishan	台山
Xinhui	Sun Wui	新会
Jinmen	Quemoy	金门
Tianjin	Tientsin	天津

People

Lao Zi	Lao-tsu	老子
Zhuang Zi	Chuang-tsu	莊子
Li Bai	Li Po	李白
Su Dongpo	Su Tong-p'o	苏东坡
Ba Jin	Pa Chin	巴金
Kang Youwei	K'ang Yu-wei	康有为
Liang Qicao	Liang Ch'i-chao	梁启超
Hong Xiuquan	Hung Hsiu-chuan	洪秀全
Shi Huang Di	Shih Huang-ti	始皇帝
Empress Dowager Cixi	Empress Dowager Tzu-hsi	慈禧
Emperor Kangxi	Emperor Kang-hsi	康煕
Emperor Yongzheng	Emperor Yung-cheng	雍正
Emperor Qianlong	Emperor Ch'ien-lung	乾隆
Emperor Guangxu	Emperor Kuang-hsu	光绪

TRADITIONAL ASSOCIATIONS
IN SINGAPORE

FROM GUANGDONG PROVINCE

Cantonese-speaking members

Singapore Kwong Wai Siew Peck
San Theng
50 Kg San Teng
Upper Thomson Road
Singapore 2057

Kong Chow Wui Kun
321 New Bridge Road
Singapore 0208

Sin Heng Wui Kun
39A Lorong 4, Geylang

Singapore Kwangtung Wui Kun
16 Church Street
Singapore 0104

Singapore Ning Yeung Wui Kun
133B South Bridge Road
Singapore 0105

Teochew-speaking members

Teochew Poit Ip Huay Kuan
97 Tank Road
Singapore 0923

Teo Ann Huay Kuan
25 Bukit Pasoh Road
Singapore 0208

Singapore Teo Yeonh Huai Kuan
341 Clemenceau Avenue
Singapore 0922

Hakka-speaking members

The Singapore Nanyang Khek
Community Guild
20 Peck Seah Street
Singapore 0207

Yin Fo Fui Kun
98 Telok Ayer Street
Singapore 0104

San Foh Whai Kuan
409A Jalan Besar
Singapore 0820

Hainanese-speaking members

The Singapore Kiung Chow
Hwee Kuan
47 Beach Road
Singapore 0718

FROM FUJIAN PROVINCE

Hokkien-speaking members

Singapore Hokkien Huay Kuan
137 Telok Ayer Street
Singapore 0106

Singapore Chin Kang Huay Kuan
27 Bukit Pasoh Road
Singapore 0208

Lam Ann Association
30 Mohamed Sultan Road
Singapore 0923

Singapore Hui Ann Association
7 Lorong 29 Geylang
Singapore 1438

Tung Ann District Guild
43 Bukit Pasoh Road
Singapore 0208

Singapore Ann Kway Association
265C New Bridge Road
Singapore 0208

Kim Mui Hoey Kuan
2A Murray Street
Singapore 0207

Eng Choon Huay Kuan
105-106 Amoy Street
Singapore 0106

Chang Chow General Association
14 Yan Kit Road
Singapore 0208

Hokchew-speaking members

Singapore Foochow Association
21 Tyrwhitt Road
Singapore 0820

Henghua-speaking members

Hin Ann Huay Kuan
35 Sam Leong Road
Singapore 0820

FROM OTHER PROVINCES

Shanghainese-speaking members

The Sam Kiang Huay Kuan
23 St Thomas Walk
Singapore 0923

BIBLIOGRAPHY

Bendix, Reinhard, *Max Weber: An Intellectual Portrait.* New York: Anchor Books, Doubleday & Company, 1962.

Bloodworth, Dennis, *The Chinese Looking Glass.* London: Secker and Warburg, 1967.

Broady, Maurice, The Chinese in Great Britain. In Morton H. Fried, (ed.), *Colloquium on Overseas Chinese.* New York: Institute of Pacific Relations, 1958.

Carstens, S. A., 'Chinese Associations in Singapore Society.' Occasional Paper No. 37, Institute of Southeast Asian Studies, 1975.

Chan Heng Chee, *The Dynamics of One Party Dominance.* Singapore: Singapore University Press, 1976.

Chen, Jack, *The Chinese of America.* San Francisco: Harper and Row, 1980.

Chen, Peter and H. D. Evers, (eds.), *Studies in Asean Sociology.* Singapore: Chopmen Enterprises, 1978.

Cheng Lim-Keak, *Social Change and the Chinese in Singapore.* Singapore: Singapore University Press, 1985.

China Reconstructs, *Finding Family Roots: Youth of Chinese Descent from America and Canada Visit Xinhui and Enping Counties.* Beijing, 1983.

Choi C. Y., *Chinese Migration and Settlement in Australia.* Sydney: University of Sydney Press, 1975.

Coughlin, Richard, *Double Identity: The Chinese in Modern Thailand.* Hong Kong: Hong Kong University Press, 1960.

Douglas, S. A. and P. Pederson, *Blood, Believer and Brothers: The Development of Voluntary Associations in Malaysia.* Ohio: Ohio University Center of International Studies, 1973.

Fairbank, John and E. Reischauer, *East Asia: The Great Tradition.* Boston: Houghton Mifflin Co., 1960.

Geiger, T., *Tales of Two City-States: The Development Process of Hong Kong and Singapore.* Washington: National Planning Foundation, 1973.

George, T. J. S., *Lee Kuan Yew's Singapore.* London: Andre Deutsch, 1973.

Gittins, Jean, *The Diggers from China: The Story of the Chinese on the Goldfields.* Melbourne: Quartet Books, 1981.

Greif, Stuart, *The Overseas Chinese in New Zealand.* Singapore: Asia Pacific Press, 1974.

Heidhues, M. F. S., *Southeast Asia's Chinese Minority.* Hawthorn, Australia: Longman, 1974.

Hoexter, Corinne, *From Canton to California.* New York: Four Winds Press, 1976.

Hsieh, Jiann, *Internal Structure and Socio-cultural Change: A Chinese Case in Multi-Ethnic Society of Singapore.* Unpublished Ph.D. dissertation, University Microfilms Inc., Ann Arbor, 1977.

Hsu F. L. K., *Clans, Caste and Club.* New York: Princeton Van Nostrand, 1963.

Hsu Hsien Chin, *The Common Descent Group in China and Its Functions.* New York: Wenner-Bren Foundation for Anthropological Research, Viking Fund Publication.

Huck, Arthur, *The Assimilation of the Chinese in Australia.* Canberra: Australia National University Press, 1970.

Huie Kin, *Reminiscences.* Peking: San Yu Press, 1932.

Hunter, Guy, *Southeast Asia: Race, Culture and Nation.* London: Oxford University Press, 1966.

Issacs, Harold, *Images of Asia.* New York: Harper Torchbooks, 1972.

Josey, Alex, *Lee Kuan Yew: The Struggle for Singapore.* Singapore: Angus and Robertson, 1974.

Kaudsky, John, *Political Change in Underdeveloped Countries*, New York: John Wiley & Sons, 1967.

Kuo, Eddie and Aline Wong, (eds.), *The Contemporary Family in Singapore.* Singapore: Singapore University Press, 1979.

Kwok S. S., *An Account of the Sources of Benevolent Assistance which are Asian in Origin and Organization.* Singapore: Academic Exercise, University of Malaya, 1954.

Lee, Rose Hum, *The Chinese in the United States of America.* Hong Kong: Hong Kong University Press, 1960.

Leong, Stephen, *Sources, Agencies and Manifestations of Overseas Chinese Nationalism.* Unpublished Ph.D. dissertation, University Microfilms, Inc., Ann Arbor.

Light, Ivan, *Ethnic Enterprises in America.* Berkeley: University of California Press, 1972.

Lim, Linda and Peter Gosling, *The Chinese in Southeast Asia*, Vols. I and II. Singapore: Maruzen Press, 1983.

Lin H. S. et. al., *Shih-lei ku-chi (Historical Ruins in Singapore).* Singapore: The South Seas Society, 1975.

Lin Yutang, *My Country and my People.* London: W. Heinemann, 1939.

Lyman, Stanford, *Chinese Americans.* New York: Random House, 1974.

Nee, Victor and Brett De Bary Nee, *Longtime Californ': A Documentary Study of an American Chinatown.* Boston: Houghton Mifflin Company, 1972.

Ng, Bickleen Fong, *The Chinese in New Zealand.* Hongkong: University of Hong Kong Press, 1959.

Ng Kwee Choo, *The Chinese in London*. London: Oxford University Press, 1968.

Peng Song Toh, *Directory of Associations in Singapore 1982–1983*. (In Chinese.) Singapore: Historical Culture Publishers, 1983.

Png P. S., 'Kuomintang in Malaya'. *Journal of Southeast Asian History*, Vol. II, No. 1 (March), 1961.

Scharfstein, Ben-Ami, *The Mind of China*. New York: Basic Books Inc. Publishers, 1974.

Skinner, G. W., *Leadership and Power in the Chinese Community of Thailand*. Ithaca: Cornell University Press, 1958.

——————, (ed.), *The Study of Chinese Society: Essays of M. Freedman*. California: Stanford University Press, 1979.

Song, Ong Siang, *One Hundred Years of the Chinese in Singapore*. Singapore: University of Malaya Press, 1967 (reprint).

Sung, Betty Lee, *Mountain of Gold: The Story of the Chinese in America*. New York: The Macmillan Company, 1967.

——————, *The Chinese in America*. New York: Macmillan Publishing Company, 1972.

Tan Giok Lan, Mely, *The Chinese in the United States*. Taipei: Orient Cultural Service, 1973.

Tan Kah Kee, *Nan-ch'iao hui-yi-lu (Memoirs of a Nanyang Overseas Chinese)*, Vol. I and II. (In Chinese.) Fuchou, Fukien: Fuchou chi-mei hsiao-yu-hui, 1950.

Tan, T. W. Thomas, *Singapore Modernization: A Study of Traditional Chinese Voluntary Associations in Social Change*. Unpublished Ph.D dissertation, University of Virginia, 1983.

——————, 'Political Modernization and Traditional Chinese Voluntary Associations: A Singapore Case Study'. *Southeast Asian Journal of Social Science*, Vol. 13, No. 2, 1985.

——————, 'Voluntary Associations and Social Change. *Southeast Asian Journal of Social Science*, Vol. 14, No. 2, 1986.

Travers, Robert, *Australian Mandarin: The Life and Times of Quong Tart*. Sydney: Kangaroo Press, 1981.

Vaughan, J. D., *The Manners and Customs of the Chinese of the Straits Settlements*. Singapore: Oxford University Press, 1971 (reprint).

Wand, David Hsin-Fu, *Asian-American Heritage: An Anthology of Prose and Poetry*. New York: Washington Square Press, 1974.

Watson, James, 'Restaurants and Remittances: Chinese Emigrant Workers in London.' In George Foster and Robert Kemper, *Anthropologists in Cities*. Boston: Little, Brown and Company, 1974.

——————, *Emigration and the Chinese Lineage: The Mans in HongKong and London*. Berkeley: University of California Press, 1975.

Wong, Aline, Thomas Tan et.al., 'Family Lifestyles Among Housing and Development Board's Residents'. In Aline Wong and Stephen H. K. Yeh, (eds.), *Housing a Nation: 25 Years of Public Housing*. Singapore: Maruzen Press, 1985.

Wong, Bernard, *A Chinese American Community: Ethnicity and Survival Strategies*. Singapore: Chopmen Enterprises, 1979.

Wu Hua, *Hsin-chia-po hua-tsu hui-kuan shih (A Survey of the Singapore Chinese Hui-Kuan or Landsmannschaften)*. Singapore: The South Seas Society, 1975 (in Chinese).

Yang C. K., *Religion in Chinese Society*. Berkeley: University of California Press, 1961.

Yen C. H., *The Overseas Chinese and the 1911 Revolution*. Kuala Lumpur: Oxford University Press, 1976.

——————, 'Early Chinese Clan Organizations in Singapore and Malaya'. *Journal of Southeast Asian Studies*, Vol. 12, No. 2, 1981.

Yeo K. W., *Political Development in Singapore, 1945–1955*. Singapore: Singapore University Press, 1973.

Yong C. F., 'Chinese Leadership in Nineteenth Century Singapore'. *Journal of the Island Society*, Vol I, 1967.

——————, 'A Preliminary Study of Chinese Leadership in Singapore'. 1900–1941, *Journal of Southeast Asian History*, 9(2), 1968.

——————, *The New Gold Mountain: The Chinese in Australia, 1901–1921*. Melbourne: Raphael Arts, 1977.

ACKNOWLEDGEMENTS

The publishers gratefully acknowledge Dr Chen Siew Min for the calligraphy of Li Bai's poem; Philip Hu for taking photographs of San Francisco Chinatown (pages 87, 88, 133, 138, 148, 149); Singapore National Archives for permission to reproduce photographs (pages 113, 114, 115, 118, 120); Singapore National Library for helping to source illustrations from the Southeast Asia Collection (cover picture and page 106); New York Public Library for a photograph from their Picture Collection (page xii); and California Historical Society, San Francisco for allowing us to use the following illustrations (frontispiece, pages vi and viii).

Many thanks also to the *Straits Times* Bilingual Section, especially Sok Chng, for assistance in obtaining research material on Chinese surnames.

Finally, the translation of 'Silent Night', Li Bai's famous poem, is attributed to Sun Yu, from the book *Li Po – A New Translation*, The Commercial Press Ltd, Hong Kong, 1982.

INDEX

ABOUT THE AUTHOR

Thomas Tsu-wee Tan studied at the University of Singapore (now the National University of Singapore) and in the United States where he earned his doctorate in 1983. Specializing broadly in the field of modernization, Dr Tan has co-authored one book, published several articles in professional journals, and delivered papers at International Conferences. He had formerly taught, on a part-time basis, in the sociology departments of the University of Virginia and the National University of Singapore.

Married to a lawyer, the Tans have one young daughter. Dr Tan now works as a sociologist in a statutory board in Singapore.